A Detective's History of Psychology

A Detective's History of Psychology

Understanding Key Theories and Concepts Through Mystery Fiction

DIANE MELLO-GOLDNER

McFarland & Company, Inc., Publishers
Jefferson, North Carolina

This book has undergone peer review.

LIBRARY OF CONGRESS CATALOGUING-IN-PUBLICATION DATA

Names: Mello-Goldner, Diane, 1968– author.
Title: A detective's history of psychology : understanding key theories and concepts through mystery fiction / Diane Mello-Goldner.
Description: Jefferson, North Carolina : McFarland & Company, Inc., Publishers, 2024. | Includes bibliographical references and index.
Identifiers: LCCN 2024024913 | ISBN 9781476686288 (paperback : acid free paper) ∞
ISBN 9781476652290 (ebook)
Subjects: LCSH: Detective and mystery stories, English—History and criticism. | Detective and mystery stories, American—History and criticism. | Psychology and literature. | Authors and readers. | Detectives in literature. | Psychoanalysis in literature. | LCGFT: Literary criticism.
Classification: LCC PR830.D4 M46 2024 | DDC 823/.087209—dc23/eng/20240610
LC record available at https://lccn.loc.gov/2024024913

BRITISH LIBRARY CATALOGUING DATA ARE AVAILABLE

ISBN (print) 978-1-4766-8628-8
ISBN (ebook) 978-1-4766-5229-0

© 2024 Diane Mello-Goldner. All rights reserved

No part of this book may be reproduced or transmitted in any form or by any means, electronic or mechanical, including photocopying or recording, or by any information storage and retrieval system, without permission in writing from the publisher.

Front cover image: © Bratishko Konstantin/Shutterstock

Printed in the United States of America

*McFarland & Company, Inc., Publishers
Box 611, Jefferson, North Carolina 28640
www.mcfarlandpub.com*

*For my parents,
Manuel and Maria,
for indulging my voracious reading
as a child and teenager
and providing me
with the opportunity and resources
to pursue my two passions:
psychology and detective fiction.*

*I would also like to thank
my husband Michael
and children Kirsten and Owen,
for their support and help.*

Table of Contents

Acknowledgments — ix

Preface — 1

1. The Psychologist as Detective — 5
2. Structuralism, Functionalism, and the Move to Psychoanalysis — 25
3. The Shift to Behaviorism and Overt Action — 54
4. The Humanistic Approach — 75
5. Cognitive Psychology — 97
6. Focus on Culture — 130
7. Neuropsychology and Forensic Psychology — 166
8. Putting It All Together — 191

Murder at the Manor: A Play in One Act — 199

Author's Notes — 211

Index — 219

Magnifying glass with psi symbol. Graphic image created by Kirsten Goldner.

Acknowledgments

This book would not have been possible without the help and support of the Pine Manor College community. The content and ideas originated from an interdisciplinary course called *Women and Detective Fiction*, which grew from lunch and tea-time discussions with my English colleague, Melinda Ponder. We discovered that we shared a love for Agatha Christie, Maisie Dobbs, and *Masterpiece Mystery*, even though we came from two different disciplines. Our discussions gradually evolved into a fully-fledged course that became part of the college's general education curriculum. During the course, I would talk about the psychological elements of the course, and Melinda would provide the literary analysis.

When Melinda retired, I co-taught the class with another English colleague, Hannah Baker-Siroty. The focus was more or less the same, but we put a much more creative spin on the course. I still focused on psychology, but Hannah, a poet, focused on the creative writing element of the stories. We decided to write a short mystery for the class to perform for the Pine Manor community at the end of the year Achievement Day, a day that recognized students' achievements and coursework. It was probably the most fun I have ever had collaborating with colleagues and students. The community loved the performance, full of college history and inside jokes.

This book owes its completion to the contributions and insights of our wonderful students. I thank the following students whose participation enriched the course and my thought process: Gisella Higuera, Natasha Kopystynsky, Iandra Mazurkevicz, Cecile Moore, Nadlyne Octavien, Melanie Rosario, Tiffanie Rosario, Sherise Rouse, Kate Holden, Margaret Roberts, Stephanie Andrade, Marlina Brown, Vivian Depina, Tasha Gonzalez, Majida Goummih, Sherry Graves, Heather Hernandez, Tatiana Mendez, Faiza Moughal, Xiara Ramos, Jordan Zoeke, Alexis Milton, Nurik Baitassov, Camarie Brantley, Erin Epps, Pamela Fernandez, Silvia Galdamez, Serena Goncalves, Ashley Leonardo, Andrea Melendez, Comfort Opokuaa, Krizabel Pastrana, Derick Speight, Gabel Williams,

Vanessa Aarons, Atazhanna Furtado-Triplett, Christina Karamitsios, Wendy Myrbell Napoleon, and Kiana Smith.

Throughout this process, I received invaluable assistance from a diverse group at Pine Manor College. Notably, colleagues Melinda and Hannah played instrumental roles, but the support extended beyond them. One experience came during a writing class on mystery stories, led by Hank Phillippi Ryan, during Pine Manor College's Solstice MFA in Creative Writing residencies. Meg Kearney, the program's Director, offered unwavering support during this period. Additionally, Ieshia Karasik contributed significantly by carefully reviewing multiple early manuscript drafts and providing insightful suggestions on the organization. Many other colleagues also contributed in various ways, reading drafts, offering reference materials, and providing helpful recommendations.

I am deeply grateful for the contributions of individuals such as Michele Ramirez, Colleen Krieser, Liz Cary Blum, Barbara Schwartz, Shelley Linso, Deborah Kronenberg, Nancy White, Michelle Wilson, Raquel Lopez, Bill Stargard, Rebecca Mitchell, and Sarah Woolf. In sum, their collective efforts have made this book a poignant tribute to the benefits of scholarly collaboration.

I also was fortunate to receive the Wean Fellowship, which provided me with a one-semester sabbatical during the spring of 2020. This opportunity allowed me to fully immerse myself in my research while my colleagues dealt with the coronavirus pandemic and a mid-semester shift to online learning. Regrettably, the pandemic brought significant financial strains upon our small college and necessitated its closure. After a two-year teach-out process, Pine Manor found a new home with Boston College (my alma mater), adopting the name "Pine Manor Institute for Student Success." I hope this book can preserve the rich legacy of Pine Manor College, evoking fond memories of the supportive and nurturing community we were fortunate to experience. The Pine Manor community will forever remain an integral part of my extended family, and I am immensely grateful for the formative experiences I encountered there.

Preface

Integrating literature and popular culture presents an intriguing and intellectually stimulating approach to invigorating courses within various academic disciplines, especially those that have traditionally struggled to pique student interest. While some courses may succeed in engaging students through conventional teaching methods, an innovative solution exists to breathe new life into more lackluster subjects. One such course facing challenges in fostering genuine enthusiasm among students is the *History of Psychology* course, a mandatory requirement in many undergraduate psychology programs.

Despite its importance, this course sometimes needs help in eliciting student excitement. However, imagine if this course were transformed into a compelling exploration through the lens of detective fiction, uncovering the history of psychological paradigms while reading or viewing the stories of Sherlock Holmes, Nancy Drew, Hercule Poirot, Precious Ramotswe, or Veronica Mars. Suddenly, the *History of Psychology* course is revitalized and becomes appealing to students of all age groups. Incorporating popular fictional detectives and their adventures infuses the curriculum with suspense and curiosity, leading to genuine engagement and passion for the subject matter.

What makes this connection between psychology and detective fiction so compelling? Psychology is a relatively young science, influenced by its scientific relatives, historical events, and societal issues. Similarly, the evolution of psychological **paradigms** (broad frameworks or sets of standards) mirrors the categorical shifts seen in detective fiction, spanning from the Victorian Era to the Golden Age and Hardboiled Era. The field of psychology is unique in that it is a "created" science based on the social construction of its early researchers. Understanding psychology requires grasping the historical and social origins that shaped its theories and research methodology (Danziger, 1990). Various genres of literature, including detective fiction, often explore those same dimensions.

The academic discipline of psychology can be combined with almost every academic subject to create an engaging and creative interdisciplinary course. Combining psychology with literature, particularly detective fiction, makes psychology more approachable. Characters in these stories offer the opportunity to apply psychological concepts in a fictional setting, making it easier for students to engage in discussions without feeling overwhelmed by real-world examples. In addition, when analyzing an effective detective's skills, you will find their[1] skills are similar to those of an effective psychologist.

Intriguingly, psychology and detective novels or mystery stories share many similarities. As psychology's focus evolved over the years due to research interests, technology, and historical events, detective fiction also experienced shifts, drawing a strong connection between the two disciplines. Through literature, readers can observe how detectives (who are professional problem solvers just like psychologists) use critical and analytical thinking to solve mysteries and then analyze the **validity** of their solutions.

In psychological research, validity refers to the accuracy of results or measures, while **reliability** refers to the consistency of results or measures (Keppel, 1982). Both concepts are essential in research and detective work. Imagine the detective who identifies the suspect who was the killer at the end of a novel—it would be important that the correct person is initially selected (validity) and that the detective continues to believe, and that other detectives also believe, that specific suspect is the killer (reliability). Reading detective fiction provides a unique opportunity to observe how fictional detectives use psychological principles to accurately and consistently analyze human behavior, solve crimes, and establish relationships.

This connection led to the creation of this book, intended to help readers to understand the historical development of psychology through the actions and behaviors of specific detectives. It caters to a diverse audience, from those with no background in psychology to seasoned enthusiasts. Moreover, it complements various high-school or college-level psychology courses, serving as a valuable resource for instructors. For example, it could serve as a supplement or a primary resource for students in an introduction to psychology or a course on the systems or history of psychology.[2] Finally, a senior capstone course could incorporate this book with the instructor providing additional content and readings to meet the course's specific learning outcomes and goals.

The ideal course structure is interdisciplinary, led by instructors from an institution's psychology and English departments who survey the detective fiction genre through a psychological lens. Not only does this approach highlight the development of the detective as a protagonist, but it also draws connections to psychological concepts and paradigms. Additionally, you can revise the course to more fully explore gender or women's studies by focusing on female or nonbinary writers and characters. Regardless of your specific purpose, the book incorporates exercises and thought-provoking questions within and at the end of each chapter. These pedagogical tools facilitate active learning by prompting students and readers to directly apply the conceptual frameworks and theories to literary examples or personal experiences. Use these exercises as guidance, changing them to suit the unique needs and interests of your different groups, classes, or individuals. Specifically, these questions and activities will help you develop the following learning outcomes:

- competence in reading, writing, and oral communication
- the ability to connect knowledge and experience to approach problem-solving
- knowledge of the history of the detective fiction genre, including different types of detective fiction within the context of psychological history, women's social history, cultural history, and literary history
- the ability to analyze examples of detective fiction given their thematic features
- understanding the historical and philosophical antecedents and contexts of the various psychology paradigms
- the ability to describe the development of psychology as a scientific discipline and a professional practice; and the ability to characterize the significant relationships between developments in psychology and other disciplines

As with the exercises themselves, these goals and learning outcomes are merely suggestions, and you should plan to adjust them to fit your needs best.

The book's organization into eight chapters aligns well with the typical college semester, allowing for structured reading and assignment schedules. Chapters 1–7 are the content-heavy chapters of this book. I would suggest assigning no more than one novel per chapter, although several short stories or excerpts from books rather than complete novels are a good alternative. You can also apply one detective fiction or mystery novel to multiple chapters to lighten the reading. For scheduling purposes, I would suggest assigning Chapters 1–7 over two weeks, more or less, depending on the number and length of readings and assignments. Each chapter links detective fiction to psychology and other non-literary interdisciplinary factors such as history, culture, and social influences.

Most writers and characters discussed within this book would likely identify as cisgender females (as a side note, these selections were made with a deliberate link to a women's studies course and the instructors' personal preferences). While these choices dominate the chapters, they are not exhaustive or exclusive. Instructors, students, or readers can substitute alternative characters and novels based on their inclinations or course requirements. Each chapter ends with a list of additional authors and detectives, thus offering a broader selection of literary options. If using this book to help guide a reading group's selections over an extended time, you may choose to read one chapter from this book with one or more accompanying novels or short stories each month. Mix it up and have different group members read different books or stories for each chapter, with individuals sharing a synopsis of their selection. Ultimately, it is your course or group, and you will know what works best for your specific group and pedagogical needs.

The final chapter ties together the concepts and insights presented throughout the text and includes an interactive activity to foster collaboration and knowledge-sharing within your broader community. It includes a one-act play, providing a unique opportunity to engage with the material. If you choose to perform the play, begin planning at your midway mark to ensure enough time to prepare and practice. Another option is to pair your course with a theater course, enlisting the theater students to perform the play for your class or community.

Whether you are an instructor looking to update your course or a reading group seeking thought-provoking material, this book offers a rich and enjoyable learning experience. By intertwining psychology with the appeal of the detective, emphasizing reader agency, and fostering diverse perspectives, it serves as a dynamic and engaging resource for exploration and intellectual growth. Lastly, what sets this book apart is its versatility and engaging nature. These characteristics allow adaptation to suit your audience's needs, promising an exciting intellectual journey that transcends traditional course structures. From the very first chapter to the last, you will find yourself drawn into the worlds of psychology and detective fiction, leaving a lasting impression that sparks a desire for lifelong learning.

Notes

1. The singular form of the gender-neutral pronoun "their" will be utilized throughout the text.
2. For a more thorough exploration of the history of experimental psychology and its critical theorists and theories, I suggest the classic books by Thomas Leahey, B.R. Hergenhahn, or Edwin Boring. Suggested contemporary textbooks on *The History of Psychology* include the following: Tracy Henley's (2018) *Hergenhahn's an Introduction to the History of Psychology*, Cengage Learning; Eric Shiraev's (2014) *A History of Psychology: A Global Perspective*, Sage Publications; and Duane Schultz and Sydney Ellen Schultz's (2015) *A History of Modern Psychology*, Cengage Learning.

1

The Psychologist as Detective

What Is Psychology?

If you had to take out a piece of paper and write what you think psychologists do on it, what would you write down? Try it now.

Investigative thinking challenge:
What does a psychologist do?

What did you write down—that they listen to people's problems and give advice? While you would not be incorrect with these statements, psychology is much more than the stereotypical image of the therapist listening to her or his client who is lying on a sofa beside them. While many psychologists are therapists who help others work through personal issues, psychology is also a science. Like other sciences, psychology can date its origin back to philosophy (Leahey, 1991). The word **psychology** comes from the Greek words *psyche*, meaning the human soul, spirit or mind, and *logos*, which means to study or "word" (Kalat, 1999; Leahey, 1991).

Aristotle, in particular, wrote about how the *psyche* is an essential component or element of life. These early Greek philosophers[1] and later contributions helped pave the way for psychology to begin studying the mind and especially brought about the ideas of introspection and nativism (Hergenhahn, 2009). Those two concepts will be explained later, but first, let us start with the definition of psychology as "the systematic, scientific study of behaviors and mental processes" (Plotnik, 1999, p.4). Let us break down that definition in this way: First, psychology involves systematic observations and methodology, like the steps followed by all scientists. Psychologists use the steps of the scientific method to develop and carry out their research. Psychology focuses on observable actions and behaviors. In addition, psychology is concerned with the mind, including thoughts, memories, and perceptions, which are often not directly observable. Furthermore, psychology focuses on the physiological or biological processes accompanying behavior and the mind.

Most psychologists study psychology from all these perspectives, especially in today's technologically and scientifically advanced times. Psychologists who conduct research also differentiate between research that is either *basic* or *applied*. **Basic research** occurs when psychologists primarily conduct research in academic, hospital, or similar research settings (Stanovich, 2007). Just because psychological researchers collect data and run experiments on *human* participants rather than animals or other living organisms does not make it less of a science. These researchers rely on scientific rigor and use analytical thinking and deductive reasoning to form conclusions (Mill, 1843). Their primary goal is to test preexisting theories, develop new approaches, and increase a particular knowledge base.

This type of research is often referred to as *shelf research* because the result is often a published journal article or book placed on a real or virtual library shelf. For example, a psychologist may conduct basic research on the strategy of self-handicapping in college students. Self-handicapping occurs when an individual creates an obstacle that may interfere with their upcoming performance to alleviate a threat to self-esteem (Arkin & Baumgardner, 1985; Berglas & Jones, 1978). The researcher (in this case, me conducting my dissertation research; see Mello-Goldner & Wurf, 1997) may design a study examining whether students are more likely to self-handicap alone (a self-protective motive) or when with others (a self-presentational motive). Psychologists, in this case, conduct this type of research not necessarily to develop strategies to decrease self-handicapping or help those who engage in self-handicapping but to increase the understanding of self-handicapping and its motivating forces.

Applied research occurs when psychologists use psychological principles and theories to solve practical problems in other fields and explain and treat people's behavior (Stanovich, 2007). These psychologists are often licensed therapists who treat people with psychological disorders but sometimes conduct research in medicine, law, sports, or education. Harvard University psychologist **Hugo Münsterberg** began the area of applied research in psychology in the early 1900s. Münsterberg's earlier research involved sensation and perception, but his later work was influential in law and forensic psychology. In his book *On the Witness Stand* (1908), Münsterberg combined experimental research and detective work skills to provide an early glimpse of how these seemingly different disciplines are similar. In 1910 Münsterberg's influence likely impacted the often-forgotten early detective fiction book by Balmer and MacHarg, *The Achievements of Luther Trant* (1910). This collection of short stories included what was likely the first fictional use of a lie detector test as well as the steps of the scientific method as a means to solving crimes (Krasner, 1983).

Luther Trant is an earlier male version of Jacqueline Winspear's (2003) **Maisie Dobbs**, psychologist and detective. Someone conducting more current-day applied research may ask members of a college sports team to track their goals, thoughts, and behaviors throughout a season to discover which factors helped enhance performance. This research would use that information to help change behavior in the future and would likely help them win more games or improve their performances. The goal of an applied researcher is to use research skills and data to solve an everyday problem.

Psychological research involves aspects of basic and applied research, both necessitating the **scientific method**. Scientific research is a type of research used to answer a question or solve a problem. Researchers use the scientific method when they: formulate a theory or develop a set or list of questions; form a **hypothesis**, an educated guess at what will happen at the end of the study; design a study; collect data; analyze the data; and make conclusions and develop new theories (Kalat, 1999; Plotnik, 1999). Does a detective do this? Absolutely! The skills of a detective mimic or parallel those of a good researcher. Both must gather large amounts of data and guess how things fit together. Detectives constantly shift through the evidence to find what is most relevant to their case. They often form a hypothesis about a suspect, which may or may not be correct when they first enter the crime scene, and then go on to collect what is necessary to support their hypothesis.

Investigative thinking challenge:
What skills do you need to be a good or effective psychologist?

Scientists must decide between several research designs before conducting their research. One method is a descriptive study or **case study** of one person or, at times, one group or event. The goal of a case study is to describe the behavior of the individual or group in as much detail as possible without looking at any relationships or comparisons. Case studies are often conducted over time with information gathered from several different sources, such as tests, interviews, or observations (Lewandowski et al., 2023). Sigmund Freud used case studies of his clients to form much of his theories. While this method is good for describing unusual things, it lacks control, objectivity, and generalization. However, when thinking about detective fiction, each mystery unfolds as a multifaceted case study. The investigator's methodology is similar to the meticulous approach of academic research. They create a detailed descriptive study of the crime (the one event) and each suspect (the person or persons involved) in order to solve the crime (diagnosis), just as Freud detailed his clients' symptoms with the goal of a diagnosis.

However, a description may not be enough for either researchers or investigators. **Correlational studies** examine the relationship between two variables or factors that happen simultaneously. Researchers examine two variables that usually happen naturally to see how they are related. In a correlational study, the researcher does not manipulate the things studied. One example is the relationship between playing violent video games and aggressive behavior. To conduct a correlational study with these two variables, a researcher might recruit a group of participants and ask them how often they usually play certain video games in a week, along with having them answer a survey measuring aggression. There is no direct manipulation by the researcher in this design. Instead, they ask participants to self-report specific behaviors or attitudes. The researcher then plots each participant's score on both variables to discover the positive, negative, or no relationship (Lewandowski et al., 2023). This method allows researchers to identify the relationship more precisely but still lacks control and is open to influence from other unintended variables **(the third-variable problem)**.

A third research design is an **experimental design**, which directly allows researchers to form conclusions about the effect of some factor on some aspect of behavior (Lewandowski et al., 2023). An experiment has two variables, the **independent variable** (the cause) is the variable manipulated by the researcher. Often, the independent variable involves two groups, one or more levels that receive treatment (**the experimental group**) and a second which does not receive the treatment or level of the independent variable (**the control group**). The researcher measures the **dependent variable** (the effect). Research participants should be randomly placed into either the experimental or control group through some method that ensures they have an equal chance of being in either group. If only these two groups existed, flipping a coin could work, with heads going to the experimental group and tails to the control group. If you are working with more than two groups, other methods, such as rolling dice or using a random number table, can be used. This **random assignment** (Lewandowski et al., 2023) helps avoid bias within the research study.

An example of an experimental design would occur when a researcher might be interested in the effects of three feedback conditions (success, failure, or no feedback) on a participant's feelings and performance on a simple task. In this example, the independent variable is the feedback (success, failure, or no performance feedback after several trial problems). The success and failure feedback groups are the experimental groups. The no feedback group is the control group. The dependent variables include feelings (measured by a self-esteem or affect survey) and performance (the number of questions correct on a final, actual trial of problems). If there is a significant difference in performance and feelings between the two groups, then the feedback did impact the participant's behavior.

In Eliot Pattison's *The Skull Mantra* (1999), the author illustrates how detectives employ a mindset deeply rooted in the cause-and-effect language of experimental design. This is exemplified by the protagonist, Detective Shan, who embraces skepticism, refusing to have blind faith in anything. To him, every aspect of an investigation is treated as suspect, constantly evolving from mere allegations to established facts, connecting causes to effects, and yet always leading to new questions or areas for research. By adopting this approach, Shan demonstrates how a successful investigator relies on logical reasoning and the scientific method to unravel complex mysteries. Chapter 6 will discuss this book again in more detail related to its cultural implications; however, early in the book, the detective, Shan, states that:

> The exceptional investigator could have no faith. Everything was suspect, everything transitory, moving from allegation to fact to cause to effect to new mystery [*The Skull Mantra*, Pattison, 1999, p. 14].

Psychologists, scientists, and researchers using these various methods possess many skills, often similar to those needed by individuals in other professions, such as detectives. Individuals should be objective and free of bias when making quantifiable and objective observations. This objectivity should extend to the process of assigning individuals to groups, such as experimental and control groups, where fairness and unbiased judgment are essential. These investigative researchers need to be able to repeat and confirm any findings or conclusions. They need to be willing to look for errors in their thinking and be willing to self-correct, ready to change faulty ideas and theories if they are incorrect. Finally, they should use controls in their actions to be sure that their conclusions accurately reflect how individuals operate. For this to occur, researchers (and detectives) might need to eliminate the other possibilities and variables to uncover the truth and safeguard against biased interpretations (Bartol & Bartol, 2018).

Investigative thinking challenge:
Thinking about the attributes of a proficient investigator, what qualities would you include in your list?

You likely mentioned some of the skills and characteristics listed below. Detectives need to be effective or "good" at the following skills and characteristics:

- observational skills
- collecting information
- analytical thinking and problem-solving skills
- ability to tell when someone is lying or not providing information
- communication skills (both written and oral communication are essential)
- listening skills (especially active listening skills)
- flexibility and open-mindedness in their thinking
- skepticism

Compare this list with the scientific method's steps. You will see much overlap and a symbiotic relationship, reinforcing the importance of objectivity, observation, confirmation, and control in both disciplines. A good detective is a good psychologist who uses the scientific method, deductive reasoning like Sherlock Holmes, and their little grey cells—like Agatha Christie's famous detective Hercule Poirot—to crack a case and solve a crime. A good psychologist uses effective observational and communication skills to work with clients to relieve stress and anxiety or talk through issues. Agatha Christie's Miss Marple is an excellent listener, gathering many clues from random bits of conversations and drawing parallels to her village experiences. Even Victorian literature, such as Charlotte Brontë's classic novel *Jane Eyre*, contains psychological and detective skills. Jane uses her observational skills and curiosity to discover the truth behind Thornfield and Mrs. Rochester's hidden mystery, although she is not entirely successful (Jung, 2007).

A good detective or psychologist should be skeptical of information until they are confirmed. Many behaviors and products, at first considered positive or effective, were revealed to be ineffective after further study (Lewandowski et al., 2023). Detectives and police should refrain from tunnel vision that restricts their lists of suspects, which may be incorrect in the end. In addition, detectives and psychologists think rationally and logically when trying to understand behaviors and uncover the truth. Psychologists and detectives use logic like the early Greek philosophers, especially the logical argument called a **syllogism,** defined by Aristotle. In a syllogism, you are presented with two truths and are asked to form a conclusion based on them (*Stanford Encyclopedia of Philosophy*, 2017). A philosopher (or anyone interested in logic) might provide individuals with the following statements that are part of Aristotle's most famous syllogism example.

"If it is TRUE that all men are mortal
and,

1. The Psychologist as Detective

it is TRUE that Aristotle is a man,
therefore?"

The correct logical answer is that *Aristotle is mortal*. The logic used in a syllogism mimics the cause-and-effect decision-making a detective uses when investigating a crime. An early detective fiction series, the Doctor Thorndyke series by R. Austin Freeman (Freeman, 1907/2004), directly links the use of syllogisms and logic by detectives.

> "But the kind of syllogism that they do make is this—
> 'The crime was committed by the person who made this finger-print.
> But John Smith is the person who made the finger-print.
> Therefore, the crime was committed by John Smith.'"
> "Well, that is a perfectly good syllogism, isn't it?" I asked.

This classic example (Thorndyke speaking with Jervis in *The Red Thumb Mark*, Freeman, 1907/2004, Chapter 8) demonstrates logical deductive reasoning—when you arrive at a conclusion based on general principles, a type of thinking made famous by Sherlock Holmes but also exhibited several years earlier in the short stories featuring the detective C. Auguste Dupin by Edgar Allan Poe.[2] Many early **Gothic novels**[3] also explored psychological issues such as mental illness, and much of the "horror" or suspense revolves around the main character essentially solving an ambiguous event (Mogen et al., 1992).

Sherlock Holmes perfected the idea of deductive or logical reasoning and used the scientific method. Holmes understands and frames the problem; he is an expert observer, seeing things at the crime scene that most others would miss; he forms a hypothesis, often using his imagination; he tests and retests his hypothesis; he forms connections and eliminates everything that cannot be true; and forms a theory. Holmes best explains this himself when he explains his process of deduction:

> That process ... starts upon the supposition that when you have eliminated all which is impossible, then whatever remains, however improbable, must be the truth ["The Adventure of The Blanched Soldier," contained in *The Case Book of Sherlock Holmes*, Conan Doyle, 1926/1980, p. 60].

Sherlock Holmes uses deductive and analytical thinking and displays much **mindfulness**, an idea that Harvard social psychologist Ellen Langer developed. Langer (1989) defined mindfulness as active observing and awareness, not just passive seeing. For example, think about the room where you might be taking this class or the location of your office or workspace at your place of employment.

Investigative thinking challenge:
How many steps and stairs do you have to take
or climb to get to the classroom or your office/workspace?

You probably take those steps several times a week, if not more, but do not actively observe the number of stairs or steps it takes you to get to your destination—"you see but do not observe." Mindful people are also constantly trying to gather as much information as possible and learn from multiple perspectives. Mindfulness helps them approach the problem from multiple perspectives and helps them develop the solution. Mindfulness is difficult to do in our multitasking world of the 21st century. However, even in the times of Sherlock Holmes, it was much easier to "see" things rather than truly observe them—which is what Watson does all the time and is more related to what Langer referred to as **mindlessness** (Langer, 1989). Mindlessness leads individuals to use preexisting mindsets as deductive methods, a kind of "focusing on the obvious," which prevents the exploration or use of alternative solutions.

Mindfulness is needed to unravel the clues and suspects of a crime or the steps of the scientific method.[4] Holmes' deductive thinking goes beyond purely logical thinking to include mindfulness. It also relates to the first two approaches to psychology covered in the next chapter. As Smith and Davis (1997) explain in their research textbook, psychological researchers follow the same steps. According to Smith and Davis, psychologists eliminate their "suspects" when conducting research by controlling extraneous or **confounding variables**, collecting their "evidence" via their data, and presenting their findings to a "jury" of their peers during the presentation and publication process. In some types of research, like experiments, confounding variables, sometimes called nuisance variables, are other factors that, if left uncontrolled, could influence the treatment conditions. They confuse the results like additional suspects or clues confuse a detective and delay a mystery's solution. As Sherlock Holmes states,

> Detection is, or ought to be, an exact science and should be treated in the same cold and unemotional manner. You have attempted to tinge it with romanticism, which produces much the same effect as if you worked a love-story or an elopement into the fifth proposition of Euclid.... Some facts should be suppressed, or at least a just sense of proportion should be observed in treating them. The only point in the case which deserved mention was the curious analytical reasoning from effects to causes, by which I succeeded in unraveling it [Sherlock Holmes in *The Sign of the Four*, Conan Doyle, 1890/1984, p. 714].

Likewise, Agatha Christie's most famous detective, Hercule Poirot, knows this very well himself and understands that he must act like a scientist or researcher to uncover the truth. He equates his deductive thinking to an archaeologist's work, like Christie's second husband, Max Mallowan, during an excavation. In *Death of the Nile* (Christie, 1937/1981), Poirot explains that detective work is like the work of an archaeologist during an excavation. Both individuals must dig deep to find something of interest (a fossil or a clue). Then, they must clear the extraneous matter from it to reveal it more clearly. In the work of an archaeologist, this reveals the fossil. Hopefully, the detective will discover the truth by clearing away unnecessary information in the case of a clue.

> You take away the loose earth, and you scrape here and there with a knife until finally your object is there.... That is what I have been seeking to do—clear away the extraneous matter so that we can see the truth—the naked shining truth [Hercule Poirot in *Death on the Nile*, Christie, 1937/1982, Chapter 27, p. 254].

Forming logical conclusions based on clear facts is a strategy also used earlier by Doctor Thorndyke in *The Red Thumb Mark* (Freeman, 1907/2004). Thorndyke and his assistant Jervis, are attempting to clear the suspect accused of theft based on the appearance of a bloody fingerprint. Thorndyke clarifies the importance of drawing conclusions from facts.

> "Impossible!" he exclaimed, with mock sternness. "Nobody but an utter fool arrives at a conclusion without data."
> "Then I must revise my definition instantly," I rejoined. "Let us say that a guess is a conclusion drawn from insufficient facts."
> "That is better," said he; "but perhaps it would be better still to say that a guess is a particular and definite conclusion deduced from facts which properly yield only a general and indefinite one. Let us take an instance," he continued. "Looking out of the window, I see a man walking round Paper Buildings. Now suppose I say, after the fashion of the inspired detective of the romances, 'That man is a stationmaster or inspector,' that would be a guess." The observed facts do not yield the conclusion, though they do warrant a conclusion less definite and more general [Thorndyke speaking to Jervis in *The Red Thumb Mark*, Freeman, 1907/2004, Chapter 10].

One final example comes from detective Roderick Alleyn, created by another of the Golden Age mystery writers, Ngaio Marsh. In *A Man Lay Dead* (Marsh, 1934), Alleyn slowly unravels the clues and puts together the evidence like a scientist collecting and analyzing data. He declares to two of the potential suspects that what he is doing is not guesswork, but he is looking for actual connections and making a note of any probabilities:

> I do not imagine; detectives aren't allowed to imagine. They note probabilities.... I'm not going to give all my tricks away, and this is such a very simple one that you ought to have seen it yourselves [*A Man Lay Dead*, Marsh, 1934/2011, pp. 117–118].

Several of the most famous fictional detectives recognize that their skills are similar to those of scientists and researchers. They form a hypothesis and collect data. They then work to analyze the data and form connections between their data or information to test their hypothesis. As readers, we should also be able to connect that the skills of these two professions, detective and psychologist, clearly overlap.

Mini-Mystery

Test your detective skills and logical thinking by solving this short mini-mystery (the solution appears in this chapter's *Notes* section[5]).

Theft at the Hess Gallery

Detective Virginia (Ginny) Henry slowed down her cruiser as she approached the Pine Manor College campus guard booth. She showed her identification to the guard, who waved her on and pointed out the correct parking lot. Henry received a call to investigate the disappearance of an Andy Warhol sketch from a locked display case in the Hess Gallery, the art gallery located within the College's Annenberg Library. After parking her cruiser in the parking lot in front of the administration building, Henry crossed the roadway and pushed through the revolving doors.

"Who is in charge here?" Henry asked a small group of uniformed security staff and library staff.

"I am," replied one of the uniformed security staff. "Captain Otto Bowie, Director of Campus Safety. This is Hazel Woolf, the Director of the Library."

"Well, I would say it's nice to meet you both, but seeing I'm here to investigate a theft of some valuable art, I'm not sure that's the right thing to say. Can someone fill me in on what happened?" replied Detective Henry.

Hazel Woolf stepped forward. "Sure, I can tell you what I know. When the morning librarian arrived, she did a quick walk-through of the library to make sure everything was in order. Her name is Emma Dane. Emma, like all the librarians, has a key to unlock the front doors of the library. At first, things seemed normal, but when she went up to the third floor, where the Hess Art Gallery is located, she noticed something was very wrong. The gallery currently contains an exhibit by local artists and our college students on the walls. There are a couple of display cases with more valuable pieces of art that have been donated to the gallery through the years. One case contained an original signed Andy Warhol sketch that would probably be worth at least ten thousand dollars. Emma said she walked by the case the first time and didn't notice anything, but when she walked back on the way downstairs, she noticed the sketch was gone. That was about 8:20 a.m. this morning, and she called me right away, and then I called Otto to help out."

"I called the on-call safety officer, Harry Ellsworth. He came over right away and secured the scene before Hazel and I arrived. The gallery and library are closed to the students and the public, so no one besides the librarians and campus safety has been in here today," answered Bowie.

As Detective Henry listened, she wrote down the details in her notebook. "Okay, before I go check out the gallery, can you tell me who was here last night and today?"

Hazel looked down to review her paper outlining the library's scheduling for the week. "I was here until 5 p.m., and then we have two evening librarians. Emma was one of them, and she was here starting around 2:00 p.m., but because the weather was getting a bit snowy, she left before closing at 8:00 p.m. because she has a long drive home. That left the other evening librarian, Helen Abercrombie, and our work-study student, Carl Ferry. Helen did a walk-through last night and didn't notice anything missing. She and Carl left when the library closed at 10:00 p.m."

"Did anyone come into the library or have access to it between 10:00 last night and 8:00 this morning?" asked Henry.

"Campus safety is supposed to do rounds every couple of hours, and they have to specifically walk into the library and check out the basement for opossums and the second floor for flooding," answered Bowie.

"Wait, what was that? You have opossums in the library and floods!"

"It's a long story, but when it gets cold out, we have an opossum who likes to sneak into the basement through a hole in a window to get warm. Last year she had seven babies, which we had to relocate, so we'd rather not have to deal with that again. And when it's really cold like last night, the heat doesn't work so well, and the old pipes can freeze and burst. They caused some flooding on the library's second floor and damaged the carpeting earlier this winter, although it's not near the Hess Gallery. We ask campus safety to walk through a few times each night to be sure another plague hasn't hit us," answered Hazel.

Henry scratched her head a bit and replied, "Okay, I guess that makes sense. Are all the librarians and safety officers here right now?"

Hazel and Captain Bowie answered together, "Yes."

"Let me check out the gallery first, and then I'd like to interview everyone," said Henry as she started walking further into the library towards the elevator doors.

Detective Henry, Hazel Woolf, and Captain Bowie entered the elevator. Hazel pushed the number 3 on the panel, and they headed up to the library's third floor. When the doors opened, Henry noticed a sign that directed people to go either left to the reference stacks and library study rooms or right to the Hess gallery. They turned right, walked down a narrow hallway, and entered a loft area which housed the Hess Gallery. Henry noticed several oil paintings and photographs on the three walls of girls and women, plus a few sculptures on some pedestals.

"The exhibit is all from female artists and is a tribute to feminism, gender equity, and when this college was an all-women's college," answered Hazel as she noticed Henry eyeing the artwork. As they all moved to a corner near the two display cases, Hazel continued, "That's where the more valuable permanent art is kept. We don't have much, but the case on the left contains a few silver cups from the late 1800s, a small sculpture called *Elegant* by the artist Beverly Benson Seamans, and a sculpture called *Primavera* by Dimitri Hadzi. Each one is probably worth only a few thousand dollars each. The case on the right contained the framed Andy Warhol sketch."

Henry walked over and looked over the empty glass case. The case looked unbroken, and there was a keyhole on the right-hand side of the front panel. "Who has a key to this case?"

"There is a key on a ring that is kept in a desk in the break room," answered Hazel.

"Who has access to that desk?"

"Well, anyone really who knew it was in that desk. The desk isn't locked. The ring has about 30–40 keys for different locks throughout the library. It's the only set we have, although I think the grounds and maintenance folks might have some spares," replied Hazel.

Henry looked around the case for any trace evidence but didn't see anything obvious. "Have the CSI techs been here yet?"

"Yes, they just finished up before you got here and didn't find any fingerprints or anything else," said Bowie.

They all returned to the elevator and returned to the first floor, entering the break room behind the circulation. Several people were in the room, Emma Dane, Helen Abercrombie, Carl Ferry, and Harry Ellsworth. Detective Henry sat in one of the chairs and asked, "I'd like to hear what you all remember from last night and this morning."

"I'll start, I guess," said Emma. "First, I'd like to say I've only just started working here since the first week in January. I moved to Boston from Indiana to start the Master in Library Science program at Simmons College. I knew about the artwork but didn't even know the drawing was by Andy Warhol. It was a normal day yesterday, I got here around 2:00 yesterday and was scheduled to be here until 10:00, but I asked Helen if she wouldn't mind staying to close because it was already snowing and my drive home takes about an hour. Helen takes the T home, so she said that was okay. This morning the roads were fine, and I got here around 8:00 and did my walk-through. I walked past the case the first time without noticing anything, but when I was heading back to the elevator, I guess something made me look again at the case, and I saw it was empty. I've never unlocked the case before, but I wasn't sure what happened since nothing was broken. I called Helen when I got back downstairs around 8:15 and asked if she had taken something out of the case. When she said no, I knew something was wrong, so I called Director Woolf right away."

Helen Abercrombie went next. "That's pretty much what I remember. Emma asked if we could switch closing nights which was fine with me. At 9:30 last night, I started walking around to see if anyone was around. No students were up on the second floor since it was Thursday night, and they were likely out having fun. I remember walking into the Hess Gallery, and everything was where it should be; the sketch was definitely in the case because I remember thinking the cases needed to be cleaned soon because they were looking dusty. When I came downstairs, Carl was coming in from smoking a cigarette outside, and since no students were in the library at all, we decided to close at 9:45, so we could catch the shuttle bus to the T station. This morning Emma woke me up a little after 8:00, asking if I had moved the sketch, which I said I didn't. I figured something was wrong, so I decided to come in right away even though my shift doesn't start until this afternoon."

Carl Ferry was next to give his version. "I came to the library at 6:00 right after eating dinner and was scheduled until closing time. I sat at the circulation desk and checked out some books for a few students. But because of the snow and because Thursdays are usually big party nights since most students don't have class on Fridays, there were no people in the library at all after maybe 8:00 p.m. When Helen said she would walk around to check on things at 9:30, I asked if I could grab a quick smoke outside. I went into the smoking booth across the road because this side of the road is a no-smoking zone. I can still see the library's front door from the smoking area, and no one went in while I was sitting there, but I did see someone walking around the back of the library near the art building right before I went inside. It was a bit smoky in the booth, so I couldn't tell who it was, but it looked like they were tall and had a dark ski jacket and hat on."

Detective Henry looked interested in that last bit of information. "Is there a back entrance to the library?"

Hazel answered, "There is a back door in the basement that leads out to the parking lot behind the building, but no one can get in the library through that door since it's always locked. The key is on the same ring as the key to the locked art case."

Henry took a deep breath and looked through all her notes. "Could I see where the keyring is kept and what the keys look like?" Emma was sitting closest to the desk, so she opened the desk drawer and pulled out the key ring. The ring did have about 30 or so rings of slightly different sizes and colors. "This is the key that unlocks the cabinet door, and this one is for the basement door," she said, pointing to a small silver key for the case key and a larger bronze key with a green cover for the back door.

Harry Ellsworth was the last person to give his version of what happened. "I was working a double shift, so I started at 8:30 p.m. and would have gone home this morning at 8:30 a.m. Last night I walked through the library around midnight, 3 a.m., and 6 a.m. and didn't notice anything out of place, and no opossums or burst pipes. I walked into the Hess Gallery at least one of those times, but I can't say I noticed if the sketch was in the case or not. I was in the front booth talking to John Cooke, who was opening the gate for drivers entering the campus. We saw Emma drive in a bit before 8:00 a.m. and saw her unlock the library and go in. She called the front booth sometime between 8:15 and 8:30, and I headed over to see what was going on. After we figured out the art was stolen, I called Captain Bowie and made sure we locked the library doors, and Emma put up a sign saying the library was temporarily closed."

Detective Henry took one more look down at her notebook, and then a small smile started to spread across her face. "You know, I think I just might have figured out who took that artwork and where it might be. One of you has definitely lied to me, and I think I know exactly what happened!"

Whodunit? Can you solve the mystery?
Who does Detective Henry know is lying and is the thief?

Maisie Dobbs, Psychologist and Detective

Among the many fictional detectives tracing their origin back to the 1800s, Jacqueline Winspear's character **Maisie Dobbs** makes the best connection between a psychologist and an investigator's skills. In her debut novel, *Maisie Dobbs* (Winspear, 2003), we learn that Maisie was trained by her mentor Maurice Blanche as what could be described today as a forensic psychologist and opened up her own detective agency in 1929 London. Maisie is successful because she uses her relationship and empathic skills to collect data or clues to solve her cases. A good therapist displays trust, empathy, warmth, and genuineness. Likewise, a good researcher displays a good knowledge base and is open-minded, diligent, focused, hard-working, resourceful, inventive, precise, and honest.

Maisie Dobbs exhibits these skills as she investigates a series of mysterious deaths and happenings at a retreat for World War I veterans. In *What Would Maisie Do? Inspiration from the Pages of Maisie Dobbs* (2019), Jacqueline Winspear states that she wanted Maisie to have the qualities of persistence, resilience, empathy, kindness, perspective, and confidence and that she should keep her values and learn from her mistakes. Her qualities match those of an effective psychologist and detective or investigator.

In her debut novel, Maisie can empathize with those involved due to her traumatic experiences as a field nurse during World War I. She uses her psychological training to understand the motivation behind those who were guilty. Maisie systematically gathers evidence and observes suspects' behaviors across several settings with the help of her assistant, Billy Beale. Maisie and Billy follow the steps of the scientific method in their approach to solving a case. They generate questions after gathering some background information, form a hypothesis about a suspect or suspects; formulate a plan of action; and collect data or evidence as they follow through with that plan. Finally, they put the pieces of information or evidence together, often reflecting on their case map, visually displaying their data and the links between them.

Maisie is concerned with not only behaviors but also with the thoughts and memories that may influence behavior. Maisie states in *Maisie Dobbs* (Winspear, 2003, p. 28) that she is concerned that the memories of World War I are still affecting the soldiers and others who experienced significant trauma during the battles. With her background in psychology, Maisie understands that people's thoughts and memories can have long-lasting effects on behavior, a concept discussed in more detail in Chapter 5.

Maisie can often mimic the verbal and nonverbal behavior of the suspects and witnesses she interacts with, a perfect example of her excellent observational, communication, problem-solving, and listening skills (this is also an example of the psychological concept of self-monitoring, discussed in Chapter 5). These are all skills that are essential for an effective therapist and psychologist. Maisie also understands the importance of her self-development, and with each case ending, she revisits significant people and locations. During her apprenticeship with her mentor and friend, Maurice Blanche, Maisie learns psychological and biological skills to help her in her career. She also knows about organization and rituals when collecting clues during an investigation and wrapping up the case.

Maurice taught Maisie to end each case by reviewing and revisiting the places and people that helped her on her detective journey. He felt this would allow her to put the old case behind her and focus her mental and physical energy on whatever came next (Winspear, 2003, p. 286). Good organization and establishing effective rituals are necessary steps in the scientific method. These examples illustrate how the character of Maisie Dobbs balances and personifies the characteristics of both psychologist and detective. Throughout this book, you will see additional examples of how other detectives demonstrate these same or similar skills, beginning with the detectives of the Victorian Era.

Suggested detective fiction/literature to accompany this chapter:
- Ann Radcliffe's Gothic novel *The Mysteries of Udolpho*
- Jane Austen's novel *Northanger Abbey*
- Daphne du Maurier's novel *Rebecca*
- Edgar Allan Poe's short story "The Murders in the Rue Morgue"
- Charlotte Brontë's novel *Jane Eyre*
- Sir Arthur Conan Doyle's Sherlock Holmes short story "A Scandal in Bohemia"
- Jacqueline Winspear's *Maisie Dobbs* series

End-of-Chapter Mind Puzzlers:
1. Thinking as a researcher or scientist, explain the concept of validity and reliability in the context of real-world applications. Discuss which you believe is more important in psychological research, providing reasoning for your answer. Do validity and reliability always occur together, or can each exist independently of the other? Illustrate situations (either in research or the real world) where both concepts coexist and instances where only one is present.
2. Test out your students' (or your book group's) detective skills by presenting them with one to five photos of different scenes for 30 seconds each. At least one photo should include one person or several people. Once the photos are no longer visible, test their observational skills by asking a series of questions about specific details in each photo. Provide the answers and then discuss why some participants may have performed better in observing details than others and if this differed by photo.
3. Explore the use of the scientific method and deductive reasoning in a Gothic novel, such as *The Mysteries of Udolpho* or *Northanger Abbey*. Provide at least one example (with page numbers) of how a character engages in basic research or applied psychology, and illustrate the connection.

4. What type of psychological skills (those associated with a good therapist or good researcher) does Dupin use in "The Murders in the Rue Morgue" by Edgar Allan Poe, or does Sherlock Holmes use in "A Scandal in Bohemia" by Sir Arthur Conan Doyle? Quote several examples that demonstrate these skills. Do the detectives Dupin or Holmes use any of the steps associated with the scientific method as they discover the identity of the murderer?
5. Think of a topic you are interested in studying. How might you study it from the case study, correlational, and experimental design approaches? Be sure to identify your variables and any groups involved. How would you recruit participants for your study?
6. Demonstrate how either Dupin or Holmes utilizes the logical thinking involved in Aristotle's classic syllogism. Create your own syllogism and share it with a partner, asking them to solve it.
7. Evaluate Maisie Dobbs' characteristics as both a detective and a psychologist. Assess whether she qualifies as an effective detective and psychologist. Identify at least two psychological concepts or techniques she employs throughout the novel or selected chapters, providing relevant examples with page numbers.
8. How does gender influence Maisie Dobbs' thoughts and behaviors? Do you think the author attempts to make an overall statement regarding gender and society?
9. Does Maisie use logical or deductive thinking? Provide at least two examples with page numbers. Explore how Maisie or Billy use mindfulness in their work, providing examples with page numbers. Additionally, assess if either of them engages in any mindlessness and include an example.
10. Demonstrate your detective and creative writing skills by writing your own short mini-mystery. The mini-mystery should be between 2,000 and 3,000 words and include at least five characters, one of whom acts as the detective or investigator.

Key Terms and People (*Introduction* and *Chapter 1*):
- **paradigm**: a broad framework or sets of standards that shape how we approach and understand certain concepts or phenomena
- **validity**: the accuracy of psychological results or measures
- **reliability**: the consistency of psychological results or measures
- **Aristotle**: the Greek philosopher who wrote about how the *psyche* is an essential component or element of life; developed the syllogism

- **psychology**: the systematic and scientific study of behavior and the mind
- **basic research**: research that is conducted in academic, hospital, or other similar research settings, aimed at testing preexisting theories, developing new ones, or increasing a particular knowledge base
- **applied research**: research that is undertaken to solve practical problems or to explain and treat people's behavior
- **Hugo Münsterberg**: a prominent Harvard University psychologist considered the father of applied psychology; with significant contributions to the field of law and forensic psychology, he authored the influential book *On the Witness Stand* in 1908
- **Maisie Dobbs**: a series of detective fiction novels by British author Jacqueline Winspear featuring the protagonist Maisie Dobbs, who is both a psychologist and a detective
- **scientific method**: the steps used by a researcher to conduct a study, collect data, and form a conclusion
- **hypothesis**: an educated guess formulated by the researcher prior to collecting data
- **case study**: a descriptive study of one person or, at times, one group or event
- **correlational study**: a type of research design that examines the relationship between two variables or factors that happen simultaneously
- **third-variable problem**: an unintended variable that might influence the relationship in a correlational study
- **experimental design**: a type of research design that directly manipulates one variable in order to determine its effect on a second variable; allows for cause and effect
- **independent variable**: the variable that is manipulated in an experiment
- **experimental group**: the group in an experiment that does receive the treatment
- **control group**: the group in an experiment that does not receive the treatment, used to compare the effects of the independent variable
- **dependent variable**: the variable that is measured in an experiment

- **random assignment**: when participants are randomly placed into either the experimental or control group (or other groups) through some method that ensures they have an equal chance of being in any group
- **syllogism**: a logical argument, as defined by Aristotle, in which a conclusion is drawn from two given true statements
- **Gothic novels**: an early genre of fiction popular in the 18th century characterized by suspense and horror, often featuring main characters (primarily women) trapped in oppressive situations, such as being confined in a castle
- **mindfulness**: a concept introduced by psychologist Ellen Langer (1989) referring to the active process of observing and being aware, in contrast to passive seeing, reminiscent of how Sherlock Holmes approaches solving cases
- **mindlessness**: also defined by Langer (1989), this refers to the act of merely seeing things without true observation, relying on preexisting mindsets and focusing on the obvious, similar to Watson's approach in solving cases
- **confounding variables**: sometimes called nuisance variables, they are other factors that, if left uncontrolled, could influence the treatment conditions and a study's results

Chapter Notes

1. For a good summary of the Greek philosophers, see *Introduction to Philosophy: Classical and Contemporary Readings* (8th edition) by Perry, Bratman, and Fischer (2018, Oxford University Press); or *The Norton Introduction to Philosophy* (2nd Edition) by Rosen, Byrne, and Cohen (2016, W.W. Norton & Company).

2. Auguste Dupin appears in three short stories by Edgar Allan Poe, "The Murders in the Rue Morgue," often called the first detective fiction story; "The Mystery of Marie Roget"; and "The Purloined Letter."

3. Horace Walpole is often credited with writing the first Gothic novel, *The Castle of Otranto*, in 1764. Ann Radcliffe was the author who popularized Gothic novels with stories featuring heroines often set within castles, such as *The Mysteries of Udolpho*, which is likewise mentioned in Jane Austen's *Northanger Abbey*. More modern examples of Gothic novels include most stories by Stephen King (Mogen et al., 1992).

4. To read more about how Sherlock Holmes used mindfulness and to develop techniques to use them yourself, see Maria Konnikova's book, *Mastermind: How to Think Like Sherlock Holmes* (2013, Viking Press).

5. The thief is Emma Dane. Emma claimed that she never opened the art case before, but she showed Detective Henry the correct key right away, as well as the key to the basement door. When she arrived that morning, instead of checking things around the library, she quickly grabbed the keyring, unlocked the case, and took out the Andy Warhol print. Emma ran down to the basement with it and went out to her car to hide it under the panel in her trunk, using the key to let herself back into the library through the locked basement door. If Detective Henry goes outside to Emma's car, she will find the stolen artwork!

6. The book's in-text citations and end-of-chapter references use APA-style formatting.

Preface and Chapter 1 References[6]

Arkin, R.M., & Baumgardner, A.H. (1985). Self-handicapping. In J.H. Harvey & G. Weary (Eds.) *Attribution: Basic Issues and Applications*. Academic Press.

Balmer, E., & MacHarg, W. (1910). *The Achievements of Luther Trant*. Small, Maynard & Co.

Bartol, C.R., & Bartol, A.M. (2018). *Introduction to Forensic Psychology: Research and Application (5th Ed.)*. Sage Publications.

Berglas, S., & Jones, E.E. (1978). Drug choice as a self-handicapping strategy in response to noncontingent success. *Journal of Personality and Social Psychology, 36*, 405–417.

Christie, A. (1937/1981). *Death on the Nile*. Bantam Books.

Conan Doyle, A. (1980, 23rd printing). *The Case Book of Sherlock Holmes*. Berkley Books.

Conan Doyle, A. (1890/1984). *The Illustrated Sherlock Holmes Treasury: Revised and Expanded*. Avenel Books.

Danziger, K. (1990). *Constructing the Subject: Historical Origins of Psychological Research*. Cambridge University Press.

Freeman, R.A. (1907/2004). *The Red Thumb Mark*. D.W. Newton.

Hergenhahn, B.R. (2009). *An Introduction to the History of Psychology (6th Edition)*. Wadsworth.

Jung, S. (2007). Charlotte Bronte's Jane Eyre, the female detective and the "crime" of female selfhood. *Bronte Studies, 32*, 21–30. https://doi.org/10.1179/147489307x157897

Kalat, J.W. (1999). *Introduction to Psychology* (5th Edition). Brooks/Cole, Wadsworth.

Keppel, G. (1982). *Design and Analysis: A Researcher's Handbook* (2nd Edition). Prentice-Hall.

Krasner, L. (1983). The psychology of mystery. *American Psychologist, 38*(5), 578–582. https://doi.org/10.1037/0003-066X.38.5.578

Langer, E. (1989). *Mindfulness*. Addison-Wesley.

Leahey, T.H. (1991). *A History of Modern Psychology*. Prentice Hall.

Lewandowski, G.W., Ciarocco, N.J., & Strohmetz, D.B. (2023). *Discovering the Scientist Within: Research Methods in Psychology*. Worth Publishers.

Marsh, N. (1934, 2011). *A Man Lay Dead: Roderick Alleyn #1*. Felony & Mayhem Press.

Mello-Goldner, D., & Wurf, E. (1997). The self in self-handicapping: Differential effects of public and private internal audiences. *Current Psychology, 15* (4), 319–331.

Mill, J.S. (1843). *A System of Logic: Ratiocinative and Inductive, Presenting a Connected View of the Principles of Evidence and the Methods of Scientific Investigation* (Book II, Chapter 3). University of Toronto Press.

Mogen, D., Sanders, S.P., & Karpinski, J.B. (1992). *Frontier Gothic: Terror and Wonder at the Frontier in American Literature*. Fairleigh Dickinson University Press.

Münsterberg, H. (1908). *On the Witness Stand: Essays on Psychology and Crime*. Doubleday.

Pattison, E. (1999). *The Skull Mantra*. St. Martin's Press.

Plotnik, R. (1999). *Introduction to Psychology* (5th Edition). Brooks/Cole/Wadsworth.

Smith, R.A., & Davis, S.F. (1997). *The Psychologist as Detective: An Introduction to Conducting Research in Psychology*. Prentice Hall.

Stanford Encyclopedia of Philosophy (2017). *Aristotle's Logic*. https://plato.stanford.edu/entries/aristotle-logic/.

Stanovich, K. (2007). *How to Think Straight About Psychology (8th Edition)*. Allyn & Bacon.

Winspear, J. (2003). *Maisie Dobbs: A Novel*. Penguin Books.

Winspear, J. (2019). *What Would Maisie Do? Inspiration from the Pages of Maisie Dobbs*. Harper Perennial.

2

Structuralism, Functionalism, and the Move to Psychoanalysis

As stated in the previous chapter, psychology is rooted in philosophy, just like all sciences. This connection may be more evident in psychology, which studies how people understand themselves, their thinking processes, and their world. Early philosophers such as Socrates, Plato, Aristotle, Kant, Nietzsche, and Descartes also focused on self-understanding in their writings and teachings. Psychology separated itself from the field of philosophy and became a separate discipline in the late 1800s. The "birthdate" of psychology is often credited as 1879,[1] when **Wilhelm Wundt** (1832–1920) set up what is considered the first psychological laboratory in Leipzig, Germany (Coon & Mitterer, 2014; Plotnik, 1999). Before Wundt, others developed some of the same experimental psychology steps and methods, such as Ernst Weber and his student Gustav Fechner.[2]

Fechner, in particular, has been credited by Edwin Boring as the first individual not only to carry out what might have been the first example of a psychological experiment but to write the first psychological textbook, *Elements of Psychophysics* (Boring, 2008; Leahey, 1991). Wundt had his new field recognized as a legitimate area of study. Students and researchers from around Europe and beyond traveled to Leipzig to obtain firsthand experience from Wundt and his students, although his theory was not without criticism. One of Wundt's most significant contributions to psychology was setting up a community of like-minded researchers who worked together rather than in isolation by establishing the first psychological laboratory. Wundt and his students constructed a social situation that set the framework for experimenters' and participants' standards of behavior that continues today (Danziger, 1990).

What Wundt studied has a minimal resemblance to what most people today think of as psychology. Wundt and his students studied sensation and perception, often testing his subjects' reaction time to respond to a **stimulus** (something introduced to a person or animal to lead to a specific reaction). Wundt's lab also studied more typical psychological topics such as attention and feelings. In his *Tridimensional Theory of Feeling* (Wundt, 1873), Wundt believed three dimensions explain the range of feelings individuals and animals can experience: pleasantness and unpleasantness, relaxation and tension, and excitement and inhibition. He found that sensations occur with feelings along these dimensions. For example, in some individuals, the taste of a strawberry is pleasant; for others, it is quite unpleasant. For most dogs, the sound of thunder is almost always unpleasant and creates great tension, while cats are more prone to ignore thunderstorms and continue their napping.

As the 20th century progressed and the political and social conflicts that led to World War I were evolving, the influence of Wundt diminished. Nevertheless, the field of psychology owes its origin and acceptance to the work of Wundt and his many students. At the very least, he deserves great praise for instructing more than 24,000 students and supervising over 200 dissertations (Leahey, 1991).

Studying the most basic element or structure of the mind to understand reactions or behaviors formed the basis of this first major paradigm of psychology, **structuralism,** a term coined by Wundt's student Edward Bradford Titchener.[3] Wundt and his followers also developed the idea of **introspection,** whereby people think inwardly to understand their sensations and resulting actions. As Europe transformed during the Industrial Revolution,[4] the new focus on science and technology impacted psychology and structuralism. Structuralism focused on scientifically studying consciousness and sensation—it explained how a stimulus, or a type of information, lead to a sensation and how people thought about them (Hergenhahn, 2009).

However, structuralism's popularity was short-lived, likely because it failed to acknowledge the importance of applied or practical psychology. Titchener and his followers were not interested in personality, development, or learning and did not consider the importance of evolution in studying human behavior (Hergenhahn, 2009). Although structuralism was not a long-lasting movement, the concepts of introspection and the focus on internal thinking expanded and became the cornerstone for another paradigm in psychology. This next movement was the **psychoanalytic** movement led by its founder, **Sigmund Freud.**

However, before Freud's rise to prominence, another school of psychology in America had risen in popularity. This school, **functionalism,** began with Harvard University psychologist **William James'** book *The Principles of Psychology* (1890). James' work occurred around the same time Titchener was developing structuralism at Cornell University, so these two movements coexisted for some time (Hergenhahn, 2009).

However, the purpose of each school of thought was quite divergent. Functionalist psychologists were more concerned with explaining what the mind did, its operations, rather than what it contained or its elements (Boring, 2008; Hergenhahn, 2009).

Functionalism and the Influence of William James

Keller (1973) explained that functionalists not only wanted to understand how the mind worked (the "why" in addition to the "what") but wanted psychology to become a more applied or practical science. Functionalists expanded psychology's area of study and its methodology, tools, and even research participants, now studying children, adults, and animals. Functionalists also accepted and recognized the importance of evolution, which influenced their focus on studying how the mind and behavior work together to help humans and animals adjust to their environments (Hergenhahn, 2009).

William James (1842–1910) is often considered the "father of American psychology," and his ideas greatly influenced the development of functionalism. James suggested that rather than studying the pure elements of thought and things like sensation, researchers should focus on individuals' stream of consciousness, which is capable of change and serves a purpose (Hergenhahn, 2009; James, 1890). James was also the first to divide personality into several parts, claiming that individuals possess two aspects of the self. One part is the "knower" that guides our thinking and decision-making (what James referred to as the "I"). The other part is the "known" (what James referred to as the "ME"), which contains the content of what makes us who we are as individuals (Brown, 1998). So, in a way, James acknowledged the importance of both structure (ME) and function (I) as influencing behavior and personality. James (1890) further defined the ME as containing three separate components: the *material me*, which contains the things that we possess, including our physical characteristics as well as items like the type of cellphone we own; the *social me*, which contains the groups we belong to and the roles we play in them; and the *spiritual me*, which contains our traits and characteristics.

James' work influenced the focus and methodology of psychology and led to the development of applied psychology. Hugo Münsterberg, James' successor at Harvard, expanded James' focus and became the "father of applied psychology" such as clinical psychology, forensic psychology, and industrial-organizational psychology (Hergenhahn, 2009). Other future functionalist psychologists who can attribute their roots back to William James include: Mary Whiton Calkins, a student of Münsterberg's who became the first female president of the American Psychological Association in 1905; G. Stanley Hall, the "father of American adolescent psychology" who taught and became the president of Clark University in Worcester, Massachusetts; Francis Cecil Sumner, a student of Hall's who was the first African American to receive his Ph.D. in psychology; and Kenneth and Mamie Phipps Clark, a married couple who were the first African Americans to obtain their doctoral degrees in psychology from Columbia University, and were influential in the study of child development and racial biases in education (APA, 2012; Hergenhahn, 2009).

These early American psychologists benefited from a switch to a more active and applied approach to studying psychology. In Europe, the field of psychology was also focusing less on structure and more on function. However, it first studied more controversial topics—the unconscious and sexuality, led by one of the most influential (perhaps some may say "infamous") psychologists of all time, Sigmund Freud.

Sigmund Freud (the "Father" of Psychoanalysis)

Sigmund Freud was born May 6, 1856, in a small Moravian town called Freiberg and died in London in 1939. Sigmund was the first child of Jakob and Amalia Freud. Amalia was Jakob's third wife and was 20 years younger than him (Amalia was only 20 years old when married). Sigmund had two brothers, Emanuel and Philipp, both more than 20 years older than Sigmund and born from Jakob's first marriage. These two older brothers were closer in age to Sigmund's mother than his father, which perhaps led to some early confusion regarding relationships and the concept of sexuality for the young Sigmund. When Anna (Freud's sister) was born when Sigmund was 2½, Sigmund thought she was his older brother Phillip's daughter, not his sister (Gay, 1988). Growing up, the young Sigmund retained a good amount of anger and resentment toward his strict father. He did have a loving relationship with his mother, which likely led him to focus his personality theory on sexual feelings and urges (Schultz & Schultz, 2016).

In 1873, Freud enrolled at the University of Vienna to study medicine. He chose sex as his foundation because he believed it had biological origins and focused on natural science and the scientific method. In 1885, he received a grant to study in Paris with Jean Charcot,[5] a famous neurologist. This experience with Charcot propelled Freud to the study of psychology. Charcot's patients came to him with physical or medical symptoms with no clear biological explanations, which Charcot identified as **hysteria**. These patients, who were primarily women, developed aversions to specific situations, anxiety, fainting, or who even had lost the use of some of their senses or mobility. Charcot used hypnosis to cure hysteria and introduced this therapeutic method to Freud, emphasizing the unconscious's importance in influencing people's thoughts and behaviors.

During the 1890s, Freud clarified his theory based on his patients' experiences and symptoms. His female patients reported incidents that Freud felt were examples of early sexual trauma (Schultz & Schultz, 2016). Freud's theory involves two basic principles. One is that all we do, think, and feel has meaning and purpose and that everything in nature is determined—what Freud referred to as **psychic determinism** (Freud, 1989). The other principle is that all behavior is unconsciously motivated, which became the main focus of not only Freud's but all psychoanalytic theorists. Freud first theorized that an individual's personality includes three distinct areas or levels: the **conscious,** containing the thoughts and feelings which that person is currently aware of; the **preconscious,** which contains thoughts and feelings that are not present in awareness but can quickly move into awareness, similar to the idea of a person waiting in a reception room before being admitted to a physical or virtual meeting; and the **unconscious,** which contains the thoughts and feelings that are not in awareness, most likely because they are perceived to be threatening.

In Freud's patients, these thoughts were mostly about sex and aggression, or even death (Mayer & Sutton, 1996). This topographical model focused on the idea that the unconscious was the most important and largest area of personality, as the conscious and preconscious were just the *"tip of the iceberg,"* according to Freud (Burger, 2018). The importance of the unconscious led Freud and his followers to develop methods to extricate those hidden motives, much like a detective uncovers the motive behind a crime. Freud found his topographical model somewhat limited in its ability to explain people's personalities fully, so he refined his theory to contain a more structural model of the unconscious, which is much more well-known. In his structural model, Freud took what he considered the largest and most important part of the mind, the unconscious, and divided it further into three distinct areas: the **id**, the **ego**, and the **superego** (Freud, 1910).

The id is the most primal part of our personality, which develops first and is buried entirely within the unconscious. The id is the self-satisfying part of our personality that ignores limitations or compromises. The id operates on what Freud called the **pleasure principle**, as it is only concerned with personal self-gratification regardless of others. Murderers, especially serial killers, personify the id, disregarding everything but their self-interest in killing a person.

The ego develops second and serves as the negotiator of the

personality, trying to satisfy the id while also monitoring the broader environment's restrictions. The ego, therefore, operates on a **reality principle**. The ego is much like the detective trying to balance what is right and others' desires (similar to how a detective tries to catch the killer using rational judgment).

The final part of the personality to develop is the superego, which contains our values, beliefs, and the conception of right and wrong. The superego, therefore, operates on a **morality principle** and possesses both the *conscience*, the little voice in our head that tells us what not to do, and the *ego-ideal*, the little voice in our head that tells us how we should want to act (Burger, 2018). The superego is like a jury deciding a killer's fate based on needs and the law.

The ego, in particular, with its rational decision-making and attempt to solve problems like anxiety, was critical to Freud. Freud, and his daughter Anna, developed a list of strategies that the ego uses (unconsciously, of course) to help defend against stress, anxiety, and unpleasantness—what he called **defense mechanisms** (Schultz & Schultz, 2016). Some of these include:

- **denial**—when someone fails to acknowledge that a problem even exists
- **repression**—when a person "forgets about forgetting" something
- **projection**—when you attribute your unacceptable characteristics to another person
- **displacement**—when you shift a negative thought or impulse onto another safer object or person
- **rationalization**—when you continually (over)analyze a problem and make excuses
- **reaction formation**—when you replace a negative or unpleasant impulse with its opposite
- **regression**—when you behave as you did in the past or when you were younger (Burger, 2018).

Investigative thinking challenge:
Engage in some investigative thought by creating examples
of the different defense mechanisms and then discuss them
in groups or with a partner.

It is often a detective's job to separate the truth from the lies of each suspect, similar to the Freudian therapist uncovering the hidden unconscious motives behind a person's behaviors or illness. How does a

2. Structuralism, Functionalism, and the Move to Psychoanalysis 31

psychoanalytic therapist go about uncovering the truth? Through the techniques of hypnosis, free association, and dream analysis.

It was Freud's experience with Charcot that piqued his interest in the technique of **hypnosis**. In hypnosis, a hypnotist or therapist guides a person into a suspended state of awareness or trance, allowing the hypnotist or therapist to ask them questions to help reveal their unconscious needs and motives (Burger, 2018). While this may seem invaluable, Freud and his followers acknowledged that not everyone could be easily hypnotized, so they began focusing on other assessment techniques.

Free association became Freud's replacement "talking cure" and involved the patient or client lying on a couch, telling Freud whatever came to their mind. The idea behind free association is for the patient or client to say whatever comes into their mind without overthinking the replies; therefore, those replies would relate to the unconscious. The therapist would be able to unravel the unknown causes of their behavior from the responses, much like the detective unravels the uncertainty of clues to discover who committed the crime, referred to often as a **whodunit**.

Freud's most well-known follower, Carl Jung, developed another technique to uncover the unconscious. In this technique, Jung would prompt his client by providing a word and asking them to say the first word to come into their mind, a **word association test**. The word association test is an example of a projective test, an assessment tool often used by psychoanalytic therapists that presents ambiguous stimuli to individuals who project their unconscious needs and conflicts onto their responses (Schultz & Schultz, 2016). For example, if I say "dog," what is the first word that comes to your mind? What if I say "tree"? There are no right or wrong answers, and your specific answers would be characteristic of your unconscious needs and conflict.

The final technique is also synonymous with Freud and his theory—**dream analysis**. To Freud, dreams were the "royal road to the unconscious" (Burger, 2018; Freud, 1900). Freud published *The Interpretation of Dreams* in 1900, and after this, interest in his theories grew, and he developed a devoted group of supporters. Most psychoanalysts interpret dreams in some manner as they believe dreams represent, in symbolic form, unconscious and repressed desires and conflicts. They are what Freud called our wish fulfillment. Every dream consists of two types of information, the **manifest content**, the actual events and people within the dream, and the **latent content**, the hidden, symbolic meaning of those actions and people (Freud, 1920). Freud and his followers were less concerned with the manifest content. They focused on interpreting dreams and uncovering their latent content, thus helping their patient identify the actual cause of their problematic behaviors.

Sir Arthur Conan Doyle published his first Sherlock Holmes novel, *A Study in Scarlet*, in 1887. The process by which Holmes and Watson solve crimes is quite similar to the process that a psychoanalytic therapist would take to uncover the true meaning of a patient's problems through dream analysis or free association. They must uncover the hidden meaning behind the clues and discard any **red herrings**,[6] just as a psychoanalyst unravels symptoms and unconscious motives. Red herrings interfere with results much like confounding variables interfere with experimental research results. Psychologists and detectives both do their job by "slowly peeling away layers of deception from a core of infantile sexual anxiety" (Priestman, 2009, p. 182). Mysteries and detective fiction maintain the tension between the unknown and the known. The process of solving the crime rather than the actual solution brings about the most enjoyment and cathartic release of anxiety for the reader (Hutter, 1975).

Detective fiction also may be popular because it relates to the unconscious needs of the readers themselves. Consider what Freud would think of the titles of these *Nancy Drew* books by Carolyn Keene[7]: *The Secret of the Old Clock; The Hidden Staircase; The Clue of the Broken Locket; The Message in the Hollow Oak; The Clue in the Jewel Box; The Clue in the Old Album; and The Clue of the Leaning Chimney*. Each title describes a boxed object or hidden location, which Freud often said symbolized female genitalia or sexual urges (Freud, 1900). Sexuality may seem like an unusual theme for a series of books geared toward preteen and teen girls. However, that age range corresponds to the latency period and genital stage of Freud's psychosexual stages of personality development[8] (Schultz & Schultz, 2016).

The latency period was when Freud believed children were less overtly focused on the sex instinct and instead concentrated on other activities, like reading. Their preferred reading choices may reflect those dormant urges. Later psychoanalytic theorists focused less on repressed sexuality as the primary determinant of personality. These other psychoanalysts (including Jung, Horney, and Erikson) are called Neopsychoanalytic Theorists[9] (Schultz & Schultz, 2016). The Neopsychoanalytic Theorists, or Neo-Freudians, agreed with Freud about the importance of the unconscious. However, they focused less on sex and aggression, Freud's pessimistic view of human nature, and Freud's ignoring of the importance of social and cultural influences on personality and behavior (Cherry, 2020).

Carl Jung

Carl Jung (1875–1961) was Freud's most famous and successful student, the person he considered the "crown prince" of psychoanalysis who

2. Structuralism, Functionalism, and the Move to Psychoanalysis

would continue his legacy. While Jung agreed with the importance of the unconscious, perhaps even more so than Freud himself, he focused less on sexuality (Schultz & Schultz, 2016). As a result, Jung chose to develop a theory that diverged from Freud's, much to Freud's chagrin. Jung's analytical psychology approach also divided personality into three levels. First is the **conscious ego,** which includes the perceptions, thoughts, feelings, and memories that we are aware of (similar to Freud's peak of the iceberg level of consciousness). Like Freud, Jung did not consider this the most important or influential element of personality as he believed most of our thoughts are unconscious.

Jung's **personal unconscious** is the level that contains the images and experiences that we are not immediately aware of but can easily become part of the conscious ego. The unawareness happens because we have either forgotten this information, perhaps because it was too insignificant, or sometimes because it was too traumatic. This level is similar to Freud's preconsciousness level and is where Jung believed people store their **complexes** (a cluster of symptoms or emotions organized around a common theme; Schultz & Schultz, 2016).

The final level is called the **collective unconscious**—Jung's most controversial level of personality, which has no parallel to Freud's theory, that contains the common experiences humans share. These memories shape our personality and motivate our behavior. For Jung, this was the most dominant part of our personality, but it continues to be the most controversial, and most personality theorists reject it (Schultz & Schultz, 2016).

Within Jung's collective unconscious, there are several subparts called archetypes. **Archetypes** are predispositions to think and act in particular ways. These are inherited and originate through our early ancestors' repeated experiences and somehow become "imprinted on our psyche" (Schultz, 1986, p. 83). The four main Jungian archetypes include the following:

- **persona**—our public mask; the image or side of our personality that we show to the outside world. This archetype may involve a sense of falseness as we can easily pretend to act in a way that is not true to our actual values, beliefs, and behaviors.
- **shadow**—the thoughts and feelings representing our "dark side." The shadow is the part of our unconscious that we try to hide from others because it may contain our inner demons and unacceptable behaviors. The shadow correlates to the evil "Mr. Hyde" side of a Jekyll and Hyde[10] personality.

- **anima/animus**—the characteristics and behaviors representing our feminine and masculine sides. All individuals have elements of the anima and animus within them.
- **self**—to Jung, this is the most crucial element of the collective unconscious and the central archetype. Jung's "self" influences individuals to strive for unity, growth, and integration of the whole personality and is always active, as we should always be in the process of self-realization. Unlike Freud and other psychoanalysts who focused on early childhood, Jung believes the self appears later in life, often in middle adulthood.

Investigative thinking challenge:
Among Jung's four primary archetypes, which exerts the most influence in motivating and guiding your behavior? Why do you believe that?

Jung's use of the word "self" was not the first time in the history of psychology that the word was defined. William James (1890) first described the self. Like James, Jung saw the self as involving both action and content and was important in motivating our behavior.

In addition to Jung's four main archetypes, he also developed several lesser archetypes observed in the actions of detectives and other literary characters. These include the **Great Mother**, which includes our preexisting concept of a typical or ideal mother, including both positive and negative elements. The Great Mother can produce and sustain life through fertility and nourishment as well as devour or neglect offspring, or cause other problems. An excellent literary example of the Great Mother is the character of "Mother Nature." The **Wise Old Man** symbolizes our preexisting knowledge of the mysteries of life, often depicted as an older man, as in God's typical image across many religions such as Buddhism, Christianity, Judaism, and Islam. This archetype embodies the all-knowing leader who captivates his audience through motivational speeches and actions. Some examples in literature may include the wizard in *The Wonderful Wizard of Oz*, the children's book by L. Frank Baum, or various depictions of kings, wizards, or magicians from fairy tales. Finally, the **Hero** is the protagonist of many stories who conquers the evil villain and overcomes darkness to save the day. In many fairy tales, the knight, prince, and sometimes princess are examples of the "hero" in stories.

Investigative thinking challenge:
Does detective fiction assist us in addressing our inherent negative impulses akin to Freud's id or our darker aspects as described by Jung's shadow? Why or why not?

2. Structuralism, Functionalism, and the Move to Psychoanalysis 35

Jung's contribution to psychoanalysis and personality theory expanded on Freud's initial approach. Jung acknowledged that we are not always purely motivated by sexual and aggressive urges but can be motivated by others and by an urge to grow or become a better person. His idea of the collective unconscious provides an interesting path to understanding many fairy tales and folk legends in various cultures. Within detective fiction, both the detectives and villains, protagonist and antagonist, exhibit archetypal behavior.

Karen Horney

The first influential female psychoanalyst was **Karen Horney** (1865–1952), the German theorist. Horney agreed with Freud about the importance of the unconscious and that early childhood influenced adult personality. However, she disagreed with exactly how the unconscious shaped personality. To Freud, we are controlled mainly through biological forces, such as sex and aggression. Horney focused more on social influences and the relationships children develop with others early in life. She did believe that needs were critical in childhood. However, Horney believed the two basic needs were *safety* (feeling secure from fear) and *satisfaction* (Horney, 1937). Children need to experience both to develop genuine love and healthy relationships with others. If parents do not satisfy their child's safety and satisfaction needs, the child may develop **basic hostility** toward the parents. Children seldom express their rage overtly to their parents; instead, they internalize it. This internalized or repressed hostility develops into feelings of insecurity that Horney called **basic anxiety**.

According to Horney's theory (called *Psychoanalytic Social Psychology*), these two feelings are the root of most unconscious conflict and psychological issues in individuals and lead to the development of neurotic needs[11] and a neurotic personality (Horney, 1937). In Horney's theory, all individuals display neurotic needs at some point in their life. Problems arise, however, when we rigidly adopt a pattern of behavior that dominates our personality and takes over our lives as a type of defense mechanism—what Horney called **neurotic trends** (Schultz, 1986).

Three Neurotic Trends

- **moving toward people**—also called the compliant personality type—involves an intense and consistent need to be loved, wanted, and protected, motivating people to move toward others. While these individuals may seek others to manipulate them, they may also do so because they feel helpless and weak and want to be controlled by others.

- **moving against people**—also called the aggressive personality. These individuals think just about everyone else is hostile and out to get them, so they must move against others almost from an evolutionary perspective to survive. Everything is a competition to them, and they must win at all costs, so they may not accept losing, at least not graciously (e.g., consider President Trump's reaction to losing the 2020 election). These individuals are difficult to interact with because they are very demanding and tend to overcriticize.
- **moving away from people**—also called the detached personality. These individuals crave isolation and try to maintain emotional distance from all people. They do not want to be involved with other people or other people's problems—they seek out and absolutely need privacy and may also deny their feelings to maintain distance from others (Horney, 1937).

Horney found that one trend or personality (above) dominates in a neurotic person, but the other two are still present to some degree and can influence behavior (Horney, 1937). As part of the neurotic and *non*-neurotic personality, Horney also felt we have a self-image, but not the same self as Jung's archetype. For Horney, individuals develop two types of self-images: the *real self* and the *idealized self* (Schultz, 1986). Typically, they coincide, but in a neurotic person, they are very different. The real self is an accurate self-image; it is who we really are. The idealized self is an unrealistically poor self-image often created for defensive purposes and is more likely to be found in neurotics.

Discrepancies between these two self-images would lead to anxiety and neuroses and their accompanying behavioral issues (this discrepancy between self-views is a theme we will see in other theories, such as humanistic psychologist Carl Rogers' theory discussed in Chapter 4). People's overestimation of their abilities can be problematic for all professions, including our fictional detectives. Even the usual infallible Sherlock Holmes' overconfidence can lead to inaccurate results, as is evidenced when he is bested by "the woman," Irene Adler, in the first of Holmes' short stories, "A Scandal in Bohemia,"[12] which he considers his one failed case (Smith, 2014).

Investigative thinking challenge:
Can detective fiction positively impact our ability to cope with anxieties surrounding topics such as loss, separation, and identity? Why or why not?

Erik Erikson and Psychosocial Development

One final psychoanalyst is **Erik Erikson** (1902–1994), an ego psychologist who studied under Anna Freud, Freud's daughter. Like Anna Freud and Heinz Hartmann,[13] ego psychologists focused on Sigmund Freud's concept of the ego and its adaptive and protective nature. Anna Freud (1936) clarified and expanded the idea of ego defense mechanisms in *The Ego and the Mechanisms of Defense*.

Erikson believed that personality developed as they aged from infancy to old age or late adulthood. What influenced the development was a conflict, or what Erikson termed a crisis, that the person would need to resolve positively or negatively. While the word crisis evokes a negative feeling, Erikson did not see this process as problematic but rather as a natural stage in a person's development from which they could acquire strength and growth. His stages are often referred to as those of Psychosocial Development because Erikson emphasized that our relationships with other people influence personality development (Erikson, 1963). The table below briefly lists Erikson's stages. (For a quick but more in-depth explanation, see the description by Saul Mcleod at https://www.simplypsychology.org/Erik-Erikson.html)

Erikson's Stages of Psychosocial Development

Crisis	*Age*	*Basic Strength (if crisis is resolved positively)*
Trust vs. mistrust	Birth–12 to 18 months (infancy)	hope
Autonomy vs. doubt	12 to 18 months–3 years (toddlerhood)	will
Initiative vs. guilt	3 years–5 years (early childhood/preschool)	purpose
Industry vs. inferiority	5 years–11 or 12 years (elementary school age)	competence
Identity vs. role confusion	11 or 12 years–18 years (tween and adolescence)	fidelity
Intimacy vs. isolation	18 years–35 to 40 years (young adulthood)	love
Generativity vs. stagnation	35 to 40 years–60 to 65 years (middle adulthood)	care
Ego integrity vs. despair	60 to 65 years+ (late adulthood/old age)	wisdom

Source Credit: (Burger, 2018; Schultz & Schultz, 2016)

> *Investigative thinking challenge:*
> *In the 21st century, is identity attainment*
> *typically accomplished by age 18?*
> *What factors contribute to this process or hinder its achievement?*

The stage of Erikson's theory that often gets the most attention is Stage 5, identity vs. role confusion, which typically occurs in adolescence and, according to Erikson, concludes by the age of 18 (Erikson, 1968). To resolve this crisis, Erikson believed that a person must successfully make three choices to achieve identity (Burger, 2018). Those choices necessitate a choice of values (*what do I believe in?*), a choice of a career (*what will I be?*), and a choice concerning sexuality (*what kind of a "sexual" individual will I be; to whom am I attracted?*). When Erikson developed his theory, homosexuality was not accepted and was still illegal in many places, so he focused only on heterosexual relationships. In today's world, one should consider healthy relationships as those involving both opposite-sex and same-sex attraction, as well as all forms of gender identity and sexual orientation.

The path to successfully make the decisions related to these three choices can be lengthy and complicated, and likely involves some trial and error. Erikson believed individuals could utilize two processes to help them resolve these choices (Schultz & Schultz, 2016). One technique is called **introspection** and occurs when an individual spends time "looking inward," thinking through their options, and considering the pros and cons of the alternatives. The second technique is **role experimentation** when an individual tries out some or all of the different possibilities for values, careers, and sexuality through a trial-and-error process.

We have already seen how psychologists such as Wundt and Freud used introspection. Erikson applied introspection to psychosocial development and decision-making. Both introspection and role experimentation are essential techniques detectives use to investigate crimes and develop their theory about the culprit's identity. Erikson's stages can also identify personal crises or dilemmas a fictional detective faces, which sometimes interfere with their ability to fully concentrate on solving the crime.

> *Investigative thinking challenge:*
> *Are you presently encountering*
> *any crises identified in Erikson's stages?*
> *Does your current crisis align with the*
> *age range that Erikson specifies?*
> *If there is any disparity, what factors could explain it?*

Psychoanalysis and Detective Fiction

Psychoanalysis presents a natural connection to detective fiction and the early detectives who employ a more introspective and reflective approach to crime-solving. Later, during the Golden Age of detective fiction,[14] detectives were more active and situationally focused. The relationship between psychological theory and detective fiction is a reciprocal one. Freud himself was a fan of detective fiction, and this interest may have influenced the development of his theories (Yang, 2010). Freud's interest in detective fiction and mysteries in general should not be surprising since we have already seen many parallels between a detective's and a psychologist's skills. Freud best explains the link between psychoanalysis and detective fiction in his remarks to a group of University of Vienna students in the early 1900s:

> In both we are concerned with a secret, with something hidden.... In the case of the criminal it is a secret which he knows and hides from you, whereas in the case of the hysteric it is a secret which he himself does not know either, which is hidden from himself.... The task of the therapist, however, is the same as the examining magistrate. We have to uncover the hidden psychical material; and in order to do this we have invented a number of detective devices [Howe, 2008, p. 2].

Freud's words demonstrate the reciprocal relationship that psychoanalysis and detective fiction have always possessed. Poe and Conan Doyle may have provided Freud with insight into deductive reasoning and even free association. At the same time, Freud's theory likely influenced the early mystery writers such as Agatha Christie and Dorothy Sayers, and later writers whose detectives are often referred to as **soft-boiled** (Panek, 2000). Soft-boiled detectives unravel clues and the killer's identity, similar to how a psychologist unravels a mental illness's symptoms to develop a diagnosis and treatment.

Soft-Boiled Detective Fiction

Soft-boiled detective fiction was most popular in the pre–World War II era, although the "cozy mystery" genre is a more recent popular trend (Stasio, 1992). The soft-boiled detective is a quiet, introspective thinker who solves the crime very much like he or she would solve a puzzle. The crime typically occurs in a village setting (most likely in England), and the suspects all live in that same village. The "detective" (who may not be a professional detective at all) uses the relationships within that small village community to help solve the crime (Charles et al., 2002). Very little violence is ever described directly in soft-boiled fiction, and the detective only rarely, if ever, carries a weapon.

Just as Sigmund Freud would sit on a chair as his patient lay on the couch recounting their dreams, so does the soft-boiled detective sit and think through the clues before the "**big reveal**" to a room full of suspects, often in the final chapter. The big reveal is the "aha moment," a plot technique disclosing previously unknown key information (e.g., the identity of the killer, motive, and important clues) to the reader (Ephron, 2005). This "denouement" occurs when the detective gathers all of the suspects together and resolves the mystery by wrapping things up, typically at the end of the novel or movie (Crombie, 2021).

A soft-boiled detective is just as likely to be female as male, a vast improvement over the male-dominated theorists and therapists of early psychology. This increase in female detectives may be because many of the most famous soft-boiled detective fiction writers were women. These early writers included Agatha Christie, Dorothy Sayers, P.D. James, and more recent writers such as Jane Langton, Amanda Cross, Lilian Jackson Braun, and, most recently, Jacqueline Winspear.

The soft-boiled detective genre coincides perfectly with the psychoanalytic paradigm's creation and rise in popularity. Soft-boiled detective fiction writers keep the reader guessing the killer's identity until the novel's end when the all-knowing detective often gathers the suspects together to explain their rationale and uncover the killer, who was among them the entire time. There is much of the hidden unconscious in soft-boiled mysteries. For example, "the killer sometimes takes on a false identity; the murder weapon is cleverly hidden; the chronology of the plot is confused; and the crime is often committed in a locked-room—a seemingly impossible situation" (Panek, 2000, p. 96). Edgar Allan Poe's short story *The Murders in the Rue Morgue* uses the locked room example.

The psychoanalyst's and detective's goals are to overcome illness or evil to restore order and coherence (Cawelti, 1976). The detective brings the solution of the crime to the surface of reality very much like Freud and other psychoanalysts bring the understanding of unconscious thoughts, impulses, and wishes to the surface of personality to explain his patients' symptoms and complexes. Many of those themes represent inappropriate or unacceptable unconscious urges, which may be why these detective fiction stories are so exciting and enjoyable. Reading about death and murder, negative unconscious urges within the id, allows us to find pleasure in the characters' fictional pain (Howe, 2008).

The Golden Age of Detective Fiction, when soft-boiled detective fiction flourished, began after the end of the "The Great War," the First World War (World War I), and ended around 1939 with the outbreak of

2. Structuralism, Functionalism, and the Move to Psychoanalysis 41

the Second World War (World War II). People in Europe suffered notable human and physical loss during World War I and perhaps were hoping for simpler, happier, and more innocent times to return. They may have turned to these soft-boiled mysteries for a fun diversion from reality. However, even before World War II, people became critical of the soft-boiled genre's formulaic and narrow views of society and crime (Chandler, 1944; Wilson, 1945) and sought more action-oriented characters, a theme in the next chapter.

Agatha Christie's most famous female detective, Miss Jane Marple, believes people behave almost all the same. Miss Marple "fixes the death and disorder in her village almost to entertain herself, like doing a jigsaw puzzle or working out a cross-stitch" (Jackson, 2002, p. 28). No matter where she is, either in her home village of St. Mary Mead or on the fictional Caribbean island of St. Honoré, Miss Marple uses village parallels to help her solve her cases. Despite never marrying or having children and hardly ever leaving her small rural environment, Miss Marple is an expert at reading people and their motives. She is skeptical of others as she knows people often lie, which a Freudian psychoanalyst would perhaps attribute to their "id." Instead, she wants to seek out the truth through her investigation. Miss Marple explains in *The Body in the Library* (Christie, 1942) that people are too trusting in others and tend to believe whatever others tell them. She says she tends to never believe other people because of her experience and understanding of human nature.

> You simply cannot afford to believe everything that people tell you. When there's anything fishy about I never believe anyone at all. You see, I know human nature so well [Miss Marple in *The Body in the Library*, Christie, 1942/1980, Chapter 16, p. 630].

Miss Marple and other female detectives are called **sleuths,** the shortened version of "sleuthhound," the Scottish word for the dogs used in hunting either animals or fugitives from justice (Merriam-Webster, n.d.). Sleuth serves as a noun when meaning the detective and a verb when meaning to search for and discover. Miss Marple uses the psychological skills of intuition and understanding of human nature to explore and discover the solution to the crimes she investigates. Likewise, Agatha Christie's more famous male detective, Hercule Poirot, uses his "little grey cells" to solve many baffling crimes. A final example of a Golden Age detective described as a sleuthhound is Ngaio Marsh's detective Roderick Alleyn, who is called that in Chapter 12 of *A Man Lay Dead* (Marsh, 1934/2011). He is described as a gentleman who is a sleuthhound not out of monetary necessity but for his interest or enjoyment in detective work.

Some detectives make the connection between psychoanalysis and detection even more straightforward. The short story "Daisy Bell" (Slung, 1975) by Gladys Mitchell features the female detective Beatrice Bradley. Bradley is a psychiatrist, a follower of Freud, and a consultant to the U.K.'s Home Office. In this short story, she mentions several psychological terms and uses her understanding of hidden motives to discover the cause of a female cyclist's crash. Remaining discreet or inconspicuous serves several early female detectives well.

In C.L. Pirkis' short story "The Murder at Troyte's Hill," the detective Loveday Brooke assumes the role of a secretary to become part of the Craven household and gather information to solve the murder of Old Sandy. As a lower member of the staff, the family largely ignored her. This "invisibility" allows her to carefully investigate the rooms and the people, helping her to solve the crime. Loveday "proceeded to make a thorough and minute investigation of every corner of the room" (Slung, 1975, p. 16). Loveday also uses the scientific method and logic to gather her evidence. When working with the (mindless) police officer she is assisting with the case, she responds to his question by saying, "put your questions in categorical order and I will answer them" (Slung, 1975, p. 31).

Pauline Hopkins was an African American writer known for novels, short stories, plays, and journalistic pieces. In her writing, Hopkins included racial and social justice, writing about racism in the post–Civil War United States (Pauline Hopkins, 2021). Her short story "Talma Gordon" (Gates et al., 2014), published in 1900, is considered by many as the first African American mystery story (Pauline Hopkins Society, n.d.). Set in Boston, where Hopkins grew up, the story takes place at a club meeting at the home of the respected Dr. William Thornton. He recounts the story of death and possible murder in the Gordon household years earlier with imagery similar to that used in gothic novels. Unlike a typical mystery, there is no detective in Hopkins' short story. However, there is deductive reasoning and hidden, unconscious conflict related to mixed blood and intermarriage. The ending also has an interesting twist and is worth reading.

Miss Marple may have a scientific attitude that helps her gather and sort through her clues, but she also successfully solves her cases because of her invisibility. She often sits in the same room during key conversations, but most people pay her very little attention. She uses this to her advantage to gather gossip and discover the village's domestic problems. In *The Murder at the Vicarage* (Christie, 1930), she explains that she is an expert in human nature. She says that while gossip may not always be kind to others, it often conveys the truth about people's behaviors.

> Observing human nature for as long as I have done, one gets not to expect very much from it. I dare say the idle tittle-tattle is very wrong and unkind, but it

2. Structuralism, Functionalism, and the Move to Psychoanalysis 43

is so often true, isn't it? [Miss Marple in *The Murder at the Vicarage*, Christie, 1930/1980, Chapter 2, p. 12].

Some people may recognize she is a "smart old pussy" as Inspector Slack observes in *The Body in the Library*, but many do not. Miss Marple is absent from most of the action in the novels featuring her. Nevertheless, she can still gather the information necessary to solve the case through her pointed questions, her intuition, and her ability to make the connections between behavior and human nature—all qualities of a good psychologist, especially a psychoanalyst. A Freudian psychoanalyst typically says very little during a therapy session and allows the client to do most of the talking to discover unconscious motives or needs. Miss Marple, and other female Golden Age detectives, employ similar techniques as they go about their business. Even in the more recent "cozy mystery" genre, female detectives and characters benefit from their invisibility and social connections. They can access private information because they can enter homes as unthreatening domestic servants, spinsters, or society gossip mongers (Dunn, 2016).

In the *Gaslight Mystery* series by Victoria Thompson, midwife Sarah Brandt works with policeman Frank Malloy to solve crime in New York City in the early 1900s. Sarah does not have a close relationship with her mother and does not choose to socialize in her mother's social circles. Nevertheless, she realizes that those connections and their endless teas and parties provide the opportunities to gain information that the police, especially male police, could never obtain. In the first novel in the series, *Murder on Astor Place* (Thompson, 1999), the importance of understanding human nature is very clear. Sarah describes how high-society women spend their days visiting each other and sharing information. While some may think this is idle gossip, Sarah recognizes these women are keen observers of behavior. Thus, her mother and the other women could help uncover the motives behind a crime.

> Women like her mother ... filled their idle hours by visiting and learning as much about their neighbors as they could.... No word or deed was too insignificant to escape their attentions, and they spent their entire lives analyzing one another's behavior [*Murder on Astor Place*, Thompson, 1999, p. 141].

As we saw in the previous chapter, the Golden Age detectives and, more recently, cozy mystery detectives use critical and analytical thinking to solve their mysteries and recognize the importance of human behavior and relationship skills to solve crimes. Like their psychoanalytic therapist counterparts, detectives uncover hidden and unconscious motives and needs influencing behavior. In addition, detective fiction, as a genre, relates to many of the unconscious conflicts psychoanalytic theorists believe individuals continually face. While the detectives and other characters may not directly assist us in addressing our inherent negative impulses like Freud's id or our darker aspects as described by Jung's shadow, they can certainly provide insights and provoke thought about these aspects of human nature. These stories typically involve characters facing personal and emotional struggles while attempting to solve the crime. Given this context, engaging with detective fiction can provide insights and coping mechanisms when dealing with our anxieties about loss, separation, or identity.

At the very least, detective fiction can be seen as a form of escapism, where readers are temporarily distracted from their real-life worries. Furthermore, detective stories often depict characters who exhibit resilience, intelligence, and determination in the face of adversity. Readers can draw inspiration from these fictional heroes and apply their problem-solving approaches to their own lives. Ultimately, the impact of detective fiction on an individual's ability to deal with their own issues could vary depending on the reader's personal connection to the themes presented in the stories. Nevertheless, detective fiction can serve as one tool individuals can use to understand themselves better via the techniques of psychoanalytic theorists. In the next chapter, we will see how changes in the world will lead to a shift, not only in the psychological paradigm prominent at the time but also in the type of detective fiction preferred by readers.

Suggested Detective Fiction/Literature to Accompany This Chapter:

- Any Agatha Christie novel, but especially those featuring the Belgian detective Hercule Poirot (suggested Poirot novels include *The Mysterious Affair at Styles*, *Death on the Nile*, and *Murder on the Orient Express*), or Christie's female sleuth Miss Marple (suggested Miss Marple novel is *The Body in the Library*)
- Sir Arthur Conan Doyle's novel *The Hound of the Baskervilles*
- Pauline Hopkins' short story "Talma Gordon"
- Dorothy Sayers' novel *Gaudy Night* featuring Harriet Vane and Lord Peter Wimsey
- Rudolph Fisher's short story "John Archer's Nose"
- Andrew Forrester's *The Female Detective,* a collection of short stories featuring Miss or Mrs. G, perhaps Miss Gladden (the book was published in 1864 and is considered the first to feature a female detective)
- The short story "The Golden Slipper" by Anna Katharine Green
- The short story "Daisy Bell" by Gladys Mitchell

2. Structuralism, Functionalism, and the Move to Psychoanalysis

- Catherine Louisa Pirkis' books and short stories featuring the detective Loveday Brooke
- Ngaio Marsh's *Roderick Alleyn series*

End-of-Chapter Mind Puzzlers:

1. Compare and contrast the actions of Mrs. G in "The Unraveled Mystery" with those of Sherlock Holmes in "A Scandal in Bohemia." Identify the shared and differing detective skills between the two characters. Analyze how gender differences, both actual and perceived, influence the portrayal of these detectives.
2. Which author, Andrew Forrester (author of *The Female Detective*) or Sir Arthur Conan Doyle (author of the *Sherlock Holmes* stories), may have been influenced by the contemporary field of psychology during the time of their published stories? Explain the possible reasons behind their incorporation of psychological elements.
3. In the story (or stories) you read, does the detective display any psychological skills associated with the scientific method or introspection discussed in the previous chapter? Why or why not? Provide specific quotes or passages from the story or stories to support your answer.
4. Identify examples of Freudian defense mechanisms, unconscious motivations, and other psychoanalytic elements in the readings related to this chapter.
5. Jungian archetypes often play an important role in many literary works, including detective fiction. Provide examples to illustrate the "hero" and other Jungian archetypes found in the stories you read.
6. Identify any of Horney's neurotic trends exhibited by characters in one of the stories you read. Evaluate whether any characters lack Horney's need for safety and satisfaction or display basic anxiety, as per Horney's theory.
7. Dorothy Sayers and Harriet Vane infer that a woman must choose between a career or a family. How does this relate to Erikson's stages of psychosocial development? How does this reflect in the behavior of Harriet Vane? How might she address Erikson's choices of values, career, and sexuality? Discuss the relevance of Erikson's stages for individuals in the 21st century.
8. In Chapter 2 of *Gaudy Night*, Harriet Vane says she has an "inferiority complex." Define an inferiority complex and identify

which specific psychologist developed the concept. Apply this idea to Harriet Vane and explain how it is relevant to her character.

9. Illustrate how Hercule Poirot and Miss Marple personify the soft-boiled detective through five examples from their respective stories. Include chapter numbers and detailed descriptions of the scenes.

10. How does Miss Marple use her skills to solve the mystery? What clues does she find important, and why does she think they are important? Does Miss Marple have a "scientific attitude," as Sir Henry says at the end of *The Body in the Library*? Give several examples to either agree or disagree with the statement.

11. Provide evidence from at least one short story and one novel to argue that a detective, like a psychoanalyst or therapist, searches for the truth in a similar manner. Draw parallels between their investigative approaches.

12. Many detective fiction short stories occur during the Victorian era or the years directly following this era. Do a little sleuthing and provide some information regarding the following:

    a. When did the Victorian era occur?

    b. What types of occupations did women have during this time in England? What about in the United States?

    c. What major historical or social events during this time were reflected in the stories?

    d. How did the Victorian era influence Freud and other psychoanalysts?

    e. How did the Victorian era influence the authors of early detective fiction stories?

Key Terms and People

- **Wilhelm Wundt**: regarded as the "father" of psychology, he established the first psychology lab in 1879, located in Leipzig, Germany
- **stimulus**: something introduced to a person or animal that leads to a specific reaction or response
- **structuralism**: the earliest major paradigm of psychology, focused on studying the most basic elements or structures of the mind to understand reactions and behaviors
- **introspection:** the process of thinking inwardly to understand sensations and resulting actions

2. Structuralism, Functionalism, and the Move to Psychoanalysis

- **functionalism**: a school of thought that focused on what the mind does, rather than its contents or structure
- **William James**: the father of American psychology, he developed the paradigm of functionalism and wrote about the concept of self in his 1890 book *The Principles of Psychology*
- **psychoanalysis**: a psychological paradigm founded by Freud that centered on the unconscious as the primary influence on personality and behavior
- **Sigmund Freud**: the first psychologist to develop a comprehensive theory of personality, focusing on unconscious motivation
- **hysteria**: physical or medical symptoms that lack clear physical explanations
- **psychic determinism**: a principle in Freud's theory stating that all our thoughts, actions, and emotions have meaning and purpose, and everything in nature is determined
- **conscious**: the thoughts and feelings that a person is currently aware of
- **preconscious**: the thoughts and feelings that are not present in awareness but can quickly move into awareness
- **unconscious:** the thoughts and feelings that are outside of conscious awareness
- **id**: the most primal part of our personality, operating on the **pleasure principle** and concerned solely with personal self-gratification, regardless of others.
- **ego**: strives to satisfy the id while also considering the limitations of the broader environment, operating on the **reality principle**
- **superego**: contains our values, beliefs, and the sense of right and wrong, operating on a **morality principle**
- **defense mechanisms**: unconscious strategies used by the ego to help cope with stress, anxiety, and unpleasantness
- **denial**: failure to acknowledge the existence of a problem
- **repression**: when a person "forgets about forgetting" something
- **projection**: when you attribute your unacceptable characteristics to another person
- **displacement**: when you shift a negative thought or impulse onto a safer object or person

- **rationalization:** overanalyzing a problem and making excuses
- **reaction formation:** replacing a negative or unpleasant impulse with its opposite
- **regression:** behaving as you did in the past or when you were younger
- **hypnosis:** when a person enters a suspended state of awareness or trance, allowing the hypnotist or therapist to ask the person questions that will help reveal their unconscious needs and motives
- **free association:** a therapeutic technique where clients share whatever comes to mind without overthinking their responses
- **whodunit:** a classic detective story where the detective unravels clues to discover who committed the crime
- **word association test:** a projective technique where a client responds to a word with the first word that comes to mind
- **dream analysis:** a therapeutic technique that interprets dreams as symbolic representations of unconscious desires and conflicts
- **manifest content:** the actual events and people within the dream
- **latent content:** the hidden, symbolic meaning behind the dream's actions and people
- **red herring:** a clue or suspect introduced in a story to purposefully mislead readers about the identity of the killer
- **Carl Jung:** Freud's most famous and successful student whose approach, called Analytical Psychology, focused less on sexuality and more on the importance of the unconscious
- **conscious ego:** perceptions, thoughts, feelings, and memories within our awareness
- **personal unconscious:** contains images and experiences not immediately conscious but can easily become part of the conscious ego
- **complexes:** clusters of related symptoms or thoughts within the unconscious
- **collective unconscious:** Jung's most controversial level of personality that contains common experiences shared among all humans
- **archetypes:** inherited predispositions to think and act in particular ways, originating from the repeated experiences of our ancestors and residing in our unconscious

2. Structuralism, Functionalism, and the Move to Psychoanalysis 49

- **persona**: our public mask or the image or side of our personality we present to the outside world
- **shadow**: the thoughts and feelings representing our "dark side"
- **anima/animus**: the characteristics and behaviors that represent our feminine and masculine sides
- **self**: Jung's most crucial element of the collective unconscious and the central archetype, driving individuals to strive for unity, growth, and integration of the whole personality
- **The Great Mother:** our preexisting concept of a typical or ideal mother, including positive and negative elements
- **The Wise Old Man:** symbolizes our preexisting knowledge of life's mysteries and what we would consider an all-knowing leader, who embodies wisdom and leadership
- **The Hero:** the protagonist in many stories who conquers the evil villain and overcomes darkness to save the day
- **Karen Horney**: an influential female psychoanalyst who focused on social forces and the relationships children develop with others early in life
- **basic hostility**: internalized or repressed hostility resulting from unmet basic needs for safety in childhood
- **basic anxiety**: feelings of insecurity arising from unresolved basic hostility
- **neurotic trends:** rigid patterns of behavior that dominate our personality and serve as defense mechanisms
- **moving toward people:** the compliant personality type; driven by a strong need for love, acceptance, and protection from others
- **moving against people:** the aggressive personality; perceives others as hostile and adopts an antagonistic stance for survival
- **moving away from people:** the detached personality; a person who seeks isolation and emotional distance from others
- **Erik Erikson:** an ego psychologist who believed that personality develops through psychosocial stages across life
- **introspection:** the process of self-reflection and inward thinking, considering options and weighing pros and cons
- **role experimentation:** when an individual tries out different values, careers, and sexualities through trial and error

- **soft-boiled detective fiction**: a type of detective fiction popular before World War II, where detectives solve crimes similar to puzzles, often in a small village setting
- **big reveal**: a plot technique where crucial information, such as the identity of the killer or important clues, is unveiled to readers, typically at the end of a novel
- **sleuth**: as a noun, refers to a detective, and as a verb, means to search for and discover information

Chapter Notes

1. This time frame coincides with the beginning of the detective fiction genre. A few years before Wundt, British author Wilkie Collins wrote what is generally considered the first detective novel, *The Moonstone* (1868), and Edgar Allan Poe published his Dupin short stories from 1841–1844.

2. Weber was a biologist who studied touch and the idea of a threshold for sensation. Along with his student Fechner, they introduced a concept or law, eventually called the Weber-Fechner law, that introduces the idea of a "just noticeable difference," which is the minimum increase in stimulation needed for a person to sense a difference in that stimulus. For example, if you were revising the amount of salt added to a recipe, the amount needed to taste a difference in salt flavor would be that "just noticeable difference" (Plotnik,1999). Fechner demonstrated that psychology could become a real science because the mind was susceptible to measurement and mathematical properties.

3. Wundt's student, Titchener, used the term structuralism to describe their research approach. Titchener also tried to determine the different components of consciousness using the tool of introspection. For example, in an experiment, a subject would be presented with an object, such as a pencil. The subject would then report the characteristics of that pencil (e.g., color or length). The subject would be instructed not to report the object's name (pencil) because that did not describe the raw data of what the subject was experiencing.

4. For a summary of the impact of the Industrial Revolution in Europe, see https://www.britannica.com/event/Industrial-Revolution.

5. Jean Charcot was a French neurologist who opened a neurological clinic in Paris in 1882. He was considered an excellent teacher who attracted many students, including Freud. Charcot was among the first to look for psychological explanations for physiological illnesses. You can read more about Charcot at https://www.ncbi.nlm.nih.gov/pmc/articles/PMC3064755/.

6. Red herrings are a type of philosophical fallacy but figure prominently in detective fiction, especially in the stories of Agatha Christie. One of her most famous novels, *And Then There Were None*, contains an excellent example of a red herring. An additional example is in Sir Arthur Conan Doyle's novel *The Hound of the Baskervilles* (http://www.literarydevices.com/red-herring/).

7. The *Nancy Drew Series* was created by children's book publisher Edward Stratemeyer in 1930. Stratemeyer developed the initial plot outlines for most of the early books but did not write them. The author named Carolyn Keene was actually a pseudonym for many different writers over the years. The first writer was Mildred Wirt, a stay-at-home mother who was paid $125 to $250 for each book she wrote. She also received one-fifth of the royalties from any book she had written. Wirt did not write all of the *Nancy Drew* novels, but she likely was most influential in determining Nancy's personality and behaviors. To read more about the development of the Nancy Drew series, I recommend Melanie Rehak's book *Girl Sleuth: Nancy Drew and the Women Who Created Her* by Harvest Books.

8. Freud's Stages of Psychosexual Development include: the oral stage (birth–1 year),

2. Structuralism, Functionalism, and the Move to Psychoanalysis 51

when children are dependent on others and learn about the environment by putting things into their mouths; the anal stage (1–3 years), when children are concerned with retention and expulsion of feces, and so toilet training may influence personality development; the phallic stage (3–7 years), when children are focused on love and sex with their opposite-sex parent and experience the Oedipus complex (males) or Electra complex (females); the latency period (7–12 years), when children repress infantile sexuality and focus on just being children; and the genital stage (ages 12 on) when individuals are focused on finding and keeping genuine and reproductive love.

9. Other Neopsychoanalytic Theorists or Neo-Freudians include Alfred Adler, who developed the theory of Individual Psychology and the concepts of inferiority and superiority complexes, and Erich Fromm, whose theory focused on the need for freedom and belonging. See Schultz (2016) or Fromm's book *Escape from Freedom* (1941, Farrar & Rinehart) to learn more about these theorists.

10. *The Strange Case of Dr. Jekyll and Mr. Hyde* is a gothic novella written by Robert Louis Stevenson and published in 1886. "The names of Dr. Jekyll and Mr. Hyde, the two alter egos of the main character, have become shorthand for the exhibition of wildly contradictory behavior, especially between private and public selves" (https://www.britannica.com/topic/The-Strange-Case-of-Dr-Jekyll-and-Mr-Hyde). The novella can be found for free online at http://www.gutenberg.org/cache/epub/42/pg42-images.html.

11. Horney's neurotic needs include: affection and approval; a dominant partner in life; narrow and constricted limits to life; power; exploitation; prestige; personal admiration; personal achievement or ambition; self-sufficiency and independence; perfection and unassailability (Horney, K. 1942. *Self-analysis* (pp. 54–60). W.W. Norton & Company).

12. "A Scandal in Bohemia" was the very first short story published by Sir Arthur Conan Doyle featuring Sherlock Holmes and Dr. Watson. Altogether there were 56 short stories written by Conan Doyle. This first story was published in *The Strand Magazine* in June of 1891, and can also be found in the collection of short stories in *The Adventures of Sherlock Holmes*, published in 1892. Project Gutenberg's electronic text of *The Adventures of Sherlock Holmes* is free at https://www.gutenberg.org/files/1661/1661-h/1661-h.htm.

13. To read more about ego psychologists and Heinz Hartmann, see Hartmann, H. (1939/1958). Ego Psychology and the Problem of Adaptation. Trans., David Rapaport. International Universities Press, Inc.

14. To read a collection of short stories from other Golden Age authors, read *Bodies from the Library* (2018), a short story collection selected by Tony Medawar (Collins Crime Club/HarperCollins Publishers).

References

American Psychological Association. (2012). *Mamie Phipps Clark, PhD, and Kenneth Clark, PhD: Featured Psychologists.* https://www.apa.org/pi/oema/resources/ethnicity-health/psychologists/clark.
Boring, E. (2008). *A History of Experimental Psychology* (volume 1 and 2). Cosmo Publications.
Brown, J. (1998). *The Self.* Mc-Graw Hill.
Burger, J. (2018). *Personality* (10th edition). Cengage Learning.
Cawelti, J.G. (1976). *Adventure, Mystery, and Romance: Formula Stories as Art and Popular Culture.* University of Chicago Press.
Chandler, R. (1944, December). The simple art of murder. *The Atlantic Monthly.*
Charles, J., Morrison, J., & Clark, C. (2002). *The Mystery Readers' Advisory: The Librarian's Clues to Murder and Mayhem.* American Library Association.
Cherry, K. (2020, May 25). *Who Were the Neo-Freudians?* https://www.verywellmind.com/who-were-the-neo-freudians-2795576.
Christie, A. (1930). *The Murder at the Vicarage.* Dodd, Mead and Company.
Christie, A. (1942). *The Body in the Library.* Dodd, Mead and Company.
Crombie, D. (2021). Plot and the bones of a mystery. In L. Child and L. King (Eds)., *How to Write a Mystery: A Handbook from Mystery Writers of America.* Scribner.

Coon, D., & Mitterer, J.O. (2014). *Psychology: A Journey* (5th Edition). Wadsworth Cengage Learning.
Danziger, K. (1990). *Constructing the Subject: Historical Origins of Psychological Research.* Cambridge University Press.
Dunn, M.D. (2016). *Transparent Interiors: Detective and Mystery Fiction on the Age of Photography.* [Unpublished doctoral dissertation]. The City University of New York.
Ephron, H. (2005). *Writing and Selling Your Mystery Novel: How to Knock 'em Dead with Style.* Writer's Digest Books: F + W Publications, Inc.
Erikson, E.H. (1963). *Childhood and Society.* W.W. Norton & Company.
Erikson, E.H. (1968). *Identity: Youth and Crisis.* W.W. Norton & Company.
Freud, A. (1936). *The Ego and the Mechanisms of Defense.* International Universities Press, Inc.
Freud, S. (1900/1913 Eng). *The Interpretation of Dreams.* The Macmillan Co.
Freud, S. (1910). The origin and development of psychoanalysis. *American Journal of Psychology, 21*(2), 181–218. Doi:10.2307/1413001. JSTOR 1413001.
Freud, S. (1920/1966). *Introductory Lectures on Psychoanalysis.* W.W. Norton & Company.
Freud, S. (1989). *The Psychopathology of Everyday Life.* W.W. Norton & Company.
Gates, H.L. Jr., Smith, V., Andrews, W.L., Benston, K., Edwards, B.H., Smith Foster, F., McDowell, D.E., O'Meally, R.G., Spillers, H., & Wall, C.A. (Eds). (2014). *The Norton Anthology of African-American Literature* (3rd Edition). W.W. Norton & Company.
Gay, P. (1988). *Freud: A Life for Our Time.* W.W. Norton & Company.
Hergenhahn, B.R. (2009). *An Introduction to the History of Psychology* (6th Edition). Wadsworth.
Horney, K. (1937). *The Neurotic Personality of Our Time.* W.W. Norton & Company.
Horney, K. (1942). *Self-analysis.* W.W. Norton & Company.
Howe, A.N. (2008). *It Didn't Mean Anything: A Psychoanalytic Reading of American Detective Fiction.* McFarland.
Hutter, A.D. (1975). Dreams, transformations, and literature: The implications of detective fiction. *Victorian Studies*, December, 181–209.
Jackson, C. (2002). *Myth and Ritual in Women's Detective Fiction.* McFarland.
James, W. (1890). *The Principles of Psychology* (Vol. 1). Macmillan.
Keller, F.S. (1973). *The Definition of Psychology* (2nd Edition). Prentice Hall.
Leahey, T.H. (1991). *A History of Modern Psychology.* Prentice Hall.
Marsh, N. (1934, 2011). *A Man Lay Dead: Roderick Alleyn #1.* Felony & Mayhem Press.
Mayer, F.S., & Sutton, K. (1996). *Personality: An Integrative Approach.* Prentice Hall.
Merriam-Webster.com Dictionary (n.d.a). Sleuth. In Merriam-Webster.com dictionary. Retrieved November 28, 2020, from www.merriam-webster.com/dictionary/sleuth.
Merriam-Webster.com Dictionary (n.d.). Whodunit. In Merriam-Webster.com dictionary. Retrieved October 9, 2020, from https://www.merriam-webster.com/dictionary/whodunit.
Panek, L.L. (2000). *New Hard-boiled Writers 1970s-1990s.* Bowling Green State University Popular Press.
Pauline Hopkins. (2021). In *Encyclopædia Britannica*. Retrieved from https://academic-eb-com.proxy.bc.edu/levels/collegiate/article/Pauline-Hopkins/2868.
Pauline Hopkins Society (n.d.). *Biography of Pauline E. Hopkins (1859–1930).* Retrieved from http://www.paulinehopkinssociety.org/biography/.
Plotnik, R. (1999). *Introduction to Psychology* (5th Edition). Brooks/Cole/Wadsworth.
Priestman, M. (Ed.). (2003). *The Cambridge Companion to Crime Fiction.* Cambridge University Press.
Rehak, M. (2005). *Girl Sleuth: Nancy Drew and the Women Who Created Her.* Harcourt.
Schultz, D. (1986). *Theories of Personality* (3rd Ed.). Brooks Cole.
Schultz, D.P., & Schultz, S.E. (2016). *Theories of Personality* (11th Ed.). Cengage Learning.
Slung, M. (1975). *Crime on Her Mind: Fifteen Stories of Female Sleuths from the Victorian Era to the Forties.* Pantheon Books.
Smith, D. (2014). *The Sherlock Holmes Companion: An Elementary Guide.* Aurum Press.
Stasio, M. (1992, October 18). Crime/mystery; murder least foul: The cozy, soft-boiled mystery. *The New York Times.*

2. Structuralism, Functionalism, and the Move to Psychoanalysis

Thompson, V. (1999). *Murder on Astor Place*. Berkley Prime Crime.
Wilson, E. (1945, June 20). Who killed Roger Ackroyd. *The New Yorker*.
Wundt, W. (1873). *Principles of Physiological Psychology. I.* (E.B. Titchener, Trans.). Sonnenschein.
Yang, A. (2010). Psychoanalysis and detective fiction: A tale of Freud and criminal storytelling. *Perspectives in Biology and Medicine* 53(4), 596–604. https://doi:10.1353/pbm.2010.0006.

3

The Shift to Behaviorism and Overt Action

The behavioristic era of psychology mainly ranged from the 1930s through the 1950s and is "The Golden Age of Theory" in the history of psychology. In the United States, during the years preceding World War I, psychology focused more on the mind's functional processes than its structural content (Leahey, 1991). Leading up to World War II, the focus shifted to more observable actions, perhaps due to the focus on the horrific global acts occurring during that time—economic depression, political unrest, and military invasions. Behaviorism was especially popular in the United States because it was "essentially a psychology of adaptation and capacity.... It ... replaced functional psychology as an active school, for it adopts functional psychology's chief tenet of showing what mind is used for" (Boring, 2008, p. 588).

Led by animal researchers, psychologists wanted to be more objective (not subjective or intuitive) in their research methodology and theories. After World War II, the behaviorist approach explained the "problems of society" (Leahey, 1991, p. 217). As a result, the paradigm of behaviorism became a more objective approach to psychology, one that did not believe in the study of the mind or consciousness. It focused on stimulus and responses—the former, a thing or event, and the latter, an observable behavior (Boring, 2008). Psychologists wanted to study people's overt behaviors and actions and be more action-oriented. Before introducing those early American behaviorists, let us consider the pioneering and groundbreaking work of Russian psychologist **Ivan Pavlov**. His methodology and theory of learning would become the foundation of the Behaviorist Movement (Leahey, 1991).

Ivan Pavlov

Pavlov (1849–1936) was a Russian physiologist who developed the idea of a conditioned reflex, first in dogs and then in humans. He won

3. The Shift to Behaviorism and Overt Action

the Nobel Prize in Physiology in 1904 for his digestive secretions research (Gantt, 2020). However, it is for his theory of **classical conditioning** that he is most well-known.

Pavlov had a "positivist's faith in objective method as the touchstone of natural science, and consequently rejected reference to mind" (Leahey, 1991, p. 172). Pavlov applied the scientific method's steps to investigate an ordinary behavior or reflex in one particular animal type. Pavlov noticed that dogs often salivated at times other than when eating, for example, during food preparation. He designed some experiments and found that a neutral object, what he called the stimulus, could cause a behavior. Pavlov conducted experiments to teach a dog how to anticipate or learn a particular behavior by introducing a specific stimulus to the dog to produce the desired behavior (Kalat, 1999; Plotnik, 1999).

The classical conditioning procedure involves three key elements: the **unconditioned stimulus**, the **unconditioned response**, and the **neutral stimulus**. The unconditioned stimulus (UCS) is an object or event that will naturally lead to or trigger a specific response or behavior. In Pavlov's experiments, he showed his hungry dogs some food. Naturally, the food made the dogs salivate—any pet owner will confirm this! This salivation is completely unlearned and is an involuntary reflex (Kalat, 1999; Plotnik, 1999; Rathus, 2013); therefore, it is called the unconditioned response (UCR).

Pavlov then identified another object that generally would not cause a dog to salivate—in his case, a bell, which became his neutral stimulus (NS). In classical conditioning, you first show your participants or test subjects your UCS several times to be sure you get the desired reaction. Then you introduce the NS before showing them the UCS again. In Pavlov's experiment, he would bring his dogs in, ring a bell in front of them, and then show them the food, which would cause salivation. After giving the participant (dog) the pairing of the NS + UCS a number of times (between 10 and 100 is a reasonable estimate), you then ring the bell for the dog without showing the food, which should still lead to salivation in the dog. At this point, the bell has become a **conditioned stimulus** (CS) because the animal has learned to respond to this previously neutral object, and the salivation has now become a **conditioned response** (CR) because it is a learned behavior. The steps of classical conditioning are as follows:

$$UCS \rightarrow UCR$$
$$NS + UCS \rightarrow UCR$$
$$CS \rightarrow CR$$

In Pavlov's experiment:

food (UCS) → salivation (UCR)
bell (NS) + food (UCS) → salivation (UCR)
bell (CS) → salivation (CR)

Classical conditioning is one of the simplest forms of learning and is relatively easy to replicate with your pets (or humans). It is important to remember that you must present the NS first when you pair the NS and UCS. Also, if given too long before the UCS, it will likely not have as strong of an effect. How long do classically conditioned responses last? Eventually, the learned behavior ends when you no longer pair the NS and UCS together. As any pet owner knows, if a dog only hears the bell, eventually, they will figure out they will not get the food anymore, so the dog will stop salivating. When Pavlov continued to ring the bell without showing the dog any meat, the dog salivated less and less, and the salivation eventually stopped altogether—what is called **extinction**.

Pavlov also found that sometimes the CR may reappear after extinction if in the same environment. Pavlov found that after he extinguished the behavior and returned the dogs to their cages the following day, they salivated again to the bell—what Pavlov referred to as **spontaneous recovery**. Pavlov also found that sometimes the dog responded to sounds similar to the original bell he used, like when a buzzer or a ticking clock also produced salivation. If a stimulus that is different yet similar to your original NS/CS produces the CR, **generalization** is the result. Generalization can lead to fears or phobias—if people are bitten by one breed of dog (for example, a chihuahua), they may learn to fear all breeds of dogs or possibly all other animals. The final concept associated with classical conditioning explains how people can become conditioned to a particular stimulus. Pavlov trained some of his dogs to salivate to a specific tone of the bell (e.g., a high-pitched bell). The dog would learn not to salivate to other sounding bells (e.g., low-pitched bells) if they never received food paired with that low-pitched bell—this final concept is what Pavlov called **discrimination** (Leahey, 1991; Pavlov, 1957).

Investigative thinking challenge:
Reflect on an example of classical conditioning rooted in pet and human behavior. Which do you think was easier to learn—the pet or human behavior? What factors contribute to the ease of learning in classical conditioning when comparing pet and human behavior?

While classical conditioning works in animals and humans, humans can take it a step further. In higher-order conditioning, the CS is paired with a neutral stimulus that takes on the CS properties. For example, if a dog bites you, you may also develop fears that will keep you away from the

3. The Shift to Behaviorism and Overt Action

dog's street. Advertising uses the same principles of classical conditioning, often pairing a celebrity and a product:

LeBron James (UCS) → respect/admiration (UCR)
Hummer (NS) + LeBron James (UCS) → respect/admiration (UCR)
Hummer (CS) → respect/admiration (CR)

A good marketing approach will pair a celebrity people admire with a specific product. The product's company hopes the consumers will transfer their positive feelings to the advertised products, thus leading them to buy the product. It is also the case that classical conditioning can prevent a behavior—either intentionally or unintentionally. Sometimes, we hate and avoid a particular food because eating it makes us sick. This learned avoidance is also the idea behind using the technique of **conditioned taste aversion** (Reilly, 2009) to help individuals stop a nuisance or unhealthy behavior—for example, smoking.

give drug (UCS) → nausea (UCR)
smoking (NS) + drug (UCS) → nausea (UCR)
smoking (CS) → nausea (CR)

The result of this example is that the person would eventually stop smoking. Sometimes, pairing the NS/CS and UCS is unintentional but can still produce strong and long-lasting reactions and behavior changes. The following is a personal example that exemplifies this:

helicopter ride (UCS) → nausea/throwing up (UCR)
eating pineapples (NS) + helicopter ride (UCS) → nausea/throwing up (UCR)
the smell of pineapples (CS) → nausea (CR)

It only took one helicopter ride and the unfortunate decision to eat pineapples for breakfast that morning, leading to my avoidance of them for nearly ten years. While this was a poor decision on my part, it is generally adaptive because people and animals would want to avoid eating food that causes nausea or other physical distress.

Thorndike and Instrumental Conditioning

Even before Pavlov, an American psychologist was conducting experiments with hungry cats—his name was **Edward Thorndike** (1874–1949). Thorndike was among the first to state that learning can occur without the influence of consciousness (Leahey, 1991). Thorndike put his cats in a puzzle box, and if the cat made the right move or behavior, a door would open, and the cat could get out and eat some fish. The cat learned the correct behavior to escape, so Thorndike called his approach to learning

instrumental conditioning because the response was instrumental in the animal escaping from the box. At first, the cats would scratch the walls, meow, or try other behaviors to escape. Then by chance, the cat would make the correct response and get the food—the cat would learn through trial and error learning. The cat would then repeat the behavior and learn what it has to do to get the food. If the animal's response does not lead to food and escape, the animal will stop making that response.

Based on his observations, Thorndike developed his **law of effect**, which states that a response leading to a satisfying consequence is increased and will occur again. In contrast, unsatisfactory responses (such as those followed by punishment) are weakened and likely will not be repeated (Encyclopædia Britannica, 2020c). The law of effect also states that "the greater the reward or punishment, the greater the change in the connection" (Leahey, 1991, p. 169).

While Thorndike is primarily connected to behaviorism, he was also influential in educational psychology. Thorndike served as a professor of educational psychology at Columbia University from 1904 to 1940 and was among the first to advocate for applying psychological principles, research methodology, and statistics in the classroom. His research during the 1920s on adult learning also helped increase the popularity of continuing education (Encyclopædia Britannica, 2020c).

John B. Watson

John Broadus Watson (1878–1958) founded behaviorism in America; it was the dominant psychological paradigm in America from the 1920s through the 1940s (Boring, 2008). In 1908, Watson began his career as a psychology professor at Johns Hopkins University, first studying animal behavior. Watson found that studying human psychology could be more objective and that he could use the same methodological techniques to obtain data rather than previous methods, such as introspection (Leahey, 1991). He claimed that animal research could teach us how humans learn conditioned responses and reflexes (Watson, 1914). Watson then expanded his research to focus on humans—particularly infants (Encyclopædia Britannica, 2020d).

Around 1919, Watson and his graduate student Rosalie Rayner conducted one of the most infamous psychological studies—the **Little Albert experiment.**[1] In this experiment, Watson trained or conditioned an 11-month-old boy called "Little Albert" to fear a white rat (Watson & Rayner, 1920). Watson and Rayner applied the same principles of classical conditioning used only previously in animals with the child, which very quickly led to his development of a fear of the white rat. In Watson's Little Albert experiment:

$$\text{loud noise (UCS)} \rightarrow \text{fear/startle reflex (UCR)}$$
$$\text{rat (NS) + noise (UCS)} \rightarrow \text{fear (UCR)}$$
$$\text{rat (CS)} \rightarrow \text{fear (CR)}$$

Little Albert also experienced the classical conditioning principle of generalization of his fear response to other objects similar to the white rat, such as a white rabbit, fluffy white beard, and a white fur coat (Plotnik, 1999). Watson and Rayner's experiment has been criticized for violating many of the current ethical guidelines for research with human participants, mainly because they did not remove or "uncondition" Little Albert's fear before returning him to his mother. Although controversial, Watson did provide evidence that humans can learn behaviors and emotional responses such as fear through classical conditioning principles. He clarifies this in his famous quote:

> Give me a dozen healthy infants, well-formed, and my own specified world to bring them up in and I'll guarantee to take anyone at random and train him to become any type of specialist I might select—doctor, lawyer, artist, merchant-chief, and, yes, even beggar-man and thief, regardless of his talents, penchants, tendencies, abilities, vocations, and race of his ancestors [Watson, *Behaviorism*, 1925, p. 10].

Watson's influence in psychology, however, was short-lived. In 1920, because of the publicity surrounding his affair with his graduate student Rayner and his divorce from his first wife, Watson was asked to resign from Johns Hopkins. Watson married Rayner in 1921. He entered the advertising business in 1921, thanks to a letter of recommendation from Edward Titchener and significantly increased marketing research. Watson's strategies helped Pond's cold cream, Maxwell House coffee, and Johnson's baby powder. Watson regretted not being able to further his psychological research, especially in child development,[2] but he will always be remembered as the initial contributor to the field of radical behaviorism in the United States (Hergenhahn, 2009).

Investigative thinking challenge:
Put yourself in the shoes of a market researcher and envision a product where you can implement the principles of classical conditioning to boost your sales. How would you approach the task?

While Watson left the field of psychology, behaviorism continued, primarily due to Watson's ability to fit his methods into the content of the field of psychology at that time (Boring, 2008). A new form of behaviorism, called neo-behaviorism, emerged, which combined Watson's behaviorism with **logical positivism,** which began in Vienna in the 1920s and focused on rational and empirical data (Hergenhahn, 2009; Kitchener, 2004). Logical positivists only accepted theoretical concepts if they could be "logically tied to empirical observations" (Hergenhahn, 2009, p. 424). Logical positivism would allow the study of observable events and include theoretical implications to explain those events, especially those related to the learning process (Hergenhahn, 2009). **Edward Tolman** (1886–1959) and **Clark Hull** (1884–1952) led the Neobehaviorist Movement.

Tolman and Hull

Tolman found Watson's stimulus-response behaviorism and study of the conditioned reflexes too limiting. However, he did believe in objective observation and using scientific and experimental procedures to conduct research. Tolman (1932) suggested that behavior is purposive and is a goal-directed act that is served and guided by cognitive processes. The Gestalt[3] school of psychology also influenced Tolman, although he mainly focused on behaviorism. His development of intervening variables (variables that intervene or come between situational events and behavior) significantly impacted the development of the paradigm of cognitive psychology, especially the idea of a cognitive map.

Tolman believed that cognitive thoughts were the intervening variables between the situation or environment and individuals' resulting behavior. Using logical positivism, Tolman linked intervening variables or theoretical concepts to observable behavior that could be measured (Hergenhahn, 2009). However, Tolman disagreed with Watson and Thorndike in that he believed learning could occur even without reinforcement. This idea would persevere in future years and would influence **Albert Bandura's** social-learning theory of **observational learning**.

Hull's theory was very influential in the 1940s–1950s, replacing Tolman's as the most regarded and cited by experimental psychologists and many students. Hull contributed to psychology mainly by developing his *approach* to studying behavior rather than his theory's specifics (Encyclopædia Britannica, 2020b). Influenced by logical positivism, Hull operationally defined all of his theoretical concepts. Like Tolman, Hull believed that behavior could be purposive and sought to attain specific goals (Hergenhahn, 2009; Leahey, 1991) and explained behavior in terms of stimulus and response (Encyclopædia Britannica, 2020e). Hull (1943) defined the stimulus-response connection as dependent on both the kind and the amount of reinforcement, which was somewhat different from Tolman.

3. The Shift to Behaviorism and Overt Action   61

Hull also believed that individuals' internal drives that arose from their needs influenced behavior.

Eventually, Hull's theory did lose popularity with research psychologists who sought to explain human behavior in more realistic and applied settings rather than in artificial laboratory settings (Hergenhahn, 2009). This section includes Hull because his "hypothetico-deductive theory," which likely influenced the development of **Piaget**'s formal operational stage,[4] also mirrors a detective's thinking. Hull states that:

> Empirical observation, supplemented by shrewd conjecture, is the main source of the primary principles or postulates of a science. Such formulations ... yield inferences or theorems, of which some may agree with the empirical outcome of the conditions in question, and some may not. Primary propositions yielding logical deductions which consistently agree with the observed empirical outcomes are retained, whereas those which disagree are rejected or modified.... Deductions made from those surviving postulates, while never absolutely certain, do at length become highly trustworthy [Hull, 1932, p. 382].

Hull's explanation closely resembles Sherlock Holmes' explanation of his deductive reasoning when solving a case discussed in Chapter 1.

B.F. Skinner

Burrhus Frederic (B.F.) **Skinner** (1904–1990) is often considered the most influential psychologist of all time. Skinner's approach, radical behaviorism, most closely followed the principles of Watson. Skinner was born in Pennsylvania to parents who instilled in him strict standards for proper behavior. Skinner's father, a lawyer, would continually warn the young B.F. what punishment would await if he did not follow the correct rules and law and even brought him to a lecture once about New York's Sing Sing prison. Skinner graduated from Hamilton College with a degree in English, and his life goal was to become a writer.[5] He was fond of reading books by Pavlov and Watson, and he eventually enrolled in graduate school at Harvard University to study psychology. He earned his Ph.D. in three years and returned to Harvard as a faculty member in 1948 (he became emeritus in 1974) until he died in 1990 (Schultz, 1986).

During the 1930s, Skinner developed **operant conditioning,** in which behavior depends on consequences or reinforcement. As a radical behaviorist, Skinner believed the relationship between stimulus and response can explain all behavior. The "science of mind" could not and should not be studied because researchers cannot directly observe and study the mind. Thus, only observable behavior should be the focus of psychological research and theory (Skinner, 1990). Skinner's approach is similar to Thorndike's.

However, Skinner called his learning or conditioning "operant" rather than instrumental because the animal acts or operates on the environment to get the wanted effect. Skinner applied his techniques to train animals to perform complex behaviors (one example was when he trained pigeons to play table tennis). One of his best-known experimental devices, the Skinner box, is often used in research to observe how drugs may affect animal behavior (Encyclopædia Britannica, 2020a). Two common behaviors seen in animals placed in a Skinner box include these examples:

Skinner Box Examples:

hungry rat presses bar → food → increases pressing, increases food
RESPONSE REINFORCEMENT RESPONSE REPEATED

pigeon pecks at key → food → increases pecking
RESPONSE REINFORCEMENT RESPONSE REPEATED

Both examples illustrate Skinner's principle of **positive reinforcement** because completing the response allows you to get more of the reinforcement—in other words, you are adding a positive or pleasant stimulus that increases a behavior. An alternative to this scenario that will increase the behavior occurs when an unpleasant stimulus is taken away from an animal or individual—what Skinner referred to as **negative reinforcement** (Myers, 2012; 2015).

Rat presses bar → decreases shock → increases pressing behavior
RESPONSE REINFORCEMENT RESPONSE REPEATED

The goal of reinforcement is to ensure that the behavior continues by adding something pleasant (positive reinforcement) or taking something unpleasant away (negative reinforcement). Students often get confused by this and focus on the word "negative" and think it must be the reinforcement that decreases behavior, but that is not the case. If you are unsure you understand the difference, consider when you enter a car and sit in either of the front seats. When the car turns on, an alarm will remind you to wear your seatbelt. The noise will not stop until you do so, and most likely, you will do it quickly. You have been operantly conditioned following Skinner's principle of negative reinforcement to buckle your seatbelt, and you likely will continue to do so every time you enter a car. In this example:

buckling seatbelt → stops alarm/noise → continue to buckle the seatbelt
RESPONSE REINFORCEMENT RESPONSE REPEATED

But what if there is a behavior that you do not want to increase or continue? Skinner outlined the principles of that as well, but instead of calling it reinforcement, he called it **punishment.** As an example,

3. The Shift to Behaviorism and Overt Action

cat jumps on a table	→	squirt it with water	→	decreases behavior/ jumping stops
RESPONSE		PUNISHMENT		RESPONSE STOPS

In punishment, either an unpleasant stimulus is presented (positive punishment) or a pleasant stimulus is withdrawn (negative punishment). In either case, the result should be a decrease in the response. (Incidentally, while the example above should theoretically work when working with cats, achieving the desired outcome can be challenging!).

It is also true that only through the direct observation of the behavior in an animal or person can you tell if a stimulus serves as a reinforcement or a punishment. If it increases behavior, it serves as reinforcement; if it decreases behavior, it serves as a punishment. For example, if a second-grade teacher yells at both Susie and Billy for talking in class, and as a result, Susie stops talking, the yelling is a punisher for her. However, if Billy increases his talking, the teacher's yelling serves as a reinforcer for him, perhaps because he likes the teacher's extra attention. The same action can be interpreted differently depending on the person, much like in detective fiction stories. The idea of murder for most characters comes with the associated consequence of punishment, such as getting arrested, possibly being put to death, or at the very least, immense guilt. But for others who could be classified as Moriarty-type[6] criminals, the murder or other crime brings a result (e.g., power, money, political gain) that makes that person want to continue with their initial action, hence a reinforcement.

When using operant conditioning with animals or humans, it is sometimes hard for the subject to know what response to make. As the researcher, you can help them achieve the task by reinforcing behavior through gradual steps approaching the desired behavior—what Skinner referred to as **shaping** (Myers, 2012, 2015).

Investigative thinking challenge:
1. Collaborate with a partner and have each of you perform a behavior secretly chosen by the other person. The first person should come up with a straightforward behavior in their mind.
2. Instruct your partner to guess the behavior and attempt different actions.
3. Provide positive reinforcement, like saying good or clapping, when they move in the right direction. 4. Observe how long it takes for both of you to execute the desired behavior, and afterward, discuss the experience and the learning process.

In the long term, Skinner's operant conditioning may not always maintain the behavior because often, when there is no longer reinforcement, the behavior stops. The classical conditioning principle of extinction is also seen here in operant conditioning. Spontaneous recovery, discrimination, and generalization can also occur with operant conditioning, just like in classical conditioning. To help prolong the duration of a reinforced behavior, even when reinforcement may not always happen, Skinner developed four schedules of reinforcement to specify different relationships between the number and timing of the responses and the subsequent reinforcement (Skinner, 1976). Not presenting the reinforcement every time after the behavior will make it more difficult to extinguish (the preferred option). These schedules of reinforcement (Myers, 2012; 2015) are:

1. **fixed ratio**: a specific number of responses is needed for reinforcement to be given, such as in the idea of piecework when workers are paid for completing a specific number of tasks (paid for every 10 baskets of apples picked at an orchard; in this case, a worker would get paid the same if they picked 10 or 15 baskets, they would have to pick 20 baskets to be paid twice what they would for picking 10 baskets)
2. **variable ratio**: an average number of responses is needed for reinforcement, such as when slot machines payout after an average number of plays by people
3. **fixed interval**: reinforcement is given after a specific time has passed, such as when workers are paid every two weeks (regardless of the actual amount of work completed by them during that time)
4. **variable interval**: reinforcement is given after an average amount of time has passed, such as when an instructor decides to assign a surprise quiz once every three weeks, but students are not sure exactly which day it will be handed out (a surprise quiz is also likely to be viewed as a reinforcement for the instructor and not the students in the class)

Skinner's schedules of reinforcement and operant conditioning principles became the foundation of activities such as animal training and, even more significantly, behavioral therapy. One of the most popular therapeutic techniques today is Applied Behavioral Analysis (ABA), which uses Skinner's techniques to help improve social, academic, communication, and adaptive skills and behaviors. ABA has been unusually effective in helping children and adults with autism (Psychology Today, n.d.). Another example of Skinner's theory put into practice involves using **token economies**, often in hospitals and schools. Individuals receive items or "tokens" for performing appropriate or desired behaviors in a token economy environment. They can exchange the tokens for other things or privileges they consider valuable (Hergenhahn, 2009; Schultz, 1986).

Ayllon and Azrin (1968) described a study of 40 institutionalized female psychotic patients who were provided tokens for successfully performing jobs or typical daily behaviors (taking a bath at the specified time, brushing their hair, or other similar activities). The tokens were collected and exchanged for things like buying candy, being able to take a walk around the hospital grounds, attending a movie, or being allowed a supervised trip into town. The women improved their behaviors and became less dependent. While using token economies is generally successful, if the tokens stop, the behavior improvement is also likely to stop (Kazdin & Bootzin, 1972). Even though other paradigms developed after this time, Skinner's techniques continue to be popular and effectively used in psychotherapy and behavioral training (Hergenhahn, 2009).

> ***Investigative thinking challenge:***
> *Identify a behavior you would like to improve or enhance, whether it is for yourself, someone else, or a pet within your home. Then, devise a token economy system aimed at accomplishing your objective. Implement the program and evaluate its effectiveness over several weeks.*

Albert Bandura and Observational Learning

Albert Bandura (1925–2021) was born in Mundare, a small farming town in Alberta, Canada (Burger, 2018). Bandura was a faculty member at Stanford University, beginning in 1953, and was one of the most influential psychologists of the past century (Albert Bandura, 2017). While Bandura was more recently known for his social cognitive theory, he first developed a theory of social learning called observational or **vicarious learning** (Bandura, 1977). Bandura agreed with Skinner that behavior is learned but proposed that learning could occur through observing and modeling others' actions without needing direct reinforcement (Mayer & Sutton, 1996; Schultz & Schultz, 2016). Bandura developed his theory based on a series of classic **Bobo doll** studies (Bandura, 1965; Bandura et al., 1963).

In the Bobo doll experiment, preschool-aged children watched a video of an adult hitting and kicking an inflatable punching bag with a clown on it (the Bobo doll punching bag). When the children were left alone in a room with toys, including a Bobo doll, the children who had watched the adults act aggressively repeated the same behavior. The children who did not watch a video of adults acting aggressively towards the doll (**a control group**) did not act as aggressively. Bandura ran many versions of the original experiment, demonstrating that the children learned behavior just by watching others perform it. The children were especially likely to repeat the behavior if their models were rewarded for the behavior rather than punished (Burger, 2018).

The real-life application of Bandura's theory of observational learning is endless. It explains behaviors resulting from watching violent television, playing violent video games, and the influences of aggressive parental behavior. Bandura's research found that children may develop aggressive "scripts" that directly lead to increased aggressive behavior as well as a tendency to interpret social interactions aggressively (Huesmann & Malamuth, 1986). These scripts can explain recent school shootings perpetrated by video game-playing teens. Bandura's research provides evidence that not only does the media influence people's behaviors but that the content of media (e.g., television shows, movies, literature) may reflect the interests of society at any given time. This connection to the media also explains how detective fiction has evolved to cater to the broader public's interests and preferences over the years.

Behaviorism and Detective Fiction

The early behaviorists wished to be less dependent on introspection as a technique of gathering data and focused on more easily seen external stimuli—they focused on more easily tracked down "clues" to behavior. This shift in approach coincided with historical events, especially in the United States, that left people looking for change, entertainment, and straightforward explanations for behavior. These events included Prohibition, the Great Depression, and the events leading up to and including World War II. This shift also happened in detective fiction. While the soft-boiled detective stories of Agatha Christie remained popular, a new and "tougher" type of writing emerged. This new genre, termed **hard-boiled detective fiction**, set its stories not in an idyllic British village but within the tough city streets of the United States—most often California.

Hard-boiled fiction used more realistic writing, including violence, sex, and colloquial language (i.e., popular slang). The first hard-boiled short story, "The False Burton Combs," was published by Carroll John Daly in 1922 (Nolan, 1985, p. 36). Like behaviorist psychologists, hard-boiled detective fiction contains stories where the situation people are involved in, and groups to which they belong (like the mob or gangs), influence their behavior. The stories involved violence and the type of

3. The Shift to Behaviorism and Overt Action

crime that was most common during that time (corruption, thefts, bootlegging). The hard-boiled detective is characterized by being: male, cynical, a street-smart professional investigator, tough; he drinks heavily, swears heavily, gets into fights, often carries a gun, and is not afraid to use it (Priestman, 2009).

No one would ever describe C. Auguste Dupin, Sherlock Holmes, Hercule Poirot, or Miss Jane Marple with any of those terms. While women are often characters in hard-boiled detective fiction, they are often the "**femme fatale**" who betrays or tricks the detective into getting what she wants or needs rescue (Rushing, 2007). Female hard-boiled detectives are currently quite popular but differ from their male counterparts. Chapter 5 introduces the female hard-boiled detectives. They became popular when thoughts and interpretations were more important to people. This shift created several female hard-boiled detectives who are tough, professional, rational, logical, and self-reflective.

However, returning to the original hard-boiled detective, there is a link between those detectives and the behaviorist paradigm. As stated earlier in this chapter, behaviorism became a more objective approach to psychology, one that did not believe in studying the mind or consciousness and focused on stimulus and responses (Boring, 2008). The hard-boiled detective does not sit around using their "little grey cells" to put clues together. Instead, the detective (or "private dick") runs out the door, often with a gun in hand, to directly confront people and find clues, sometimes engaging in criminal behavior themselves. In *Farewell, My Lovely* (Chandler, 1940/1988), detective Philip Marlowe is about to solve the case when he boards a boat, climbs in through the ventilation shaft, and carries his gun, which he is ready to use if needed.

The hard-boiled detective carefully formed associations between the clues (or stimuli) and the received reinforcement or reward throughout the investigation. The hard-boiled detective uses trial-and-error learning and often makes mistakes before heading off on the right path, particularly regarding the intentions of the femme fatale. At the end of *The Maltese Falcon* (Hammett, 1929/1992), Sam Spade explains how reinforcement and reward are essential to him as a detective. He describes how catching the criminal at the end of a case is like a dog that catches a rabbit. Letting the rabbit go would not be natural for a dog, and likewise, as a detective, the idea of releasing the killer would not be his idea of the proper ending of a case.

> I'm a detective and expecting me to run criminals down and then let them go free is like asking a dog to catch a rabbit and let it go. It can be done, all right, and sometimes it is done, but it's not the natural thing [Hammett, *The Maltese Falcon*, 1929, reprinted 1992, p. 214].

Hard-boiled detectives also learn by operant conditioning by watching others, following Bandura's observational learning. Two of this time's more popular detective fiction series—the *Hardy Boys* and *Nancy Drew* series—also employ many elements of behaviorism. Publisher Edward Stratemeyer created both series by writing the story outlines and then having ghostwriters, using a pseudonym, complete them. Leslie McFarlane wrote many of the *Hardy Boys* novels, and Mildred Wirt Benson wrote many of the *Nancy Drew* novels (Rehak, 2005). Reinforcement and reward are important to both the *Hardy Boys* and *Nancy Drew*. They often solve a case to get some reward for themselves or someone they know—as when Nancy Drew is given the old clock at the conclusion of her first mystery, *The Secret of the Old Clock* (1930, reprinted 2010).

The "sleuths," as they were often called, employed analytic and observational skills they learned from their fathers to solve cases: Mr. Hardy is a former New York detective turned private investigator, and Mr. Drew is a lawyer. Both parents reinforce and encourage their children's sleuthing, with Nancy even stating, "Dad depends on my intuition" (Keene, 1930/2010, *The Secret of the Old Clock*, p. 1), and when Mr. Hardy said to his sons at the start of their first mystery, *The Tower Treasure*, "…I suppose it is about as good a chance as any to watch a crime investigation from the inside" (Dixon, 1927/1987, *The Tower Treasure*, p. 52). Both detective series focus on the sleuths directly going into their communities and finding the evidence to form the stimulus-reinforcement (S-R) connections between clues and solutions.

There is much overt observation of behavior and action and less introspection, often placing the young detectives in danger. Overall, the behaviorist paradigm's influence evolved with detective fiction, particularly in the emergence of hard-boiled detective stories that emphasized observable stimuli and behavior. These connections between psychology and literature reflect their respective times' broader societal interests and influences, contrasting the themes and foci of the paradigm discussed in the following chapter.

Suggested Detective Fiction/Literature to Accompany This Chapter

- Raymond Chandler novels *Farewell, My Lovely,* or *The Big Sleep*—I would also recommend watching the Humphrey Bogart/Lauren Bacall movie version of *The Big Sleep*
- Dashiell Hammett's Sam Spade Series, especially *The Maltese Falcon* (which could be paired with the Humphrey Bogart movie version)
- Chester Himes' Harlem hard-boiled novel, *A Rage in Harlem*

3. The Shift to Behaviorism and Overt Action

- The *Nancy Drew* series by Carolyn Keene, especially the first book, *The Secret of the Old Clock,* or *The Hidden Staircase*—either novel could be combined with different movie versions of Nancy Drew over the years featuring Bonita Granville (1938–1939), Emma Roberts (2007), and Sophia Lillis (2019).
- *The Hardy Boys* series by Franklin Dixon, particularly book one, *The Tower Treasure* (although several television series have featured the Hardy Boys, there has never yet been a full-length movie adaptation; the 2020 series adaptation of the Hardy Boys on Hulu received positive reviews).
- For contemporary hard-boiled fiction, read the *Cormoran Strike* series by Robert Galbraith (aka J.K. Rowling).

End-of-Chapter Mind Puzzlers

1. Identify at least two instances of operant conditioning in the stories you read. Provide supporting quotes and corresponding page numbers for each example. Specify whether each instance illustrates reinforcement or punishment.
2. Explain how the detective in one of the narratives employs the techniques of instrumental conditioning and trial-and-error learning in their efforts to solve the case.
3. Evaluate the portrayal of the hard-boiled detective by examining five specific examples from one of the assigned stories. Each instance should be accompanied by the respective chapter number, scene description, and a comprehensive explanation of how it embodies the attributes of a hard-boiled detective.
4. What psychological elements do the Hardy Boys or Nancy Drew demonstrate in their behaviors and thoughts? What skills do they use to solve their mystery?
5. Analyze the portrayal of Nancy Drew in various film adaptations, taking into consideration the historical and contextual factors surrounding each version's release. Which psychological paradigm fits best with the character—the psychoanalytic or behaviorist paradigm? Provide at least three examples to support your answer.
6. Consider the relationship between Frank and Joe Hardy, Nancy Drew, and their respective fathers. Do both fathers satisfy the sleuths' need for safety and satisfaction, or do they experience some basic anxiety? (See previous chapter section on Horney.)

7. Compare Sam Spade or Philip Marlowe to the Hardy Boys or Nancy Drew. Provide at least one example illustrating similarities and differences in their behaviors, actions, and detective methods.

Key Terms and People

- **Ivan Pavlov**: a Russian physiologist renowned for pioneering the learning technique of classical conditioning
- **classical conditioning**: a learning technique where a behavior is learned by pairing stimuli to solicit a specific response
- **unconditioned stimulus (UCS)**: in classical conditioning, the stimulus that naturally triggers a given response without any prior learning
- **unconditioned response**: in classical conditioning, the response or behavior that naturally results from the UCS
- **neutral stimulus (NS)**: in classical conditioning, the stimulus that gets paired with the UCS to solicit the desired response
- **conditioned stimulus**: in classical conditioning, the NS becomes a conditioned stimulus when it is consistently paired with the unconditioned stimulus to elicit the desired response
- **conditioned response**: in classical conditioning, the learned response that results from pairing the NS and UCS
- **extinction**: in classical conditioning, when the desired behavior decreases or stops because the CS is presented without the UCS
- **spontaneous recovery**: in classical conditioning, the reappearance of the desired behavior after a period of absence, following extinction
- **generalization**: in classical conditioning, the occurrence of the same response to a similar stimulus or object as the original CS
- **discrimination**: in classical conditioning, the learned ability to respond to a specific CS while not responding to other similar stimuli
- **conditioned taste aversion**: a technique based on the principles of operant conditioning, employed to help individuals stop a nuisance or unhealthy behavior
- **Edward Thorndike**: an American psychologist who developed the idea of instrumental conditioning
- **instrumental conditioning**: a learning technique where behavior is reinforced if it leads to a positive outcome

3. The Shift to Behaviorism and Overt Action

- **law of effect**: Thorndike's law that states that responses followed by satisfying consequences are strengthened and likely to recur, while unsatisfying responses weaken and are less likely to be repeated
- **John Watson**: considered the founder of behaviorism in America who is known for the Little Albert experiment
- **Little Albert experiment**: the infamous experiment by Watson and Rayner in which they conditioned an infant to develop a fear of a white rat
- **logical positivism**: a philosophical stance that accepts theoretical concepts only if they are directly observable
- **Edward Tolman**: an American psychologist who developed the idea of a cognitive map and believed that learning could occur even without reinforcement
- **Clark Hull**: American psychologist who led the Neobehaviorist movement
- **Albert Bandura**: a Canadian-American psychologist who developed the learning principle of observational learning
- **observational or vicarious learning**: learning by watching others and imitating their behaviors
- **Piaget**: a Swiss developmental psychologist who developed a theory of cognitive development in children
- **B.F. Skinner**: one of the most influential American psychologists of all time who developed the theory of operant conditioning and wrote the fiction book *Walden Two*
- **operant conditioning:** a type of learning developed by Skinner, where behavior is dependent on consequences or reinforcement
- **positive reinforcement**: in operant conditioning, the addition of a positive or pleasant stimulus to increase a behavior
- **negative reinforcement**: in operant conditioning, the increase of a behavior by removing an unpleasant stimulus
- **punishment**: in operant conditioning, the reduction of a behavior either by presenting an unpleasant stimulus (positive punishment) or withdrawing a pleasant stimulus (negative punishment)
- **shaping**: reinforcing behavior through a process of gradual steps approaching the desired behavior
- **fixed ratio**: a reinforcement schedule where a specific number of responses is required to receive reinforcement

- **variable ratio**: a reinforcement schedule where an average number of responses is needed to receive reinforcement
- **fixed interval**: reinforcement is given after a specific time has passed
- **variable interval**: reinforcement is given after an average amount of time has passed
- **token economies**: a system where individuals receive tokens or items for exhibiting appropriate or desired behaviors, which can later be exchanged for valuable items or privileges
- **Bobo doll experiment**: Bandura's famous experiment where preschool-aged children watched a video of an adult hitting and kicking an inflatable punching bag with a clown (Bobo) on it
- **control group**: the group in an experiment that does not receive the treatment, used to compare the effects of the independent variable
- **placebo**: an inert substance often presented to a control group
- **hard-boiled detective fiction**: a genre of detective fiction characterized by a more realistic style of writing, including violence, sex, slang, and featuring a male detective who is cynical, street-smart, a professional investigator, tough, prone to violence, and carries a gun
- **femme fatale**: the female protagonist of a classic hard-boiled detective story who is linked to the crime, either as the perpetrator or the victim, and who often exhibits a physical attraction to the male detective

Chapter Notes

1. There is much speculation about what happened to Little Albert after he left Watson and Raynor's lab and his identity. In 2009, Beck et al. claimed that Little Albert was a child named Douglas Merritte, who died at age 6 in 1925 of hydrocephalus. A few years later, Powell et al. (2014) contested this and stated that Little Albert better matched the characteristics of another infant named William Albert Barger. We likely will never know Little Albert's identity for sure, but the impact of his experience is far-reaching.

2. Mary Cover Jones (1897–1987) was a well-known developmental psychologist and considered the "mother of behavior therapy" for her famous "Little Peter" studies (Jones, 1924). With the help of her mentor Watson, Jones found a 3-year-old boy named Peter who was afraid of white rabbits, among other things. Jones tried to countercondition Peter of his rabbit phobia by slowly introducing the white rabbit to Peter at closer distances while he was eating. Eventually, he could touch the rabbit without fearing it, and this technique became the groundwork for future examples of behavior therapy (Hergenhahn, 2009).

3. Gestalt psychology is a school of psychology popular in the early 1900s, primarily in Europe, and was associated with sensation and perception. Gestalt psychologists believed individuals perceived things by organizing their elements into a meaningful whole pattern and believed that "the whole is more than the sum of its parts (Plotnik, 1999)." For

3. The Shift to Behaviorism and Overt Action

more about gestalt psychology, please read *Ash, M.G. (1995). Gestalt Psychology in German Culture, 1890–1967: Holism and the Quest for Objectivity. Cambridge University Press* or Kohler, W. (1992). *Gestalt Psychology: An Introduction to New Concepts in Modern Psychology*. Liveright Publishing Corporation.

    4. Piaget's theory will be explained in more detail in Chapter 5. the formal operational stage is the fourth stage in Piaget's theory and typically begins in adolescence.

    5. In 1948, Skinner published a novel, *Walden Two* (Skinner, 1962), which describes a fictional utopian community completely modeled on his operant conditioning theory.

    6. Professor James Moriarty is the arch-nemesis of Sherlock Holmes and directly appears in two of Sir Arthur Conan Doyle's detective stories—the short story "The Adventure of the Final Problem" (contained in the book collection *The Memoirs of Sherlock Holmes*) and the full-length novel *The Valley of Fear*. Moriarty is briefly mentioned in several other short stories—"The Adventure of the Empty House," "The Adventure of the Norwood Builder," "The Adventure of the Missing Three-Quarter" (all contained within *The Return of Sherlock Holmes*), "The Adventure of the Illustrious Client" (contained in *The Case Book of Sherlock Holmes*), and "His Last Bow" (a short story contained in the collection also titled *His Last Bow*) (Arthur Conan Doyle Literary Estate, n.d.; Encyclopædia Britannica, 2020f).

References

Albert Bandura (2017). *Albert Bandura*. https://albertbandura.com/index.html.
Arthur Conan Doyle Literary Estate (n.d.). *Professor Moriarty*. https://www.arthurconandoyle.com/professormoriarty.html.
Ayllon, T., & Azrin, N. (1968). *The Token Economy*. Appleton-Century-Crofts.
Bandura, A. (1965). Influence of models' reinforcement contingencies on the acquisition of imitative responses. *Journal of Personality and Social Psychology*, 1, 589–595.
Bandura, A. (1977). *Social Learning Theory*. Prentice Hall.
Bandura, A., Ross, D., & Ross, S.A. (1963). Imitation of film-mediated aggressive models. *Journal of Abnormal and Social Psychology*, 66, 3–11.
Beck, H.P., Levinson, S., & Irons, G. (2009). Finding little Albert: A journey to John B. Watson's infant laboratory. *American Psychologist*, 64(7), 605–614. https://doi.org/10.1037/a0017234
Boring, E. (2008). *A History of Experimental Psychology* (volume 1 and 2). Cosmo Publications.
Burger, J. (2018). *Personality* (10th edition). Cengage Learning.
Chandler, R. (1940, reprint 1988). *Farewell, My Lovely*. Vintage Books.
Dixon, F.W. (1927, reprint 1987). *The Tower Treasure*. Grosset & Dunlap Publishers.
Encyclopædia Britannica. (2020a). *B.F. Skinner*. https://academic-eb-com.proxy.bc.edu/levels/collegiate/article/BF-Skinner/68114.
Encyclopædia Britannica. (2020b). *Clark L. Hull*. https://academic-eb-com.proxy.bc.edu/levels/collegiate/article/Clark-L-Hull/41455.
Encyclopædia Britannica. (2020c). *Edward L. Thorndike*. https://academic-eb-com.proxy.bc.edu/levels/collegiate/article/Edward-L-Thorndike/72241.
Encyclopædia Britannica. (2020d). *John B. Watson*. https://academic-eb-com.proxy.bc.edu/levels/collegiate/article/John-B-Watson/76286.
Encyclopædia Britannica. (2020e). *Logical Positivism*. https://academic-eb-com.proxy.bc.edu/levels/collegiate/article/logical-positivism/48766.
Encyclopædia Britannica. (2020f). *Professor Moriarty*. https://academic-eb-com.proxy.bc.edu/levels/collegiate/article/Professor-Moriarty/485799.
Gantt, W.H. (2020). Ivan Pavlov. *Encyclopædia Britannica*. https://www.britannica.com/biography/Ivan-Pavlov. Retrieved December 19, 2020.
Hammett, D. (1929, reprint 1992). *The Maltese Falcon*. Vintage Books.
Hergenhahn, B.R. (2009). *An Introduction to the History of Psychology* (6th Edition). Wadsworth.
Huesmann, L.R., & Malamuth, N.M. (1986). Media violence and antisocial behavior: An overview. *Journal of Social Issues*, 42(3), 1–6. https://doi.org/10.1111/j.1540-4560.1986.tb00239.x.

Hull, C. (1943). *Principles of Behavior: An Introduction to Behavior Theory*. Appleton-Century Company, incorporated.

Jones, M.C. (1924). A laboratory study of fear: The case of Peter. *The Pedagogical Seminary, 31*(4), 308–315. https://doi.org/10.1080/08856559.1924.9944851.

Kalat, J.W. (1999). *Introduction to Psychology* (5th edition). Brooks/Cole, Wadsworth.

Kazdin, A.E., & Bootzin, R.R. (1972). The token economy: An evaluative review. *Journal of Applied Behavior Analysis, 5*(3), 343–372.

Keene, C. (1930, reprint 2010). *The Secret of the Old Clock*. Grosset & Dunlap Publishers.

Kitchener, R. (2004). Logical positivism, naturalistic epistemology, and the foundations of psychology. *Behavior and Philosophy, 32*(1), 37–54. Retrieved December 28, 2020, from http://www.jstor.org/stable/27759470.

Leahey, T.H. (1991). *A History of Modern Psychology*. Prentice Hall.

Mayer, F.S., & Sutton, K. (1996). *Personality: An Integrative Approach*. Prentice Hall.

Myers, D.G. (2012). *Psychology in Everyday Life* (2nd Edition). Worth.

Myers, D. (2015). *Psychology* (11th edition). Worth Publishers.

Nolan, W.F. (1985). Behind the mask: Carroll John Daly. In W.F. Nolan (Ed.), *The Black Mask Boys: Masters in the Hard-Boiled School of Detective Fiction* (pp. 35–74). William Morrow & Company.

Pavlov, I.P. (1957). *Experimental Psychology and Other Essays*. Philosophical Library.

Plotnik, R. (1999). *Introduction to Psychology (5th Edition)*. Brooks/Cole/Wadsworth.

Powell, R.A., Digdon, N., Harris, B., & Smithson, C. (2014). Correcting the record on Watson, Rayner, and little Albert: Albert Barger as "psychology's lost boy." *American Psychologist, 69*(6), 600–11.

Priestman, M. (2009). *The Cambridge Companion to Crime Fiction*. Cambridge University Press.

Psychology Today (n.d.). *Applied Behavior Analysis*. https://www.psychologytoday.com/us/therapy-types/applied-behavior-analysis.

Rathus, S.A. (2013). *Psychology: Concepts and Connections* (9th Edition). Cengage Learning.

Reilly, S. (2009). *Conditioned Taste Aversion: Behavioral and Neural Processes* (T.R. Schachtman, Ed.). Oxford University Press.

Rehak, M. (2005). *Girl Sleuth: Nancy Drew and the Women Who Created Her*. Harcourt.

Rushing, R. (2007). *Resisting Arrest: Detective Fiction and Popular Culture*. Other Press.

Schultz, D. (1986). *Theories of Personality* (3rd edition). Brooks/Cole Publishing Company.

Schultz, D.P., & Schultz, S.E. (2016). *Theories of Personality (11th Ed.)*. Cengage Learning.

Skinner, B.F. (1962). *Walden Two*. Macmillan Company.

Skinner, B.F. (1976). *About Behaviorism*. Vintage Books.

Skinner, B.F. (1990). Can psychology be a science of mind? *American Psychologist, 45*(11), 1206–1210.

Tolman, E.C. (1932). *Purposive Behavior in Animals and Men*. Century/Random House.

Watson, J.B. (1914). *Behavior: An Introduction to Comparative Psychology*. Henry Holt.

Watson J.B. (1925). *Behaviorism*. People's Institute Publishing Company.

Watson, J.B., & Rayner, R. (1920). Conditioned emotional reactions. *Journal of Experimental Psychology, 3*(1), 1–14. https://doi.org/10.1037/h0069608.

4

The Humanistic Approach

Psychology as a discipline was moderately crowded during the early 20th century. The schools of structuralism, functionalism, psychoanalysis, and behaviorism were all active and had many followers (Hergenhahn, 2009). Beginning in the 1930s, in addition to studying overt behavior, psychologists also began to look into other human issues, such as the self, love, creativity, and meaning. In particular, World War II led to a greater focus on understanding human behavior and its motivation, transforming psychology into, according to Leahey, "a profession increasingly concerned with human welfare" (Leahey, 1991, p. 266). By the 1960s, behaviorism and psychoanalysis were the primary schools of thought. However, neither focused on human welfare or meaning (Hergenhahn, 2009). Psychology needed a new viewpoint, and fortunately, a group of psychologists emerged to lead this change movement that transformed psychology forever.

The new movement created a **third-force psychology** (Goble, 1980) as an alternative to the two main paradigms of psychology at that time—behaviorism (considered the first-force psychology) and psychoanalysis (second-force psychology). The new group felt the first two paradigms were inadequate in explaining human thoughts and behavior (Hergenhahn, 2009; Leahey, 1991). Two individuals, Abraham Maslow and Carl Rogers, led this shift. Both began as behaviorists but became similarly dissatisfied with behaviorism's limitations (Leahey, 1991). The third-force movement psychologists did not like how the behaviorists equated human behavior with the actions of animals and also felt psychoanalysts developed their theories primarily by the behaviors of psychologically unhealthy individuals (e.g., neurotics) (Hergenhahn, 2009). Third-force psychologists did not necessarily want to eliminate all of the previous ideas but instead wanted to explain the complexities of human behavior more fully.

Abraham Maslow

Beginning at the start of the 1960s, **Abraham Maslow** (1908–1970) became the leader of this transformative group. Maslow was born in New York City, the son of Russian-Jewish immigrants. He attended one year of law school before losing interest in that career (Hoffman, 1992). Maslow first became interested in psychology because of Watson's work in behaviorism. He attended the University of Wisconsin for both undergraduate and graduate school. Maslow earned his Ph.D. in 1934 and began his career as an animal behaviorist under the supervision of his doctoral advisor, Harry Harlow.[1] After graduating, Maslow worked at Teachers College, Columbia University, as a research assistant for Edward Thorndike from 1935 to 1937. He then moved to Brooklyn College for 14 years, where he interacted and learned from leading psychologists such as neo-psychoanalysts Karen Horney, Alfred Adler, and Erich Fromm; anthropologist Ruth Benedict; and Gestalt psychologist Max Wertheimer.

Maslow eventually moved to Brandeis University in Waltham, Massachusetts, about 15 miles west of Boston, where he remained affiliated until he died in 1970 (Burger, 2018; de Carvalho, 2000). Maslow's theory of personality and behavior changed through his conversations and work over the years, and the birth of his first daughter especially influenced his theory. After her birth, Maslow experienced some of the feelings of awe and wonder that he would describe and add to his theory in the coming years. He no longer considered behaviorism the most appropriate or adequate way to explain behavior (Burger, 2018).

Maslow moved from focusing on animal needs to those of humans and added the study of new factors, like creativity, that were not part of animal research (Leahey, 1991). Eventually, this approach came to be known as **Humanistic Psychology**. Maslow became an influential theorist and leader within the psychology community, becoming the president of the American Psychological Association and the smaller regional organization, the New England Psychological Association (NEPA).

The Principles of Humanistic Psychology

The humanistic paradigm is a much more optimistic approach than psychoanalysis in particular. These researchers study the healthy personality, not those with dysfunctions, mainly studied in psychoanalysis. Humanistic psychologists believe individuals are inherently good and strive to grow. Every person strongly desires to realize their full potential or reach a self-fulfillment level. Humanists want people to live in the present, not in the past, which often contains much conflict, unhappiness, and unfulfillment.

Five basic principles often summarize the humanistic psychology perspective: Human beings are more important than the sum of their parts; human beings have a uniquely human existence; human beings are aware and aware of being aware—i.e., they are conscious; human beings have some choice and, with that, responsibility; and human beings are intentional, aim at goals, are aware that they cause future events, and seek meaning, value, and creativity (adapted by Association for Humanistic Psychology, 2006, from Bugental, 1964, pp. 19–25).

All five principles focus on individuals as active beings, not machines or animals. Although Maslow is credited with being the "father of humanistic psychology," the ideas of a feminist psychologist, **Charlotte Bühler**, predate Maslow, perhaps bestowing upon her the title of "mother of humanistic psychology." Born in Germany in 1893, Bühler and her husband Karl (also a psychologist) escaped Nazi persecution by moving to the U.S. in 1940. The Bühlers moved to California in 1945, and Charlotte worked as a clinical psychologist at the Los Angeles County Hospital until 1953 (Derobertis, 2006; Gavin, 1990). Even before this time, when she was still working in Europe, she developed her ideas of humanistic psychology and incorporated the developmental principles of studying the whole person throughout life.

Bühler was one of the first psychological researchers to value using diaries as data. Using the narrative feedback from diaries helped her form the idea that by late adolescence, individuals are asking questions related to "What is my purpose in life?" Bühler may have been conceptualizing an adolescent identity crisis even before Erik Erikson developed his crisis of identity vs. role confusion within the adolescent age. Bühler's research with infants saw "intentional behavior and distinctive personal styles... (and) found evidence of curiosity, social interest, delight in achievement and distinctive individual styles in the activity of infants no older than a few months" (Gavin, 1990, p. 51).

Bühler's theory of life goals emphasizes the end goal of personal fulfillment, achieved through reasonable life goals organized according to individuals' gifts (Gavin, 1990), again very similar to Erikson's stages of psychosocial development. According to Bühler (1967), people face continuous challenges throughout life and must balance four basic tendencies. The four tendencies are "the tendency to strive for personal satisfaction in sex, love, and ego recognition; the tendency toward self-limiting adaptation to fit in, belong, and gain security; the tendency toward self-expression and creative accomplishments; and the tendency toward integration or order-upholding" (Bühler & Allen, 1972, p. 48).

Charlotte Bühler emphasized the distinction between her humanistic psychology and the Freudian psychology that dominated the discipline earlier in her career. She noted that psychoanalysts like Freud and Adler were psychiatrists and developed their theories from the psychologically "unhealthy" patients they treated. Bühler writes that "...Freud and Adler, as psychiatrists, sought to explain the human mind from a starting point based on illness, while we, as psychologists, chose the healthy mind as our baseline" (Bühler, 1974, p. 199). She also clarified that while psychoanalysts' idea of homeostasis or balance of urges and instincts is one's end goal, humanists believe life's end goal is self-realization or fulfillment (Bühler & Allen, 1972; Bühler & Marschak, 1968).

Investigative thinking challenge:
How does the humanists' emphasis on personality growth compare and contrast to the psychoanalytic and behaviorist approaches previously examined?

Maslow's Hierarchy of Needs

Like Bühler, Maslow thought there was more to humans than the balance of physiological urges or needs. In psychology, a **need** arises when a state of deprivation generally propels the organism to action (Rathus, 2013). Maslow considered human needs important, but he did not believe they were solely physiological or primitive. Instead, he arranged human needs into a hierarchy, with the more basic needs at the bottom, and the higher, more distinctly human, needs at the top (Hergenhahn, 2009). Maslow's hierarchy of needs is often displayed in a pyramid shape.

From bottom to top, Maslow's needs are:

1. **Physiological Needs**: The most basic needs, without which survival would become difficult. This level includes food, water, sex, sleep, and shelter.
2. **Safety Needs**: This level includes physical safety (such as living where we do not feel concerned about crime or danger) and a sense of security regarding resources (such as money, employment, and housing/property).
3. **Love and Belonging Needs**: This level, which involves more of a psychological need, involves our interactions with others and the feeling that we have a support network of family and friends to associate with and that we feel accepted by others or the groups to which we belong (such as clubs, book groups, work groups,

4. The Humanistic Approach

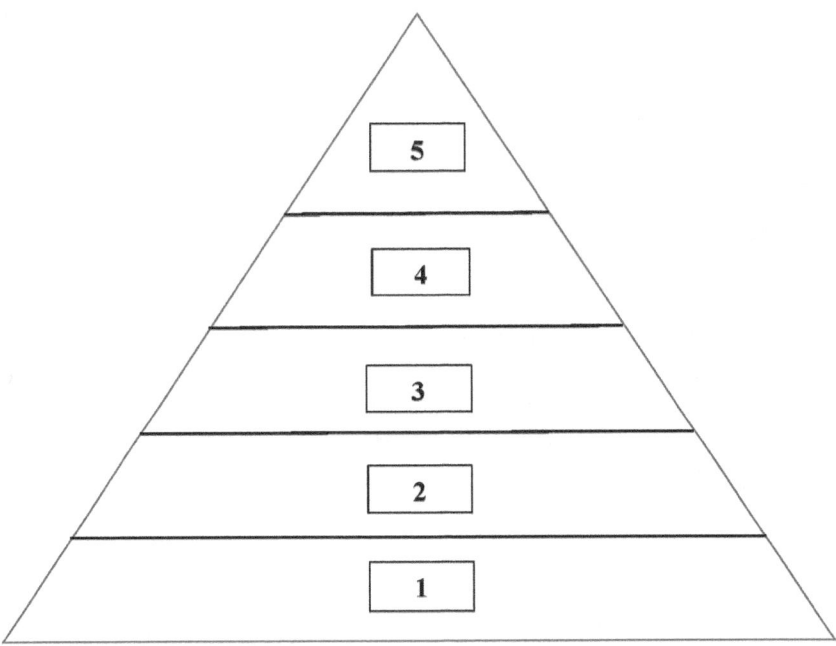

Maslow's Hierarchy of Needs

or sports teams). These relationships involve both platonic and romantic intimacy.

4. **Esteem Needs**: These psychological needs relate to our feelings of achievement, approval, respect, and recognition by others and ourselves. Individuals can develop a sense of self-esteem (how we feel about ourselves) and social-esteem (how others feel about us).
5. **Self-Actualization**: At the top of Maslow's hierarchy is the need for self-fulfillment in which individuals must feel like they have fulfilled their potential, are content with their lives, and have few or no regrets. These individuals have become all they ever wished to be and fully accept themselves and others.

Investigative thinking challenge:
Should individuals follow Maslow's original sequence of needs progression, or can they bypass certain requirements and focus on higher-level needs without fully satisfying the lower ones first?

Maslow revised his theory over the years, and while he may have been more rigid about the order or sequence of his levels at first, later on, he became more flexible, recognizing that individuals may move up or down his hierarchy, sometimes bypassing one level altogether based on their individual needs (Maslow, 1987).

Maslow's hierarchy of needs also can be divided into two broader groups: **deficiency** needs (*D-needs*) and **growth** needs (*B-needs*). The first four levels are called deficiency needs; the top level is the growth (or being) need. Deficiency needs (D-needs) will dominate a person's or animal's actions because of a lack of resources or deprivation. Thus, D-needs motivate people to act when they feel some unmet needs. It is also true that motivation to fulfill unmet needs becomes stronger with time, which may lead to more frantic attempts to obtain a critical resource like food, water, or safety. For example, the longer a person goes without food, the hungrier they become, which leads to more desperation and a greater sense of urgency to fill the deficient need. Unfortunately, this may lead to actions such as stealing, looting, or mob violence.

At the top of Maslow's hierarchy is the growth or B-need, self-actualization. Maslow (1987) listed the following characteristics of individuals who achieve self-actualization:

- an unusually accurate ability to perceive reality, judge others, and detect dishonesty in others "correctly and efficiently" (Maslow, 1987, p. 128)
- self-acceptance and acceptance of others, even recognizing that both may involve shortcomings
- spontaneous in their external behavior and even more so in their inner life or thoughts
- externally problem-centered rather than internally problem-centered
- a preference for solitude and privacy
- a strong degree of autonomy or independence from their environment and others
- a novel or fresh appreciation of their experiences, even if it is something they have experienced many times
- they sometimes will experience a **peak experience**, what Maslow defined as an intense, almost mystical experience where there is almost a loss of self in the person coupled with feelings of awe and wonder—the person becomes one with the experience and gains a sense of clarity about themselves and the world (an example I always offer is when a person drives to the rim of the Grand Canyon for the very first time and, after finally driving to the top

of the mountain, they gaze with wonder and awe at the red rocks and beauty of the canyon below)
- a deep feeling of connection to all people, not just those they directly or personally know
- a sense of humility and respect that allows them to interact and work with others regardless of class, gender, race, color, ethnicity, religious beliefs, education, or political beliefs
- deeper interpersonal relationships than most individuals; however, they have these with only a few select people, meaning they have a smaller circle of friends than most other people
- a strong sense of right and wrong and ethics; however, their beliefs of good and evil may not always be the conventional ones shared by the majority
- more concerned with the *ends* rather than the *means* of behavior
- a good sense of humor that is never hostile or aggressive (they would never put down another person or laugh at others' behavior or characteristics)
- display creativity, originality, and inventiveness that is greater or different from most people
- resist enculturation in that, while they do get along with the majority culture, they can detach from the culture to preserve their autonomy and sense of right and wrong

The investigators and other characters found within detective fiction experience many of these elements, just as real-world individuals experience them. One clear example of a peak experience appears in *The Skull Mantra* (Pattison, 1999). The reluctant investigator, Shan, is searching for clues to a murder on a Tibetan mountainside and comes to a spot where he can see Mount Everest, called Chomolungma by the locals.

> It wasn't just the awesome top-of-the-world view that stretched so far he could glimpse the shimmering white cap of Chomolungma, highest mountain of the Himalayas, more than a hundred miles away. It was the clarity. For a moment it seemed he had not only reached the top, but entered a new dimension. The sky wasn't just clear, it was like a lens, making everything seem larger and more detailed than before. The clutter in his mind seemed to have been stripped away by the wind [*The Skull Mantra*, Pattison, 1999, p. 95].

> ***Investigative thinking challenge:***
> *Have you ever encountered a "peak experience,"*
> *as defined by Maslow? If so, where did it take place,*
> *and what were the sensations you experienced?*

Why doesn't everyone get to the top of Maslow's pyramid and have peak experiences? In a few words, because it is not easy. Maslow believed few people ever reach the top of his hierarchy of needs and develop self-actualization—less than one percent of the world's population. Some famous individuals who likely reached self-actualization include Abraham Lincoln, Eleanor Roosevelt, Albert Einstein, Mahatma Gandhi, and Mother Theresa. It would be hard for most people to consider equating themselves with any individuals on that list, but one does not need to be world-famous to become self-actualized.

The quest for self-actualization, however, is a daunting one. Self-actualization is the highest need but also the weakest in its power or necessity for survival and well-being. The path to self-actualization is easily interfered with by events that may happen in your life. Some of these interferences include loss of employment; a family member's death; a change in marital status; an experience of natural disasters that lead to a loss or change of living conditions; or troubling events occurring within the community such as political unrest or riots.

It is hard to focus on reaching your full potential when, for example, you have lost your job and may not know how you will be paying your monthly rent or buying food for your family. Besides these interfering events, even if an individual is not necessarily experiencing great hardships, self-actualization takes a lot of effort, discipline, and self-control. Fear and doubt about one's abilities and potentialities may slowly creep into an individual's thoughts. The individual may be excited and thrilled about the possibilities but afraid of not reaching their potential and perhaps disappointing others. Individuals can fear success just as much as failure, and Maslow called this fear of reaching one's full potential the **Jonah complex**[2] after the biblical figure (Hergenhahn, 2009; Maslow, 1971).

In his later life, Maslow worked to develop a "fourth-force psychology" called **transpersonal psychology** that embodied much of his previous theory's mystical and spiritual elements (Hergenhahn, 2009). Perhaps because this subfield focuses on spiritual experiences, religious conversion, and altered states of consciousness, the American Psychological Association (APA) has never acknowledged it as a separate division. However, the British Psychological Society (the U.K. equivalent of the APA) established a Transpersonal Psychology Section (Daniels & McNutt, 1997).

Thinking about transpersonal psychology should not be limited to thoughts of fortune-tellers and other superstitious behaviors and ideas (Taylor, 1992). An overview of the themes most commonly found in its studies includes states of consciousness; highest or ultimate potential; beyond ego or personal self; transcendence; and the spiritual (Lajoie & Shapiro, 1992). People define the field as "concerned with the study of humanity's highest potential, and with the recognition, understanding, and realization of unitive, spiritual, and transcendent states of consciousness" (Lajoie & Shapiro, 1992, p. 91). Regardless of this later focus, Maslow's hierarchy of needs and his study of motivation and personality remain popular today and cross into other fields beyond psychology, such as business and education.

Carl Rogers

Carl Rogers (1902–1987) is the second psychologist most associated with the humanistic paradigm. Rogers attended the University of Wisconsin as an undergraduate and earned his Ph.D. in clinical and educational psychology from Teachers College of Columbia University in 1931. His first job was with New York's Society for the Prevention of Cruelty to Children, where he worked with underprivileged children or those with behavioral problems. He joined the Ohio State University faculty in 1940 and stayed until 1945, when he moved to the University of Chicago. At Chicago, Rogers also helped set up their counseling center in addition to his teaching duties. In 1957, he returned to the University of Wisconsin as a professor and developed his theory or personality and approach to counseling, which remains extremely popular today (Schultz & Schultz, 2016).

Rogers' approach to humanistic psychology stressed the way people view themselves. His theory is upbeat, believing that individuals want to strive to make the most of their potential, to "be all that they can be," like the slogan for the U.S. Army. The self is central to most humanistic theories, and Rogers' theory is no exception. He believed that self-perception is the most important characteristic of personality, which is why his theory is called **self-theory** or **self-actualization theory**. Central to Rogers' theory is the belief that the motive to self-actualize drives most behaviors. People have an inherent need to survive, grow, and enhance themselves, which is the definition of self-actualization. This process can involve struggle and pain, but individuals persist because the self-actualization urge is stronger than their hardships.

Rogers believed that an **organismic valuing process** is inherent in people and tells them how well something serves the self-actualization tendency. It pushes us towards self-actualization. People are always interpreting ongoing experiences in terms of their actualizing tendencies. Whether or not self-actualization is helped or hindered by new experiences depends on those experiences (Schultz & Schultz, 2016). Rogers (1961) calls this way of living the **process of becoming** because it describes how a healthy personality continually evolves to become a **fully functioning person**. The characteristics of a fully functioning person include an increase in three areas: being open to new experiences, existential living (living fully in the moment), and trust in one's decisions of how to behave in situations.

According to Rogers, the organism is the part of an individual's personality that contains their experiences and everything accessible to awareness. For a person to have what Rogers considers a healthy personality, there must be congruence between the organism and the self. In other words, people need to perceive themselves accurately. Rogers makes a distinction between two important types of self—the **actual self** (who we really are) and the **ideal self** (who we would like to be) (Mayer & Sutton, 1996). When individuals experience a discrepancy or conflict, the result is **incongruence** between these two self-perceptions. Rogers believed that incongruence leads to anxiety, psychological distress, and an unhealthy personality.

Why does this occur? When others share negative opinions and evaluations about a person, those opinions become internalized. If incongruence of the self occurs, the self is fragmented or disorganized, and a person's behavior may seem odd. The example I always provide is to describe this despair like Edvard Munch's (1893) famous painting, *The Scream*. The artwork offers a powerful image of a disorganized self trying to defend itself from distortion. Helping his clients regain congruence in the self became essential to **person-centered** or **client-centered therapy**. Rogers focused on the client, who was not necessarily an unhealthy patient typical in psychoanalytic treatment, and centered on the individuals and their unique problems. Researchers adopted the **Q-sort**[3] procedure, a self-reporting card-sorting technique, to assess this discrepancy and to gain information about how individuals see themselves (Burger, 2018; Schultz & Schultz, 2016).

> *Investigative thinking challenge*:
> *What characteristics, actions, or inquiries should be incorporated in a Q-sort to explore the distinction between one's ideal and actual self? Can this method effectively discern between these two self-perceptions? What alternative approaches could be used to evaluate the gap between the actual and ideal selves?*

The second major component of Rogers' theory is that all people need **positive regard**—feelings of acceptance, respect, warmth, and love. This need first develops based on how others treat a person or child. Later in life, it will help them develop this need about themselves, or a sense of positive *self-regard*. Positive regard is reciprocal in that it comes from others, but when an individual gives another person positive regard, they receive it too. However, this is not an easy task to achieve. Individuals primarily receive positive regard for specific behaviors—we are much more likely to be praised after doing well—which sets up a scenario where conditional positive regard is more likely to exist. Early on, children may understand that their parents might not love them unless they do what their parents want.

The child perceives their parents have placed **conditions of worth** on them—provisions preventing them from following the organismic valuing process and becoming fully functioning (Hergenhahn, 2009). The child or adult may behave how others want, not how they want. Client-centered therapy consists of trying to heal the damage done by conditional regard. Rogerian therapy aims to help the individual understand that positive regard can be given independently of the worth or value placed on an individual's actions—meaning that we should treat others with a sense of **unconditional positive regard.** By treating others with such regard, we learn to treat others without expectations for who they are, not what they do or accomplish. This behavior should be the model for all parental love.

Providing unconditional positive regard is not only crucial in the relationship between parents and their children, but it is also vital in therapeutic relationships. For client or person-centered therapy to work, three factors must be present in the relationship between therapist and client (Corey, 2005). First, the therapist must be *genuine* in their interactions with their clients. The therapist should never act in a phony way with their client; they need to be open.[4] Second, the therapist should display a sense of *empathy* by understanding their clients and seeing the world from their view. Finally, the therapist should provide the client *unconditional positive regard*, accepting them with no conditions of worth. Only by doing this will the client be able to express who they really are.

In general, Rogerian therapy is non-directive and supportive. The goal is to help the client become a fully functioning person and move to self-actualization. Rogers' therapy has helped people overcome psychological or emotional issues and works in other settings. For example, managers can use Rogerian therapy principles to develop better employee relationships (Schultz & Schultz, 2016). Rogerian therapy also benefits religion, law enforcement, and cultural relations (Hergenhahn, 2009; Levant & Schlien, 1984). Eleanor Criswell founded the Humanistic Psychology Institute (now called the Saybrook Graduate School and Research Center in San Francisco) in 1970 to train future humanistic psychologists (Milner, 1986). She also is a past president of Division 32 (Humanistic Psychology) of the American Psychological Association (APA) and past president of the Association for Humanistic Psychology (AHP). Criswell (2003) clarifies the importance that humanistic psychology has even now in the 21st century:

The need for humanistic psychology in the world is greater than ever. All our organizations and institutions need to work together toward global well-being. We need to blend the individualistic tendencies of humanistic psychology with a more collaborative model for dealing with world situations. We need to foster a balanced global, environmental context with appreciation of cultural diversity and interspecies well-being at the forefront. This is the challenge to humanistic psychology [Criswell, 2003, p. 51].

As expected, the field of humanistic psychology has a long list of criticisms, most notably that it rejects traditional scientific research methods and ignores animal research (Hergenhahn, 2009). The order of Maslow's hierarchy is another area of contention—do all people need to fulfill Maslow's groups of needs in the same hierarchy that he initially established? Do people move up and down the hierarchy as needed throughout their lifetime? Nonetheless, the humanistic paradigm provides psychologists, and therapists in particular, with another means to study and understand human nature. Humanistic psychology also encouraged researchers to study psychological distress and illness and the more positive aspects of behavior. The recent popularity of positive psychology[5] and mindfulness can be traced back to concepts within the humanistic paradigm. Because of its focus on needs and motivation, the humanistic paradigm also can be used to explore the behaviors of many of the characters within various detective fiction series, especially those featuring women as the protagonist.

The Humanistic Approach and Detective Fiction

The exploration of basic needs and their fulfillment, or lack thereof, forms a central theme in numerous detective fiction stories. The crimes themselves involve the theft of basic physiological needs, a loss of safety, and a loss of love and belongingness. In many novels, the protagonists embark on a quest to reach the higher levels of Maslow's hierarchy of needs or strive to become a fully functioning person, as defined by Rogers. Detectives not only seek to solve crimes for professional advancement but also to bolster their self-esteem and achieve a sense of fulfillment. Reaching Maslow's top need, individuals must be content with their lives and have few or no regrets. Reaching the pinnacle of Maslow's hierarchy necessitates contentment with one's life and the absence of significant regrets. For a detective who may not have solved every case, whose actions may have resulted in the death of others, or who allowed a murderer to escape, this task can prove particularly challenging. Even Hercule Poirot, Agatha Christie's self-proclaimed greatest detective in the world, occasionally engages in soul-searching and expresses a few regrets in the novels featuring him, such as in *Curtain* (Christie, 1975), Poirot's final case.

However, detectives typically grow in character, success, and celebrity throughout more extended series. Harriet Vane recognizes the importance of striving to reach her potential and establishing strong self-awareness. She talks about this early on in *Gaudy Night*: "As one gets older, as one established one's self, one gained a new delight in formality" (Harriet Vane, *Gaudy Night*, Dorothy Sayers, 1936/2012 p. 5).

Harriet Vane, created by Dorothy L. Sayers, is a wonderfully complex character who grapples with the constraints imposed on women during the early 20th century despite being a successful detective fiction writer. *Gaudy Night* takes place in 1935 England, and the five novels featuring Harriet Vane are set between 1930 and 1939. The setting for *Gaudy Night* is Shrewsbury College, a fictional all-women's college that is part of Oxford University, and the term "gaudy night" refers to a festival or reunion for the college's alumnae (Merriam-Webster, n.d.). Sayers attended Somerville College, one of Oxford's first women's colleges (Brabazon, 1981; Reynolds, 1997). The first three Harriet Vane novels revolve around a fiercely independent Harriet, who continues to decline Lord Peter Wimsey's offer of marriage. The final two novels (spoiler alert!) occur after the two are married. Wimsey appears in several other novels and short stories without Vane.[6]

In *Gaudy Night*, Sayers perhaps borrows from personal experiences and can describe the struggles in Harriet's mind as she tries to find a place as an educated woman in the society and class system of the time. Like Sayers, Harriet Vane struggles to balance her intellect and emotions, mirroring the experiences of many ambitious and intellectually gifted women of her era. She wonders to herself what she and others like her should do, people who are "cursed with both hearts and brains" (Sayers, 1936/2012, p. 74).

Harriet Vane also faces questions about her celebrity status and abilities as she investigates a mysterious poison-pen mystery at Shrewsbury College without Peter's assistance or without reconsidering his marriage proposal. However, Peter does appear several times in the novel. Harriet ponders several levels of Maslow's hierarchy of needs in Chapter 3 of *Gaudy Night* (Sayers, 1936/2012). She thinks that being at Shrewsbury College should have given her time away from thinking about marrying Peter (love and belonging needs). Harriet is annoyed that people still consider Peter more well-known than her (esteem needs). She is also bothered that others would rather interact and get to know him than herself (a struggle for identity or self-fulfillment related to esteem or possibly self-actualization needs).

Harriet Vane's quest for self-fulfillment and actualization is not unique to her or Dorothy Sayers. Many historical detective fiction stories, particularly those featuring female investigators or partnerships with reluctant male partners, revolve around similar themes. In Anne Perry's Charlotte and Thomas Pitt series, which takes place in Victorian London, the headstrong and independent Charlotte assists her husband, Thomas, a police inspector who becomes a superintendent and then joins the Special Branch (Perry, 2019–2020). Charlotte and Thomas first meet when he is investigating several murders in *The Cater Street Hangman* (Perry, 1979). She is headstrong and intent on helping Thomas, whether he likes it or not, and the two fall in love and get married. Thomas grudgingly accepts that Charlotte can help him gather information that would otherwise be unavailable, and they form a partnership in their personal and professional lives. Charlotte recruits the help of other strong female characters and is often assisted by her sister, her mother, and her housemaid throughout the series, with the final book in the series published in 2017.

Similarly, Kerry Greenwood's *Phryne Fisher* series depicts a wealthy English noblewoman who establishes a private detective agency in 1920s Melbourne, Australia (Phryne Fisher, n.d.). The first novel, *Cocaine Blues* (Greenwood, 1989), introduces Miss Fisher and explains her move to Australia from London. The book introduces the reader to her reluctant "partner" in crime-solving, Detective Jack Robinson, along with other supporting yet essential characters. The series is a fun and engaging depiction of how one wealthy English noblewoman goes against convention to set up her own private detective agency but also refuses to marry and has many lovers throughout the series. Miss Fisher's self-esteem and self-worth are never dependent on others' beliefs. She is the perfect example of Rogers' fully functioning person—she is always open to new experiences, she lives fully in every moment, and generally trusts her decisions of how to behave in situations.

A television series, *Miss Fisher's Murder Mysteries* (Cox, 2012–2015), and a feature film, *Miss Fisher and the Crypt of Tears* (Tilse, 2020), were created based on the book series. While the actions and dialogue of Phyrne and the other characters differ slightly from those within the books, the episodes and movie are just as good, if not even better, entertainment. They also are an excellent match to the humanistic paradigm, thanks mainly to the acting of Essie Davis, who portrays Phryne Fisher. Watching an episode as a supplement to this chapter is highly recommended.

Jacqueline Winspear's character Maisie Dobbs struggles with Rogers' process of becoming throughout the series. Maisie succeeds professionally as a detective, but emotionally, she has difficulty letting go of the past and her first love, Simon (Winspear, 2004). Because of her modest background, she is reluctant to enter into a relationship with a character of a higher class. Maisie has difficulty with two of the three characteristics of a fully functioning person. She has difficulty engaging in new experiences and fully living in the moment. Fortunately, her best friend Priscilla tries to help her in this area since Priscilla is the epitome of someone who lives fully in the moment. Maisie generally does trust her instincts about how to behave in situations since she is a high self-monitor (a concept explained in the next chapter) and adapts her behavior to fit a situation best.

In *A Dangerous Place* (Winspear, 2015), Maisie returns to England after a four-year journey (or escape) following a personal tragedy. She trusts her decision to get off the ship traveling from India and stops in Gibraltar, a dangerous place because of the Spanish Civil War. Maisie is at a personal crossroads (Winspear, 2015). However, because of her training in India and before with her mentor Maurice, she can use the principles of humanistic psychology to help her progress on her road to self-fulfillment and even self-actualization.

Several other novels with female investigators—such as the Cordelia Gray mystery, *An Unsuitable Job for a Woman* by P.D. James (1977), the Kate Fansler mystery, *Death in a Tenured Position* by Amanda Cross (1981), and for a lighter and more amusing read, *Her Royal Spyness* by Rhys Bowen (2007)—explore similar themes of female investigators' pursuit of self-fulfillment and professional success. However, series featuring male investigators or co-investigators also explore humanistic needs. In the *Cormoran Strike* series, beginning with *The Cuckoo's Calling* (Galbraith, 2013), investigator Cormoran Strike and his assistant (later partner) Robin Ellacott constantly question their feelings for each other. They worry that giving in to their love needs may compromise their friendship (belongingness needs) and work success (esteem needs).

Their "will-they-or-won't-they" interactions are reminiscent of two popular TV series *Moonlighting* (Caron, 1985–1989), starring Bruce Willis and Cybill Shepherd, and *Castle* (ABC Studios, 2009–2016), starring Nathan Fillion and Stana Katic. All of these series demonstrate how the collaborative nature of the humanistic paradigm enriches the backdrop of detective fiction and offers insights into the human need for meaning, growth, love, and fulfillment. Moreover, the humanistic approach serves as a bridge to the next major paradigm within psychology—the cognitive paradigm—bringing a more cerebral and social approach to understanding need fulfillment, human nature, and behavior in psychology.

Suggested Detective Fiction/Literature to Accompany This Chapter

- Dorothy Sayers' novel *Gaudy Night* featuring Harriet Vane and Lord Peter Wimsey

- Anne Perry's *Thomas Pitt* series
- Kerry Greenwood's *Phryne Fisher Mystery* series
- The *Nancy Drew* or *Hardy Boys* series
- The *Maisie Dobbs* series
- P.D. James' novel, *An Unsuitable Job for a Woman*
- Amanda Cross' novel, *Death in a Tenured Position*
- Rhys Bowen's *Molly Murphy Mysteries* series
- Rhys Bowen's *Her Royal Spyness* series
- Alyssa Maxwell's *Murder at the Breakers, A Gilded Newport Mystery*

End-of-Chapter Mind Puzzlers

1. Evaluate Maisie Dobbs in relation to Maslow's hierarchy of needs. Identify the levels she has already fulfilled and the ones still remaining. Provide examples to support your answers. Additionally, explain which level of Maslow's hierarchy you believe you are currently working on in your life and justify your selection.
2. Describe the relationships between Nancy Drew or the Hardy Boys and their fathers. Determine whether these relationships are positive or negative, and provide reasons for your assessment. Discuss the humanistic needs that you believe these relationships help the young sleuths develop.
3. Dorothy Sayers wrote in 1929 that "there have been a few women detectives, but on the whole, they have not been very successful. In order to justify their sex, they are obliged to be so irritatingly intuitive as to destroy that quiet enjoyment of the logical which we look for in our detective reading" (Sayers, 1929, pp. 15–16). Select TWO main female detectives from the discussed stories (Nancy Drew, Miss Marple, Harriet Vane, or Maisie Dobbs) and provide arguments supported by examples, either agreeing or disagreeing with Sayers' complaint. Analyze the similarities and differences between these female detectives. Explore the representation and roles of women in the stories and explain the author's presentation of them. Compare these female detectives to the male detectives in the readings.
4. Dorothy Sayers' novels are "…long and do not age well. Yet intellectually they are resourceful and highly refined" (Merry, 1983, p. 18). Do you agree with this statement? *Gaudy Night*

presents the reader with many story plotlines that can relate to Maslow's hierarchy of needs. Provide at least one example from the novel corresponding to each of Maslow's levels.
5. Do you believe any of the detectives or characters in the stories you have read have reached self-actualization, as defined by Maslow or Rogers? Provide examples (with chapter and page numbers) of the characteristics you see in them that indicate self-actualization.
6. Choose one of the main characters and explore their Q-sort for their actual and ideal selves. Identify the traits or behaviors they would place in each pile and determine if their self-concept is congruent or disorganized, according to Rogers. Provide explanations to support your assessment.
7. Assess whether the parents of Nancy Drew and the Hardy Boys treat them with unconditional positive regard or place conditions of worth on them. Support your answer with examples from the stories.
8. Please select any novels or stories you have read involving a detective and his assistant or **foil**.[7] Describe the relationship between these two individuals and whether it is positive. Analyze whether the relationship involves the three factors Rogers believes must be present in an effective relationship between a therapist and client. Provide examples to support your analysis.
9. Explore the relationship between social class and justice within the humanistic paradigm, particularly in connection to Maslow's hierarchy. Analyze how class and gender are reflected in the relationship between the detective and police in the *Thomas Pitt* series or any other novel you have read. Provide several examples from at least one novel to illustrate this relationship.

Key Terms and People

- **third-force psychology**: a new movement created as an alternative to the two main paradigms of psychology in the early 20th century—behaviorism (considered the first-force psychology) and psychoanalysis (second-force psychology)
- **Abraham Maslow**: often credited with being the "father of humanistic psychology" who is known for developing his hierarchy of needs
- **humanistic psychology**: a more optimistic approach to studying human behavior, focusing on understanding the healthy

personality rather than those with dysfunctions—humanistic psychologists believe that individuals are fundamentally good and possess a strong desire to realize their full potential

- **Charlotte Bühler**: a feminist psychologist predating Maslow, often regarded as the "mother of humanistic psychology," who believed the ultimate goal in life for individuals is self-realization or fulfillment
- **need**: arises when there is a state of deprivation, motivating the organism to act
- **physiological needs**: the most basic requirements for survival, including food, water, sex, sleep, and shelter
- **safety needs**: basic needs that includes both physical safety and a sense of security regarding resources
- **love and belonging needs**: needs tied to our interactions with others and the feeling of having a support network of family and friends; they involve the sense of acceptance by others or groups we belong to, including both platonic and romantic relationships
- **esteem needs**: needs related to feelings of achievement, approval, respect, and recognition by others and ourselves—individuals can develop a sense of self-esteem (how we feel about ourselves) and social-esteem (how we feel others feel about us)
- **self-actualization**: the top of Maslow's hierarchy, this represents the need for self-fulfillment, contentment with one's life, and minimal regrets
- **deficiency needs (*D-needs*)**: the first four levels of Maslow's hierarchy, which dominate actions when resources are lacking or in short supply
- **growth need (*B-need*)**: the top of Maslow's hierarchy, representing the need for growth and self-actualization
- **peak experiences**: a strong, almost mystical experience where individuals feel a sense of awe and wonder, losing themselves in the experience
- **Jonah complex**: a fear of reaching one's full potential, based on the biblical story
- **transpersonal psychology**: Maslow's later idea of a fourth-force psychology that embodied the mystical and spiritual elements of his previous theory, concerned with studying individuals' highest potentials

4. The Humanistic Approach

- **Carl Rogers**: the second psychologist most associated with the humanistic paradigm who developed a theory and therapeutic approach focused on the self and helping clients reach their full potential
- **self-theory/self-actualization theory**: Rogers' theory that focuses on self-perception as the key characteristic of personality
- **organismic valuing process:** an inherent mechanism guiding individuals on what is good or bad for them, and how well something serves their self-actualization tendency, motivating them towards self-actualization
- **process of becoming:** the way people interpret ongoing experiences in terms of their actualizing tendencies, where new experiences can either help or hinder self-actualization depending on their impact.
- **fully functioning person**: Rogers' view of a healthy personality
- **actual self:** according to Rogers, who we really are
- **ideal self:** according to Rogers, who we would like to be
- **incongruence**: a discrepancy between the actual and ideal self, which can lead to anxiety, psychological distress, and an unhealthy personality
- **person-centered therapy,** or **client-centered therapy**: Rogers' therapeutic approach focused on helping his clients regain congruence in the self
- **Q-sort:** a card sorting assessment tool used by humanistic psychologists for measuring differences between individuals' actual and ideal selves
- **positive regard**: feelings of acceptance, respect, warmth, and love
- **conditions of worth**: provisions under which a child or adult will be accepted, and which will prevent them from following the organismic valuing process to become a fully functioning person
- **unconditional positive regard**: treating others without expecting them to conform to specific criteria based on their actions or accomplishments
- **foil**: in literature, a character presented to contrast with another, often the main character or protagonist

Chapter Notes

1. Harry Harlow was an American psychologist who, during the 1950s, showed that monkeys raised in isolation (i.e., in cages without maternal stimulation) displayed abnormal development. Baby rhesus monkeys were reared alone in the cages and could interact with either a "wire mother" or a "terry cloth mother." The monkeys preferred the terry cloth mothers and their softer touch. Harlow concluded that this demonstrated a preferred and advantageous need for infant stimulation, eventually leading to programs and techniques to promote normal development (Encyclopædia Britannica, 2021).

2. The Jonah complex is named after the biblical figure Jonah. *The Book of Jonah* is a short four-chapter Old Testament (OT) book. Unlike the other OT books named for prophets, *The Book of Jonah* is a narrative story describing the adventures of Jonah as he tried to disobey God. God told Jonah to go to Ninevah to warn them that their wickedness would destroy the city. Jonah did not want to go, and he disobeyed God and set out on a ship with a group of sailors in the opposite direction of Ninevah. A great storm frightened the sailors, and they threw Jonah into the sea to try to calm the storm. A large fish (usually portrayed as a whale in visual images) swallows Jonah, and he remains inside the fish/whale for three days, praying to God for forgiveness. Jonah promises to go to Ninevah to prophesy against the people's behavior, and, as a result, the fish/whale spits Jonah out onto the beach. Jonah walks for three days, arrives at Ninevah, and tells the people that God will destroy their city in 40 days unless they stop worshipping idols and disobeying God. The people believed in Jonah and repented, so God did not punish them. Jonah was angry that God did not destroy the city and goes outside, sits, and waits to see what happens. God made a plant grow over him to provide him some shade which Jonah appreciated, but the next day a worm destroyed the plant, angering Jonah again. God asks Jonah why he is angry and provides the final moral of this story: "This plant grew up in one night and disappeared the next; you didn't do anything for it and you didn't make it grow—yet you feel sorry for it! How much more, then, should I have pity on Ninevah, that great city? After all, it has more than 120,000 innocent children in it, as well as many animals!" (American Bible Society, 1978, p. 1006).

3. The Q-sort can help therapists understand how their clients see themselves. Initially developed by William Stephenson in 1935, it was refined in 1953 to assess different psychological concepts (Stephenson, 1953). The Q-sort is a card-sorting assessment tool that worked well for measuring individuals' actual and ideal selves, and so was used frequently by Rogers. In this research strategy, people are given a set of cards, each card with a particular trait printed on it, such as lazy, domineering, religious, or friendly. The client sorts the cards into piles according to how characteristic each trait is for them or the degree to which the card fits them. The client completes this sorting twice, once asking them to sort the cards into those that describe their actual self and a second time using the same cards to describe their ideal self. Congruence or incongruence of these self-views is identified by looking at the two piles of cards and the difference between them (Burger, 2018; Schultz & Schultz, 2016).

4. For an example of when a therapist is not always genuine or empathetic within the therapeutic relationship, read Yalom's (1989) case study "The Fat Lady" in his book *Love's Executioner*.

5. *Positive psychology* is a term first used by Abraham Maslow to describe a field of psychology that focuses on positive or adaptive subjective experiences, traits, behaviors, and social institutions that enhance well-being and quality of life (American Psychological Association, n.d.). For a good review of positive psychology, see Seligman, M.E., & Csikszentmihalyi, M. (2000). Positive psychology: An introduction. *The American Psychologist*, 55(1), 5–5–14. https://doi.org/10.1037/0003-066X.55.1.5 or Seligman, M.E. (2019). Positive psychology: A personal history. *Annual Review of Clinical Psychology*, 15(1), 1–23. https://doi.org/10.1146/annurev-clinpsy-050718-095653.

6. Dame Harriet Walter portrayed Harriet Vane in a 1987 BBC adaptation of *Gaudy Night*, a highly recommended adaptation if you can find it at your local library.

7. In literature, a foil (2021) is a character presented so that they contrast with a second,

most often the main, character. The foil's behaviors typically lack the qualities that the main character excels in, so the reader can better understand the main character. The foil is not necessarily the story's antagonist since the foil and main character, the protagonist, often work together to solve the crime. The prototypical example of a foil is Arthur Conan Doyle's Dr. Watson, whose lack of observations makes Sherlock Holmes's deductions seem even more impressive. Other examples of a classic foil in detective fiction include Agatha Christie's Captain Hastings, the foil to detective Hercule Poirot; Rex Stout's Archie Goodwin, the foil to detective Nero Wolfe; and Janet Evanovich's Lula, the comical foil to bounty hunter Stephanie Plum.

References

ABC Studios. (2009–2016). *Castle* [Television series]. Beacon Pictures, Experimental Pictures, ABC Studios.
American Bible Society. (1978). *Good News Bible: The Bible in Today's English Version*. American Bible Society.
Association for Humanistic Psychology. (2006). Five basic postulates of humanistic psychology. *Journal of Humanistic Psychology, 46*(3), 239.
American Psychological Association (n.d.). *Positive Psychology*. Retrieved January 24, 2021, from https://dictionary.apa.org/positive-psychology.
Bowen, R. (2007). *Her Royal Spyness: A Royal Spyness Mystery*. The Berkley Publishing Group.
Brabazon, J. (1981). *Dorothy L. Sayers: A Biography*. Scribner.
Bugental, J.F.T. (1964). The third force in psychology. *Journal of Humanistic Psychology, 4*(1), 19–26. https://doi.org/10.1177/002216786400400102.
Bühler, C. (1967). Human life goals in the humanistic perspective. *Journal of Humanistic Psychology, 7*(1), 36–52. https://doi:10.1177/002216786700700105.
Bühler, C. (1974). Humanistic psychology as a personal experience. *Interpersonal Development, 4*, 197–214.
Bühler, C., & Allen, M. (1972). *Introduction to Humanistic Psychology*. Brooks/Cole Publication Company.
Bühler, C., & Marschak, M. (1968). Basic tendencies of human life. In C. Bühler & F. Massarik (Eds.), *The Course of Human Life* (pp. 92–102). Springer.
Burger, J. (2018). *Personality* (10th Edition). Cengage Learning.
Caron, G.G. [Executive Producer]. (1985–1989). *Moonlighting* [TV series]. American Broadcasting Company (ABC).
Christie, A. (1975). *Curtain: Poirot's Last Case*. Dodd, Mead and Company.
Corey, G. (2005). *Theory and Practice of Counseling and Psychotherapy*. Thomas Learning.
Cox, D. [Producer]. (2012–2015). *Miss Fisher's Murder Mysteries* [TV series]. Australian Broadcasting Company (ABC) TV.
Criswell, E. (2003). A challenge to humanistic psychology in the 21st century. *The Journal of Humanistic Psychology, 43*(3), 42–52. https://doi.org/10.1177/0022167803043003004.
Cross, A. (1981). *Death in a Tenured Position*. The Ballantine Publishing Group.
Daniels, M., & McNutt, B. (1997). Questioning the role of transpersonal psychology. *Transpersonal Psychology Review, 1*(4), 4–9.
de Carvalho, R.J. (2000). Maslow, Abraham Harold. *American National Biography*. https://doi.org/10.1093/anb/9780198606697.article.1400858.
Derobertis, E.M. (2006). Charlotte Bühler's existential-humanistic contributions to child and adolescent psychology. *Journal of Humanistic Psychology 46*(1):48–76. https://doi.org/10.1177/0022167805277116.
Foil. (2021). In *Encyclopædia Britannica*. Retrieved from https://academic-eb-com.proxy.bc.edu/levels/collegiate/article/foil/125185.
Galbraith, R. (2013). *The Cuckoo's Calling*. Mulholland Books/Little, Brown & Co.
Gavin, E.A. (1990). Charlotte M. Bühler (1893–1974). In O'Connell, A.N. & Russo, F.F. (Eds.) *Women in Psychology: A Bio-bibliographical Sourcebook*. Greenwood Press.
Goble, F.G. (1980). *The Third Force: The Psychology of Abraham Maslow*. Pocket Books.

Greenwood, K. (1989). *Cocaine Blues*. McPhee Gribble.
Hoffman, E. (1992). Overcoming evil: An interview with Abraham Maslow, founder of humanistic psychology. *Psychology Today*, https://www.psychologytoday.com/us/articles/199201/abraham-maslow/.
Hergenhahn, B.R. (2009). *An Introduction to the History of Psychology* (6th Edition). Wadsworth.
Infant stimulation program. (2021). In *Encyclopædia Britannica*. Retrieved from https://academic-eb-com.proxy.bc.edu/levels/collegiate/article/infant-stimulation-program/604974#313844.toc.
James, P.D. (1977). *An Unsuitable Job for a Woman*. Faber & Faber.
Lajoie, D.H., & Shapiro, S.I. (1992). Definitions of transpersonal psychology: The first twenty-three years. *The Journal of Transpersonal Psychology, 24*(1), 79–98.
Leahey, T.H. (1991). *A History of Modern Psychology*. Prentice Hall.
Levant, R.F., & Schlien, J.M. (Eds.). (1984). *Client-centered Therapy and the Person-centered Approach: New Direction in Theory, Research and Practice*. Praeger.
Maslow, A.H. (1971). *The Farther Reaches of Human Nature*. Penguin Books.
Maslow, A.H. (1987). *Motivation and Personality* (3rd edition). Harper & Row.
Mayer, F.S., & Sutton, K. (1996). *Personality: An Integrative Approach*. Prentice Hall.
Merriam-Webster. (n.d.). Gaudy night. In *Merriam-Webster.com Dictionary*. Retrieved January 24, 2021, from https://www.merriam-webster.com/dictionary/gaudy%20night.
Merry, B. (1983) Dorothy L. Sayers: Mystery and demystification. In Benstock, B. (Ed.), *Essays on Detective Fiction*. Palgrave Macmillan. doi.org/10.1007/978-1-349-17313-6_2.
Milner, T. (1986). Humanistic psychology: Saybrook Institute Graduate School and Research Center. *The Humanistic Psychologist, 14*(1), 38–41. https://doi.org/10.1080/08873267.1986.9976751.
Munch, E. (1893). *The Scream* [Painting]. National Gallery and Munch Museum., Oslo, Norway.
Pattison, E. (1999). *The Skull Mantra*. St. Martin's Press.
Perry, A. (1979). *The Cater Street Hangman*. St. Martin's Press.
Perry, A. (2019–2020). *Books by Anne Perry*. Retrieved from https://anneperry.us.
Phryne Fisher (n.d.). *Phryne Fisher: The Books*. Retrieved from http://phrynefisher.com/books.html.
Rathus, S.A. (2013). *Psychology: Concepts and Connections* (9th edition). Cengage Learning.
Reynolds, B. (1997). *Dorothy L. Sayers: Her Life and Soul*. St. Martin's Press.
Rogers, C.R. (1961). *On Becoming a Person: A Therapist's View of Psychotherapy*. Houghton Mifflin Company.
Sayers, D.L. (1929). *The Omnibus of Crime*. Harcourt, Brace.
Sayers, D.L. (1936/2012). *Gaudy Night*. Bourbon Street Books.
Schultz, D.P., & Schultz, S.E. (2016). *Theories of Personality (11th Ed.)*. Cengage Learning.
Stephenson, W. (1953). *The Study of Behavior: Q-sort Technique and Its Methodology*. University of Chicago Press.
Taylor, E. (1992). Transpersonal psychology: Its several virtues. *The Humanistic Psychologist, 20*(2–3), 285–300. https://doi.org/10.1080/08873267.1992.9986796.
Tilse, T. (Director). (2020). *Miss Fisher and the Crypt of Tears* [Film]. Every Cloud Productions.
Winspear, J. (2003). *Maisie Dobbs: A novel*. Penguin Books.
Winspear, J. (2015). *A Dangerous Place*. HarperCollins.
Yalom, I.D. (1989). *Love's Executioner & Other Tales of Psychotherapy*. Harper Perennial.

5

Cognitive Psychology

By the middle of the 20th century, more researchers and theorists were questioning the applicability of the paradigm of behaviorism. Earlier theorists such as Ebbinghaus, Fechner, and James had already begun studying topics such as memory and thoughts about the self (Hergenhahn, 2009). During the 1950s, an alternative approach began to attract more attention and became the new "leader" in psychology. This new **cognitive psychology approach** focused on people's thoughts, including memories, and how we process information as causes of behavior and personality. Two influential researchers in the popularity of this new approach included Noam Chomsky and George Miller. Chomsky's work revolved around language as a uniquely human, biologically based cognitive capacity (Chomsky, 2021). Miller (1956) published a very influential study on the capacity limits of short-term memory (seven things, plus or minus two), which continues to be a classic study taught in Introduction to Psychology courses. Their contributions to the field of cognitive psychology helped bring about a "cognitive revolution" within the disciple of psychology that continues today (Chomsky, 2021). However, even before Chomsky and Miller's contributions to the field of cognitive psychology, a developmental psychologist was working on his theory to understand how children's thinking changes over time. That influential researcher was Swiss psychologist **Jean Piaget**.

Jean Piaget

Jean Piaget (1896–1980) was born in Neuchâtel, Switzerland on August 9, 1896. In 1923, he married Valentine Châtenay, and they had three children, Jacqueline, Lucienne, and Laurent, who helped Piaget form his theory of intellectual development (Piaget, 1952). Piaget's theory is one of psychology's most influential cognitive development theories. Piaget's (1929) theory focuses on understanding how knowledge grows and changes systematically over time, from infancy to adulthood. Through the observations of his children, Piaget believed that children's way of thinking is different from adults' thinking processes. Piaget initially trained as a biologist, so he felt the differences and changes in children's thinking were a biological adaptation to the environment that develops as the child tries to make sense of the world (Plotnik, 1999; Santrock, 2018).

The central concept of Piaget's theory is the concept of a **scheme** (what we may call a schema), a cognitive structure that allows children to make sense of the world and their experiences by organizing information into a mental representation (Hughes et al., 1996; Santrock, 2018; Shaffer, 1996, 2008). An infant's first schemes are simple but get more complex as they get older and have more experiences where they encounter new stimuli and events. For example, an infant's first scheme may involve how to suck and shake a rattle. Two characteristics for understanding the environment help shape the child's cognitive development: **organization** (when abilities or concepts are combined and used in a coordinated and integrated way); and **adaptation** (a cognitive tool for dealing with tasks and demands presented by the environment by trying to adjust to them).

Piaget further explained that two processes allow adaptation to occur. One, **assimilation**, occurs when new information is taken in and incorporated into existing knowledge and schemes. The other, **accommodation**, occurs when new information is again taken in and applied to the existing knowledge. However, the old scheme must be adjusted or modified because the new information does not easily fit into previous ideas and concepts (Santrock, 2018; Shaffer, 1996, 2008). As a child, and even later into adulthood, when individuals enter a new situation, they first apply an old scheme. If the recent experience fits well, the individual is satisfied, and nothing else needs to transpire. If the new experience or knowledge does not work well with that previous scheme, the individual will need to change the old scheme if the required change is small or develop a new scheme if there is a significant discrepancy.

For example, imagine you have a two-year-old child who has just learned to call your four-legged pet a "kitty." What do you think will happen when the child sees a dog for the first time? First, the child is likely to call the new animal a kitty because they are assimilating a new animal into an old scheme. If the child's parents correct that answer, the child will need to modify the kitty scheme to smaller furry four-legged animals that meow and creates a new scheme, "doggy," for larger furry four-legged animals that bark. The child has now used accommodation to create a new scheme.

Investigative thinking challenge:
Describe a situation in which you used both assimilation and accommodation when faced with a new experience, item, or person. How did you apply these processes, and which one was more straightforward for you? Why do you think that was the case?

Piaget's theory is qualitative in that he believed that the quality of children's thinking changes as they age. Older children think about different *things* than younger children, and they think in different *ways*. While this may seem fairly obvious today, it was a new idea during the 1920s and 1930s when Piaget developed his theory. Children differ in how quickly or slowly they create new ways of thinking, but Piaget did propose a sequence of four stages of cognitive development that children go through at their own pace. Children can progress through them at different speeds, but the stages are successive, and each new step builds on the skills developed in the previous stage. Because of this, a child cannot skip a stage but progresses through them in the sequence Piaget indicated (Santrock, 2018; Shaffer, 1996, 2008).

Piaget's Stages of Cognitive Development

Piaget developed four stages to explain how children's thinking changes qualitatively as they age (Hughes et al., 1996; Kalat, 1999; Plotnik, 1999; Santrock, 2018; Shaffer, 1996, 2008).

1. **Sensorimotor Stage** (from birth to about age 2): In this initial stage, babies explore their environment primarily through looking, hearing, touching, mouthing, and grasping new objects—they learn from input from their senses and resulting motor responses. The primary skill a child must develop to move to the next stage is **object permanence** when a child understands that an object out of sight still exists.
2. **Preoperational Stage** (from about age 2 to about age 7): This is the crucial stage in which children develop and improve language. It is also during this stage that the importance of play emerges. Children learn through pretend play by using one object to represent another. However, children still cannot perform mental operations that require more concrete logic, and they also have difficulty imagining another person's point of view, what Piaget referred to as **egocentrism**. During this stage, children develop a "theory of mind,"[1] the ability to understand that other people have

their own thoughts, reactions, feelings, intentions, and even mistaken ideas or "false beliefs" (Wellman & Wooley, 1990).

Developmental psychologists interested in false beliefs study how 3- and 4-year-old children would respond to the following scenario: Robin, the child participant in the study, observes the experimenter place a piece of candy in a green trash can, while a stuffed bear observes this action. The experimenter takes the bear from the room for a few minutes. In the meantime, the experimenter moves the candy to a yellow trash can. The bear returns to the room and is placed before the colored trash cans. The experimenter asks the child, "Where will the bear look for the candy?" If Robin is 3 years old, they will likely answer "in the yellow trash can" because they saw it moved and believe the bear has their same perspective or viewpoint. If Robin is 4 or 5 years old, they will likely answer in the original "green trash can" because they understand that the bear only saw the candy where it was first placed, not where it was later moved. A child older than three understands that beliefs can influence behavior, even if those beliefs are incorrect (Wellman & Wooley, 1990).

3. **Concrete Operational Stage** (between ages 7 to about 11): Children can think logically about concrete events and can now think reversibly. Thus, it is this age range (generally elementary and middle school years) when children fully gain the ability to understand simple math and the concept of **conservation**. Conservation allows the child to realize that the amount of an object does not change even if its appearance slightly changes. For example, look at the two rows of alligators on the next page. Which row has more gators in it, the top or bottom row?

You probably answered that both rows have the same number of gators. A child who lacks conservation would likely respond "the top row" because it appears longer because of the spacing. Lack of conservation prevents a child or adult from understanding more complex mathematical operations, essential in cognitive development.

4. **Formal Operational Stage** (starts around age 11 or 12 and continues throughout life): During Piaget's final stage, a child's reasoning ability expands from concrete thinking to abstract, logical, analytical, and hypothetical thinking. They can now use symbols and imagined realities to reason systematically, which helps them learn more complex math and science subjects.

Piaget's Conservation Task

Investigative thinking challenge:
To assess your ability to engage in hypothetical reasoning, take on the one-leg scenario challenge: Imagine a world where all human babies are born with just a single leg. What adaptations would be necessary?

Piaget based his theoretical ideas on natural observations and interviews with his three children. Although critics contend that Piaget's reliance on observing and interviewing his offspring might have introduced biases, the vast body of research conducted worldwide over the years consistently supports the fundamental notion that human cognition follows the sequence he delineated. Thus, while acknowledging the potential limitations of his methods, it is essential to recognize the enduring impact of Piaget's pioneering work on our understanding of cognitive development. Moreover, beyond simply elucidating the stages of cognitive growth, Piaget's theory served as a catalyst for subsequent researchers, who, inspired by his initial ideas, developed more rigorous and systematic techniques to investigate and comprehend the intricate process of cognitive maturation. Consequently, his work laid the foundation for a robust and expanding body of literature that seeks to unravel how cognitive development intricately shapes and guides child and adult behavior.

Moral Development

As a child progresses through Piaget's stages of cognitive development, the child acquires the ability to reason at a higher level. One of the advantages of this is that it helps them make decisions about the appropriateness of certain behaviors. **Morality** includes the rules or ideals that guide social and interpersonal behavior and help us distinguish right from wrong (Shaffer, 1996, 2008). As children's cognitive thinking advances, so does their ability to reason at a "higher" or more complex level of morality. While various theories of moral development existed, the theorist most recognized for his contributions in this area was **Lawrence Kohlberg** (1927–1987).

Kohlberg's Theory of Moral Development

Kohlberg (1963, 1981), a prominent figure in developmental psychology, felt that part of children's social development includes their moral development. He sought to explore the evolution of individuals' moral perspectives as they matured. His original research is limited because he only used boys between ages 10 and 16 to resolve a series of moral dilemmas; no girls were part of the original study. While the original study may have limitations, its lasting impact on the field is a testament to his research's enduring significance. Kohlberg presented his participants with several hypothetical dilemmas and asked them how they would solve them. He was less concerned with the answer and more interested in the boys' reasoning. His best-known dilemma is referred to as the *Heinz dilemma* and can be described as follows (Shaffer, 1996, 2008):

> In Europe, a woman was near death from a special kind of cancer. There was one drug that doctors thought might save her. It was a special form of radium, and a druggist in the same town that Heinz lived in had discovered it. It was expensive to make, but the druggist was charging $2000 or 10 times the cost of the drug for a small (possibly life-saving dose). Heinz, her husband, borrowed all he could but only collected $1000 or half of what he needed. He told the druggist his wife was dying and asked him to sell the drug cheaper or let him pay later. The druggist replied, "No, I discovered it, and I'm going to make lots of money from it." Heinz became desperate and broke into the drug store and stole the drug. Should he have done it? Why or why not?

Again, Kohlberg was less interested in the yes/no answer than its reasoning. He was interested in how the boys would consider things like the importance of the wife's life, Heinz's duty as a husband, the behavior of the druggist, or other factors. Kohlberg found a series of stages representing a sequential-like method of thinking about this and similar dilemmas. He identified three levels of thinking, each containing two distinct but similar stages (Colby & Kohlberg, 1987; Hughes et al., 1996; Shaffer, 1996, 2008).

- *Level I Preconventional Morality*: This is the earliest and most self-serving level of moral thinking. A child (or adult) will follow the rules and laws so that they can either avoid being punished (Stage 1) or receive some reward in return (Stage 2). Some of the reasoning might include: "He shouldn't steal the drug because it's breaking the law and he will go to jail" (Stage 1); or "He should steal the drug because if he does, his wife will not die so she will be able to continue to take care of him and cook for him" (Stage 2).
- *Level II Conventional Morality*: The child obeys the rules to either gain the approval of others by living up to their expectations

(Stage 3) or maintain the correct social order by conforming to authority or complying with the law to avoid censure or guilt (Stage 4). Reasoning in this level may be: "Heinz should definitely steal the drug because his family is going to be really mad at him for not stealing it and letting his wife die" (Stage 3) or "Heinz shouldn't steal it because he will always feel guilty for breaking the law" (Stage 4).

- *Level III Postconventional Morality*: According to Kohlberg, this is the most advanced level of moral reasoning. At this level, an individual's moral reason is more principled, and their decision may go against the law or authority. Individual rights and democratically decided rules guide thinking (Stage 5), or, at the highest level, one's conscience guides decisions (Stage 6). Examples of the reasoning in this level include: "Heinz needs to think about everything, if he lets her die, it will be out of fear and not thinking it through" (Stage 5); or, "Heinz needs to think about the ends justifying the means, and the universal principles we all agree to follow. If Heinz doesn't steal the drug, he disobeys the external law, but he hasn't lived up to his own conscience" (Stage 6).

Incorporating a discussion of morality is essential in this context, as it may aid law enforcement or detectives identify the correct suspect in a criminal investigation. The moral reasoning of a criminal can shed light on their motivations, a facet often revealed in the final chapter of most mystery novels. The detective should be well-versed in how individuals might solve hypothetical and real-life dilemmas. Critics have taken issue with Kohlberg's theory for its cultural and gender biases, particularly concerning the post-conventional level of morality. Responses from females or non–Western cultures are often not categorized within Stage 5 or Stage 6, but this does not imply that they are less moral. Instead, it highlights the limitations of Kohlberg's theory in explaining all aspects of moral reasoning and behavior. Therefore, research must encompass the consideration of individual and group differences.

For example, Shweder et al. (1987) conducted a study with Indian and American children between the ages of 5 and 13 and adults. They asked the participants if various situations were wrong and how severe. Two of these scenarios included a married woman whose husband beats her after going to a movie without asking for permission, and the oldest son in a family going out the day after his father died to get a haircut and some food at a restaurant. American children and adults considered the wife-beating the most serious and morally wrong. In contrast, the Indian children and adults (who were Hindu) found the son who went out the day after his father's death more morally offensive and did not consider the wife-beating as wrong at all. This research supports recognizing the situation's or context's power in influencing people's behaviors and thoughts. Part of an individual's situation or environment includes their culture and religion. Culture influences moral reasoning, ideas, and behaviors, and another social construct, gender, may also be associated with differences. Two decades after Kohlberg, psychologist **Carol Gilligan** (1936–) developed an alternative theory focusing on how girls and women approach moral reasoning differently from males.

Gilligan's Theory of Moral Development

Gilligan (1982) believes there is a gender-based difference in how girls and women approach ethical dilemmas, whether they are hypothetical scenarios like those in Kohlberg's studies or real-life situations. This disparity stems from societal expectations regarding appropriate behavior for each gender. In Western-centric cultures, boys are raised with a focus on assertiveness and tend to view dilemmas as conflicts between individuals, suggesting that resolution should primarily be sought through the lens of law and justice. On the other hand, girls are socialized to be more nurturing and compassionate, leading them to base their moral judgments on interpersonal relationships and concern for the well-being of others.

While some studies conducted by other researchers have not consistently supported Gilligan's perspective, her theory offers an alternative viewpoint. Gilligan's research on women's concepts of self and morality significantly improved one particular aspect of Kohlberg's study. Unlike the traditional approach of using solely hypothetical dilemmas, Gilligan presented female participants in her research with a real-world situation that had significant relevance to their lives at the time, specifically the decision to have an abortion. This approach provided a more nuanced understanding of how women approach ethical challenges in their everyday lives.

Gilligan's 1982 study focused on the belief that a decision to have an abortion involves a conflict between the self and others. She was interested in examining how women think about various issues and dilemmas. She interviewed 29 women between the ages of 15 and 33 who were from different ethnic and social classes. The participants were referred by pregnancy or abortion counseling services, and the circumstances of their pregnancies varied. The researchers interviewed the participants twice, once when the participant was making the abortion decision and a second time at the end of the following year. Gilligan and her colleagues asked them about their abortion decision and presented them with three hypothetical moral dilemmas, including the Heinz dilemma. After analyzing the results, Gilligan also constructed a set of three stages, with one transition occurring between the first and second levels and another between the second and third levels.

- *Level 1 Orientation of individual survival*: decisions are made based on what is best for the self and do not consider the interests of others.
- *Level 2 Focus on goodness as self-sacrifice*: decisions are made because girls or women sacrifice their wishes for what others want because they consider themselves responsible for and dependent on others which may cause feelings of guilt.
- *Level 3 Morality of nonviolence*: care is now the most critical strategy or mechanism for resolving conflicts in human relationships. This care is directed toward the self and others, with both perspectives equally important when solving these moral dilemmas.

Again, even though other researchers find that females perform comparably to males when reasoning through Kohlberg's dilemmas, Gilligan did provide evidence that a difference may exist when faced with real-world difficulties (Hughes et al., 1996; Jaffee & Hyde, 2000). Gilligan's findings that women focus more on care than justice are interesting from both a psychological and a literary perspective. This research may explain the behavioral differences between female and male suspects and between female and male detectives and perhaps demonstrates how we can process information based on the individual and the context of a situation.

Information Processing

Newell et al. (1958) redefined human problem-solving in terms of **information processing**, shifting the focus of the study of human problem-solving. This approach defined problem-solving by stating that humans process input from the environment and then produce an output (Hergenhahn, 2009).

Investigative thinking challenge:
Which "invention" do you believe impacted people's fascination with information processing?

Newell et al. (1958) posited that humans think like simple computer programs. These early cognitive theorists were interested in how individuals understand their surroundings and how their interpretations influence their behavior and their thoughts about themselves. In a way, early cognitive theorists reverted to Skinner's ideas in that they focused on conscious thought, which is more easily studied, if not directly observed (Schultz, 1986). However, terminology more relevant to computer programming replaced behaviorist language. Rather than a stimulus, there is an *input*; rather than using the term *response*, information processing theorists use the term *output*. Thus, an information-processing theorist studies "normal, rational thinking and behavior and views the human as an active seeker and user of information" (Hergenhahn, 2009, p. 632), much like someone writing a computer program to execute a task or function. Here is another excellent example of how other disciplines and historical events influenced psychology.

Like the computer programming analogy, personality theorist **George Kelly** (1955) believed that people behave like naive scientists by making and testing hypotheses, which he called **personal constructs**. Personal constructs are idiosyncratic cognitive structures that interpret and predict events and differ on three dimensions. These include the **range of convenience**—a set of circumstances or topics to which a personal construct applies; the **focus of convenience**—a set of events it best applies to; and **permeability**—the degree to which it can be applied to new events.

Kelly's approach showed that people construe or interpret the world differently, which leads to differences in personality and perhaps psychological problems. Kelly was a researcher and a therapist who believed that faulty personal constructs and flawed information processing caused most psychological problems (Burger, 2018). Information processing focuses on some of the nativist beliefs seen earlier in psychology. Modern nativism is most associated with the work of Jerry Fodor, Noam Chomsky, and Steven Pinker. They argue that humans from birth have specific cognitive modules (specialized genetically inherited psychological abilities) that allow them to learn and acquire certain behaviors and skills, such as language (Hergenhahn, 2009).

Pinker, one of the most influential contemporary cognitive psychologists,[2] wrote: "The mind ... is not a single organ but a system of organs, which we can think of as psychological faculties or mental modules" (Pinker, 1997, p. 27). Using information processing techniques, more contemporary cognitive psychologists have studied cognitive structures (e.g., memory) and a structure first defined by William James in 1890—the self. These researchers clarified that the self, or the self-concept, works like other cognitive structures (Higgin et al., 1988; Greenwald & Banaji, 1989).

The self can, therefore, be defined as an ordinary structure with some "special" aspects associated with it (Greenwald & Pratkanis, 1984)—for example, the self can create and use future or possible selves (Markus & Nurius, 1986).

The Self and Information Processing

Throughout the 19th and 20th centuries, scholars continued to study the self more extensively. William James first recognized the dual and reflexive nature of how people perceive themselves (Brown, 1998). James (1890) conceptualized the self as both an object containing self-descriptions and an active subject enabling individuals to reflect on their actions. In a way, he provided an early information processing approach to the self—individuals take in information, reflect upon it, and then act based on their reflections.

Fast-forward nearly a century: Kihlstrom et al. (1988) expanded on this idea, describing the self from a cognitive information processing perspective. Kihlstrom depicted the self as a complex cognitive knowledge structure that guides our processing of information, akin to the declarative and procedural knowledge guiding information processing theories. In their model, nodes representing the self link to other nodes representing semantic information like "lives in MA" and episodic information like "helped an elderly lady cross the street" or "went to the store." For instance, someone might have a node representing "athletic" linked to another node representing "basketball," indicating that they see themselves as both athletic and a basketball player.

Cantor and Mischel (1979) took a similar approach, organizing social categories into an information-processing hierarchy. Different levels become activated depending on how a person interprets a situation before deciding how to act. Building on these models, Kihlstrom et al. (1988) emphasized the significance of information processing in studying the self, as it sheds light on hidden aspects of mental structures and processes that influence behavior. Furthermore, this approach aligns with procedures and outcomes employed by both social and nonsocial psychologists. In essence, the self guides the processing of that information, which in turn influences behavior. Because the self resembles other cognitive structures, its functions are also similar. As a mental structure, the self is a reservoir of information that also uses this information to influence behavior. The self-concept guides our behavior through data stored in our minds. The self is structured to serve as the location for this self-relevant information. When we encounter familiar situations, specific nodes within our self-concepts become activated, reminding us of how we have acted in the past and how we are likely to act in the future. This link between the structure of the self and its function is fundamental, as it enables us to draw upon our self-relevant information to activate and guide behavior.

In the work of **Hazel Markus** (1977), the self is a collection of representations of the self that she refers to as a **schema**. She defines the self-concept as a personal schematic system that guides our processing of self-relevant information (Markus, 1977; Markus, 1990). These schemas are cognitive structures that encompass knowledge about specific concepts or domains, including the attributes and relationships between those attributes (Fiske & Taylor, 1991)—they are an *active* information processing structure (Greenwald & Pratkanis, 1984). Like Piaget's schemes in children, schemas are active information processing structures crucial in guiding our processing of self-relevant information.

Markus (1977) differentiated between individuals with schemas for a particular domain and those without such structured knowledge (aschematic). Both the structure and functioning of the self for these two groups differed, with schematics possessing a well-developed knowledge structure for a particular domain (e.g., shyness, independence). These schemas would then guide information processing about that domain, influencing how the individual would act in certain situations. Individuals with shy schemas will use previous knowledge and experiences from similar situations when deciding how to behave in new situations—probably exhibiting characteristics of shyness. On the other hand, aschematics lacked this structured knowledge, leading to more varied and inconsistent behaviors in domain-specific situations. For example, an aschematic would not have a set response pattern for a "party situation" or "school situation." Because of this distinction, schematics are more likely to be consistent in their behavior and are more likely to show **cross-situational consistency** on that dimension.

Schemas are continually constructed from our life experiences, determining what aspects of ourselves we should consider, especially in ambiguous situations. They serve as both "objects of knowing" and "agents" within our mental landscape. Self-schemas are "cognitive generalizations about the self, derived from past experience, that organize and guide the processing of self-related information contained in the individual social experience" (Markus, 1977, p. 63). Self-schemas are complex, highly integrated structures containing information organized into a unified system (Markus, 1990). These complex and integrated structures motivate and enable individuals to act in line with the information they possess. Thus, individuals' unique set of self-schemas shapes how they perceive and respond to the world around them, contributing to the diversity of human behavior.

5. Cognitive Psychology

Investigative thinking challenge:
Which traits or characteristics do you consider yourself to be schematic? Now identify those aspects that you feel are lacking or are aschematic. Contemplate how these different facets influence and guide your behaviors and decisions.

Linville (1982) added to the existing body of research concerning the cognitive aspects of the self by defining its "complexity." In this context, complexity refers to the number of knowledge dimensions an individual possesses within a specific domain. Greater complexity means that an individual possesses more knowledge dimensions in that domain. Her model illustrates that the complexity of a person's knowledge structure connects to the extremity of their responses to stimuli or information related to that domain. When a person's representation of a domain is less complex, their emotional responses to stimuli in that domain tend to be more extreme. Conversely, if their representation is more complex, their thoughts and actions become more moderate.

Linville's research demonstrates that self-representations, like schemas, guide our actions and thoughts. Linville believes the self is structured around the number of dimensions a person has in a certain domain. Thus, two individuals who both exhibit schematic behavior for shyness may differ in the complexity of their schemas due to varying experiences. Consequently, self-complexity affects these individuals differently, with greater complexity leading to less extreme emotional responses. Moreover, self-views can be compartmentalized, separating positive and negative content to protect the self (Showers, 1992a). As a result, differences in the structure of self-representations lead to functional distinctions in the self.

Linville's model deviates slightly from other information processing approaches, presenting self-representations as multiple aspects or schemas and emphasizing the consequences of individual differences in self-representations. Her theory primarily concentrates on the affective implications of the self, while Markus' approach leans more toward cognitive aspects. Despite these differences, both methods aim to elucidate behavior by examining the contents of the self.

Investigative thinking challenge:
Answer the question "Who am I?" in as many unique ways as possible. How many distinct ways did you answer? If you can provide 20 or more unique responses, your self-concept is more complex than if you answered fewer times.

These information-processing approaches show the relationship between the structure and function of the self. The structure of the self contains knowledge arranged efficiently (as in a hierarchy, for example) to make retrieval of that information relatively quick and automatic. By organizing self-knowledge into certain domains, the self can process information about new situations and guide future behavior. Greater complexity in the self (representing differences in the content of the self) influences how individuals experience emotions and behave differently. This complexity directly impacts behavior by using its intricacies in various situations.

The debate over the structure and function of the self has a long history in psychology, with roots dating back to the pioneering work of William James. One perspective views the self as an object of knowledge (structural), while another viewpoint portrays the self as the knower (function). Epstein (1980) proposed an integrative theory, suggesting that self-theories include both objects of knowledge and executives of that knowledge. Greenwald and Pratkanis (1984) likened the self to a computer with data (the content of cognitive processes) and a program (the cognitive process itself), supporting the duality notion of the self. Just as a computer cannot effectively use its data without an operating program, the self must possess executive functions to process and act upon the self-knowledge effectively. This metaphor highlights the intricate interplay between the structural and functional elements of the self, suggesting that understanding the self necessitates considering both its content and the cognitive processes involved. In this framework, the self is not merely a passive repository of information but an active processor and executor of knowledge, shaping our perceptions, emotions, and behaviors.

Expanding on the content of the self-concept, it encompasses not only personal identities, representing our individual traits and characteristics, but also social identities, which reflect our roles within society and the various groups to which we belong. This dual nature of the self underscores the significant influence of our interactions with others on how we perceive ourselves and behave in different social contexts. By recognizing the complex interplay between self-knowledge, cognitive processes, and social influences, researchers gain valuable insights into the intricate mechanisms that underlie human identity and behavior.

Once considered relatively stable and unifaceted, the self-concept is now seen as malleable and multifaceted (Markus & Wurf, 1987). While some aspects of the self-concept (e.g., self-schemas) are relatively stable and may be chronically accessible, other parts of the self-concept are more temporary. Different situations may activate specific aspects of the self-concept, leading to varying perceptions of oneself. An individual's **working self-concept** (Markus & Nurius, 1986) is that part of the individual's self-knowledge activated at any particular time.

5. Cognitive Psychology

The malleability of the working self-concept can result in fluctuating views, swinging between positive and negative self-perceptions. Research on self-esteem maintenance motives (Rhodewalt et al., 1991; Tice & Baumeister, 1990) suggests that people employ strategies to preserve a positive self-concept. However, after facing personal failures, individuals may adopt self-protective strategies to cope with negativity and preserve positive feelings about themselves. Some of these strategies are collectively identified as **self-protective** strategies because they attempt to protect an individual from feeling negative about themself and maintain the person's positive feelings about the private self-image. Other **self-presentational** strategies try to preserve people's positive feelings and impressions of a person's public self-image (Mello-Goldner & Wurf, 1997).

One example of a self-defeating strategy used to protect the self is **self-handicapping**. Berglas and Jones (1978) first defined self-handicapping as a cognitive strategy in which individuals create (unconsciously) obstacles to performance. If the person does not perform well, they can blame the barrier and still protect and maintain positive self-views. For example, a swimmer who decreases practice time during the week before a big swim meet can have this serve as an excuse for failure. The individual is willing to do this because they are concerned with how others "see" them and is willing to maintain the optimistic impression others have of them. Self-handicapping research is one example of how recent research in cognitive psychology has focused on "social cognition."

Defensive pessimism is another example of a cognitive strategy utilized by individuals concerned with maintaining their self-esteem and ensuring positive performances in uncertain or risky situations (Cantor, 1990). Defensive pessimists strategically set low expectations for themselves before beginning an upcoming event (Norem, 1989; Cantor, 1990). Individuals with successful performance histories can use this strategy, but they nonetheless set unrealistically low expectations for themselves in new situations. Defensive pessimists can be easily spotted in the classroom—they are the people who, after every exam, claim that they have failed when it turns out that they typically get the highest grade in the class. These individuals may feel highly anxious and out of control before their performance and therefore play through "worst-case" scenarios of the upcoming situation, even if that outcome does not seem likely (Norem, 1989). Thus, defensive pessimism is more of a "confronting" coping strategy than an avoidant one because it helps individuals directly imagine their failure and subsequent consequences.

Defensive pessimists use their cognitive strategy to help them work through the possibility of a negative outcome before it happens, in anticipation of failure, allowing them to focus their anxiety more constructively

(Cantor, 1990). Defensive pessimism enables individuals to prepare for disappointment, which may increase their motivation by preventing negative scenarios (Showers, 1992b). This negative focusing style is advantageous to defensive pessimists. Showers (1992b) compared negatively focused and positively focused defensive pessimists. She found that the negatively focused defensive pessimists actually felt more relaxed, positive, and prepared for an upcoming social situation than the positively focused defensive pessimists.

Self-handicapping and defensive pessimism are cognitive strategies that help individuals avoid negative self-evaluations by attributing failure to external factors. These strategies protect self-esteem and "save face" in the eyes of others. Constructing hindrances to successful future performance helps individuals who fear failure to avoid negative self-evaluations by creating less esteem-threatening explanations for the failure (Kimble et al., 1990). In essence, these individuals attempt to deflect the blame for their perceived personal inadequacies from internal to more external factors.

Individuals constantly interpret the behaviors of others, often using cognitive strategies such as self-handicapping or defensive pessimism. These strategies, however, can lead to attributional errors. The **fundamental attribution error** involves attributing others' behavior to personal characteristics rather than considering situational factors (Greenberg et al., 2018; Jones & Harris, 1967). For example, suppose you saw a person enter a room and trip. In that case, you might automatically say to yourself, "What a klutz!" attributing their tripping to an internal trait rather than the uneven carpeting you may not have noticed from across the room. When making attributions for your behavior, this is typically not the case, as people are more likely to explain their behavior with external causes in contrast to the internal causes they attribute to others' behavior—what Jones and Nisbett (1971) called the **actor-observer effect**. Why do people make these errors, and how often do they make them? The answer to the latter question is: very often! Why they make these errors vary, but one reason is due to what may very well be my favorite phrase in all of social psychology.

Individuals are naturally error-prone in their thinking, likely because they have so much to think about daily. People frequently make attributional errors because they are **cognitive misers**. Individuals are generally lazy thinkers and want to expend only a little effort when making inferences or attributions about a person or situation, taking shortcuts instead (Greenberg et al., 2018). During a typical day (think before the months of Covid-19 pandemic home isolation), we can encounter dozens to hundreds of different people as we go about our daily business. It would be impossible to go up to each person and ask them why they enacted a specific behavior or what made them trip. We watch the action from a distance and make a quick attributional decision. These mental shortcuts, or **heuristics**, help us make decisions quickly. Sometimes we make a judgment based on how quickly we can think of similar situations, the **availability heuristic**, or how much it is similar to a typical example of that situation, the **representativeness heuristic** (Lewandowski et al., 2023). Why do people make these errors? Because we are all cognitive misers!

> *Investigative thinking challenge:*
> *Can you imagine an example of when you behaved like a cognitive miser? Have you observed others demonstrating similar behavior? Describe the situation.*

Imagine a detective acting like a cognitive miser and making attributional errors for behavior. Using these shortcuts could lead to the wrong person's arrest. Other errors or biases that could strongly interfere with a detective's or the police's work include **confirmation bias**, when people only look for evidence that supports their beliefs, or **hindsight bias**, when people feel like they knew the answer all along after learning the solution, or whodunit (Lewandowski et al., 2023). In detective fiction, confirmation bias is often present when the investigators and police seek evidence against only one particular person they feel is the killer. Detective fiction readers are often guilty of the hindsight bias, thinking they knew who the killer was before the big reveal at the end of the book. These biases occur frequently in literature and the real world when explaining other people's behaviors. Additionally, these cognitive strategies and attributional errors may be employed to protect one's self-esteem or different aspects of their self-concept.

Public and Private Self

A person's self-concept has two components—a **private self** and a **public self**. The private self is like a schema, serving as a mental structure and process that guides thoughts and behaviors (Schlenker, 1986). The private self also refers to the thoughts people have that are "inherently unobservable by another person" (Tedeschi, 1986, p. 2) and can be generally described as how we see ourselves. Baumeister and Tice (1986) see this private self as being composed of three different parts: the private self-concept (who we think we are), the actual self (who we truly are), and the ideal self (the person we aspire to be). Thus, the self is not a solitary or unchanging concept but is multidimensional (Markus & Wurf, 1987).

On the other hand, the public self is the aspect of ourselves active in social situations and is the self that others can "see" (Schlenker, 1986) and to which they respond (Carver & Scheier, 1981). The public self also includes how we present ourselves to the outside world, how others see us, and our different social roles (Baumeister & Tice, 1986). Thus, the private self is the self that can be hidden from the view of others, while the public self can be observed and evaluated by others (Schlenker & Weigold, 1992; Tedeschi, 1986). At times, how we view ourselves coincides with how others view us. However, in threatening situations (e.g., being evaluated), individuals may use strategies to present a better picture of themselves to others or themselves. In other words, these individuals are engaging in self-protective (when the private self is more relevant) or self-presentational strategies (when the public self is more relevant) to protect their self-images (Mello-Goldner & Wurf, 1997). Audiences influence these strategies, and those audiences can be either private or public.

A private audience refers to the individual themselves or internally represented significant others, while a public audience includes other individuals who are physically present and can observe and evaluate the person's behaviors (Baldwin & Holmes, 1987). Audiences observe the actions of an individual (Baldwin & Holmes, 1987) and evaluate those actions. Individuals are concerned about appearing positively to an audience that is present at the time. Therefore, an audience is a critical variable influencing a person's behavior. The audience influences which aspect of the self becomes more relevant and dominant in motivating the individual's behavior (Baldwin & Holmes, 1987; McKillop et al., 1992; Schlenker, 1986).

If a private audience (e.g., the self) influences a person to pursue individual achievement, then protecting the private self would be an important concern for that person. In other words, the person would likely be motivated to engage in self-protection. On the other hand, if a public audience leads a person to be concerned with public evaluation, then that person's public self would be much more important to protect. Because internal audiences are not objective situations like the number of people in a room, they may be more relevant in motivation because different individuals can interpret them differently.

Investigative thinking challenge:
Can you recall a situation in which you behaved to safeguard your inner or "private self" due to self-protection and another instance where you behaved in a way to shield your outer or "public self" for a self-presentational reason? What motivated you to behave in these ways?

All individuals are concerned with both their private and public selves to some degree, but some people are more naturally concerned about one or the other.[3] Some people are more naturally concerned with their public self, leading them to adapt their behavior to fit the expectations of others in different social situations. This ability to constantly monitor and change behavior in a public setting is what Snyder (1974) called **self-monitoring**.[4] High self-monitors gather information about the situation and adjust their behavior to meet the perceived expectations, similar to performers who adapt their actions based on their roles. In contrast, low self-monitors tend to stay consistent with their private self and act according to their internal ideals and standards. They stick to their private self and act consistently with their inner ideals and standards (Brown, 1998). Self-monitoring is a perfect example of how information processing guides people's behaviors, especially high self-monitors. A high self-monitor enters a room, for instance, looks around to see who is there and what they are doing (inputting the situational information), and then acts accordingly (processing the information to produce an output or appropriate behavior). This strategy can benefit many of the detectives popular throughout the years.

Cognitive Psychology and Detective Fiction

So far, you have read about research that supports the idea that the self-concept guides what behaviors a person chooses or wishes to enact while mediating and regulating this behavior. In other words, the self-concept is **dynamic**, meaning it is active, forceful, and capable of change (Markus & Wurf, 1987). Your self-concept very likely helped you decide what job you currently have or which college to attend. The self-concept can also prevent you from attempting certain skills or experiences because you believe you lack the skills, such as explaining the misguided beliefs that girls cannot do math or women should not be detectives. Chapter 3 introduced you to hard-boiled detectives. Most of those early detectives were male, but beginning in the late 1970s, a new type of detective became popular—the *female* hard-boiled detective. These female detectives are especially good at demonstrating cognitive flexibility that allows them to imagine the suspect or criminal's motivations and behaviors on the path to solving their cases (LaGrand & Mattson, 2007). They may also use their experiences as women when considering the motivation behind a crime.

Morality in Detective Fiction

Detectives constantly battle moral dilemmas by investigating cases and collecting evidence to convict suspects. Often convictions lead to the death of the convicted criminal, which adds another layer to the moral dilemma. However, since it is the detective and police's job to discover who is behind a crime, many might not experience the moral ambiguity of the Heinz dilemma. One example which takes the reader through the moral or ethical thinking process is Susan Glaspell's one-act play *Trifles* (1916). Glaspell based the play on an actual murder (the John Hossack murder; Iowa Cold Cases, n.d.) that she covered when she was a reporter for the *Des Moines Daily News* (Susan Glaspell, 2021).

The suspicious death described in *Trifles* (Glaspell, 1916) occurs in a farmhouse, and most of the dialogue and action occur after the fact in the kitchen. There are only five characters: an attorney; a sheriff; a neighboring male farmer; and two women, Mrs. Peters and Mrs. Hale (the neighbor's wife). The males dismiss the women and consider their behavior (and that of women generally) as "trifles." But the women are the better detectives, and they piece together the evidence and discover the manner and motive of the death. The ending contains a bit of a surprise and provides an excellent prompt for discussing morality and justice across many different behaviors. Glaspell adapted the play into the short story "A Jury of Her Peers," initially published in 1917 (Heckel & Glaspell, 1980).

Female Hard-Boiled Detectives

Remember that the early stories featuring hard-boiled detectives included violence and sex and involved a cynical, street-smart professional who was also tough, a heavy drinker, and willing to use a gun when necessary. This description is true for both male and female hard-boiled detectives, although female hard-boiled detectives tend to use violence only when necessary (Priestman, 2009). A hard-boiled detective engages in much self-talk, describing to the reader what they are doing and feeling, and this seems especially true of female hard-boiled detectives. In detective fiction, female hard-boiled detectives have emerged as prominent characters. The first book to feature a more contemporary female hard-boiled detective was M.F. Beal's (1977) *Angel Dance* (Davidson et al., 1995). The detective, Kat Guerrera, is a radical feminist and Latina; however, this book and author did not receive much attention or popularity.

Marcia Muller, considered the "mother of the woman private eye novel" (Jackson, 2002, p. 130), debuted the Sharon McCone series with *Edwin of the Iron Shoes* in 1977. The Sharon McCone series did receive positive reviews and is one of the first ongoing series to remain very popular for decades (there have been 40 books in the series so far). Beal, Muller, and other novelists who came after them integrated gender awareness into the hard-boiled detective genre (Klein, 1995). Muller's series shows that a hard-boiled detective can be female without losing any of the enjoyable and popular components of the genre (Priestman, 2009). Muller's stories often link mystery-related plots with elements of romance (similar to the Gothic novels discussed in Chapter 1).

Sharon McCone engages in much self-talk within the series, explaining her thoughts on the case and her feelings, especially when interacting with the many male characters. In Chapter 11 of *Edwin of the Iron Shoes* (Muller, 1977), McCone is annoyed when her colleague Marcus questions her thinking, calling it intuition, but not in a positive way. Through her actions and thoughts, the reader can clearly see and possibly relate to her anger and annoyance.

> "Sounds more like a woman's intuition than logic." I shifted on the stool and started fiddling with my hair, as I always did when angered.... Why did Marcus feel he must oppose everything I said [*Edwin of the Iron Shoes*, Muller, 1977, p. 86].

McCone is a strong female character who has many positive self-views and does not need to have a romantic relationship with someone to find her purpose or identity (Muller, 1977). She is a professional private investigator who carries a gun and fits the tough hard-boiled detective persona, seen in this exchange between Mr. Hood and McCone in the second Sharon McCone novel, *Ask the Cards a Question* (Muller, 1982). McCone describes herself as tough and able to defend herself against the thugs she often encounters. McCone personifies the hard-boiled detective in that she is willing to use a gun when necessary—as an example, she shoots the killer to death at the end of the novel *Ask the Cards a Question*; however, she does this out of necessity to save another person. McCone uses self-talk and constantly cues the reader to her thought processes as she investigates a crime. The character of Sharon McCone is part Native American, and Muller includes ethnic and cultural differences to some degree in the novels. Calling attention to such differences is an important component that will be discussed in the next chapter.

Muller's Sharon McCone character may have been the first truly popular and note-worthy female hard-boiled detective; however, the two quintessential examples of a female private eye are Sue Grafton's Kinsey Millhone and Sara Paretsky's V.I. Warshawski (Jackson, 2002). Both Millhone and Paretsky embody the characteristics of a traditional hard-boiled detective and the characteristics of the cognitive psychology paradigm. Paretsky's V.I. (Vic) Warshawski uses information processing techniques to collect, organize, and synthesize her evidence. Vic recognizes the importance of others and the situation during her investigations. In *Shell*

Game (Paretsky, 2018), V.I. Warshawski also borrows a bit from Agatha Christie's Hercule Poirot, stating that her detective work is like an archaeologist's work in that both look for facts and context. "Detecting is like archaeology, I guess—we need facts and we need a context for them before they have any value" (Paretsky, 2018, p. 122).

Vic also brings up an essential social topic found in many of Agatha Christie's Miss Marple stories—the concept of invisibility. Miss Marple's invisible status helps her gather information to help her solve the mystery at hand. In *Shell Game* (Paretsky, 2018), Vic sneaks into an office dressed as a cleaning woman to look for information related to her case. As she looks for clues in the office, someone approaches her, and she bends her head to avoid being seen and possibly recognized. However, she realizes that is unnecessary because, as a maid, no one notices her or sees her as an individual. She realizes this invisibility could be helpful to her at later points in her investigation. "I dropped my cloth, bent over, head hidden. It didn't matter—I was a maid; none of the trio even noticed me.... Anyone who's cleaning up after you is part of your furniture, not a person" (Paretsky, 2018, pp. 154–155). Here, invisibility relates to occupation and social class, not old age. Chapter 6 will discuss invisibility related to race.

Kinsey Millhone is a tough talker, which serves as an "exercise of power—the power to express her emotions and sensibilities, and power over situations" (Christianson, 1995, p. 130). Grafton's first novel in the series is *A Is for Alibi* (Grafton, 1982), where we are quickly introduced to Kinsey's personality. Kinsey is independent, stubborn (or, as she describes herself, sometimes "downright bitchy"), has some anger issues, and is a bit neurotic. However, she also is fiercely loyal to her friends and compassionate, has a good sense of humor, and is quirky in a good way. Her favorite food is a peanut butter and pickle sandwich, and her closest friend is her elderly landlord Henry Pitts (Kaufman & Kay, 1997). Kinsey does not have a good track record with men and is twice divorced by the age of 32.

In the first chapter of *N Is for Noose* (Grafton, 1998), Kinsey admits to the reader that not only is she not good with relationships, but that they can lead to many emotional problems if her significant other leaves or disappoints her. She explains that she prefers being alone, which she also admits may not be the most psychologically healthy strategy. Regardless, Kinsey is a strong, resourceful character. She is unlike the femme fatale characters in the male-dominated hard-boiled detective fiction. Kinsey, instead, personifies the characteristics seen in traditional male hard-boiled detectives. Like her earlier male counterparts, she works in a profession that often involves violence, crime, and power, sometimes overlapping with a plotline involving sex and betrayal (Johnson, 2004).

Besides seeming like a fun person to go out and have a drink with,

5. Cognitive Psychology

Kinsey is a successful detective who is organized in her approach to solving her cases. As she collects evidence to solve her cases, Kinsey often writes down facts and other bits of information on index cards. Grafton's alphabet series continued for 25 novels and is set in the 1980s (her death in 2017 prevented its completion, and there will not be a "Z" book in the series). Therefore, Kinsey cannot use technology like cell phones and the internet. When she finalizes the facts, she will take her index cards and fit them together like a puzzle or a case map. Kinsey uses the techniques of information processing and schemas to organize and perceive the case information. People use schemas to manage current information and provide a framework for future understanding and interpretations of new situations. This technique is precisely how Kinsey approaches each case.

In the third chapter of *A Is for Alibi* (Grafton, 1982), Kinsey describes how she writes notes on her index cards. Kinsey's written information includes the witnesses and background facts and sometimes includes notes to remind her to research some unknown terms or facts. This system allows for a more straightforward process of writing her final reports to her clients. She can also hang the cards on her bulletin board with push pins, enabling her to move them around to fit the information into a story. This technique is a three-dimensional version of the information processing in her head, demonstrating that she has the skills of an excellent cognitive psychologist.

> I have a system of consigning data to three-by-five index cards…. I tack them up on a large bulletin board above my desk and stare at them, telling myself the story as I perceive it. Amazing contradictions will come to light, sudden gaps, questions I've overlooked [*A Is for Alibi*, Grafton, 1982, p. 20].

Kinsey is aware of her private and public self and also understands that thoughts influence how people behave and interact with each other and with other groups. This is reflected in some of the social and political issues in Grafton's novels. Female hard-boiled detectives engage with these thought-provoking and contemporary issues more frequently than their male counterparts. Kinsey deals with social class, family issues (including with her own family), domestic violence, child abuse, health care issues, issues in the courts or judicial system, sex and gender roles, ageism, sexual orientation, and problems with large American corporations Kaufman & Kay, 1997). Sara Paretsky's *Shell Game* (2018) involves murder and a missing person but also deals with the issues of immigration, Middle-Eastern prejudices, the conflict in Syria, and fear of the actions of the U.S. Immigration and Customs Enforcement Agency (ICE).

A final example of how detective fiction includes elements of cognitive psychology is Jacqueline Winspear's character of *Maisie Dobbs*

(Winspear, 2003). Like Kinsey Millhone, Maisie uses a case map to link bits of evidence and information. Whereas Kinsey uses index cards, Maisie uses bits of old wallpaper, allowing her to spread them apart and tack them to a wall if needed. Maisie and her assistant Billy Beale will mark the paper with colored crayons creating connections between the key pieces of evidence, much like how activation nodes spread during memory use. A spreading activation theory of memory (Anderson, 1983) explains how the brain processes connected or associated ideas to retrieve information. The individual concepts within our memory serve as cognitive units, with each node containing associated characteristics connected to memories or behaviors.

Maisie Dobbs, Kinsey Millhone, and V.I. Warshawki use a similar technique to link their evidence procedure when working on their case maps. Maisie uses wallpaper scraps, Kinsey uses index cards, and Vic uses an artist's sketch pad to visually lay out a case's names and information. Each then explains to the reader their thought processes and how the information is connected, providing a much more detailed look into a detective's thinking process than the early male hard-boiled detectives ever offered. This focus on information processing is a distinguishing feature of the more recent female hard-boiled detectives.

Like their male counterparts, the females put themselves in danger when they rush around to collect information and confront suspects. They experience violence but are more often the victims of violence (e.g., getting attacked, shot, stabbed) rather than the perpetrators of violence against others. But what stands out is that we, as readers, are much more "in the heads" of Kinsey, Vic, and Maisie than we are with Philip Marlowe or Sam Spade. The female hard-boiled detectives actively explain each step in their thinking as they solve the case. This approach or style contrasts sharply with the "big reveal" endings of traditional soft-boiled detectives, as we are often left in the dark until the end regarding the killer's identity and motivation. The soft-boiled big reveal, or "aha moment," typically occurs at the novel's end and is similar to a magician successfully orchestrating a magic trick (Clark, 2012).

How a magician performs the trick is often never disclosed; it is, after all, supposedly magic. The audience watches the trick in awe with little interaction. Soft-boiled detectives similarly solve their cases, although they explain how they performed their "trick" (solving the case) to the assembled audience and readers at the end of the novel or movie. Male hard-boiled detectives sometimes explain their reasonings, but they more often solve their cases by rushing around and confronting individuals. Female hard-boiled detectives employ a very different approach. They explain to the reader (typically their only audience for most of the story) how they put the information together, ostensibly divulging the secret behind their magic trick.

Maisie, and her assistant Billy, engage in another type of information-processing technique—they perform what they refer to as a grid search when investigating a crime scene and gathering evidence. Billy Beale describes Maisie's grid-search technique in *The Consequences of Fear* (Winspear, 2021). Maisie walks around a specific crime scene or important area in her investigation in an organized way, similar to following a map's grid lines. She does this physically to avoid missing any clues or information. It also helps her thinking process to separate evidence and clues or group-related information. Like Kinsey Millhone, Maisie's grid search is a three-dimensional representation of the information processing in her brain.

Maisie Dobbs not only uses the cognitive technique of information processing, but she also is keenly self-aware, likely from her training as a psychologist and her interest in spirituality, self-awareness, and mindfulness. Maisie recognizes the importance of creating the right environment and behaving differently based on how she perceives her environment. In *Birds of a Feather* (Winspear, 2004), she explains why she avoids questioning individuals in enclosed spaces, as that might prevent them from opening their minds to more possibilities: "Maisie knew that an enclosed area encouraged an enclosed mind.... Space broadens the mind and gives the voice room to be heard" (*Birds of a Feather*, Winspear, 2004, p. 22).

As a high self-monitor, Maisie is good at changing her behavior, including her accent, to fit the situation and the individuals she may be interviewing. In *Elegy for Eddie* (Winspear, 2012), Maisie changes her accent and style to match Jack Barker, a newspaper vendor, as she makes small talk with him at the start of her day in the book's first chapter. Maisie also mimics those around her to ingratiate herself and win their trust to gain critical information. In *An Incomplete Revenge* (Winspear, 2008), Maisie emulates the posture of the gypsies she speaks with, even dancing a gypsy dance at one point to show her connection with the community. She goes to their encampment to learn from them, eating their food and acting like them so that she will be accepted and gain critical information related to the mysterious fires she initially investigates.

One final example of Maisie's self-monitoring skills occurs in the more recent Maisie Dobbs novel, *The Consequences of Fear* (Winspear, 2021). Maisie describes how she learned to change her tone and word choice to fit the situation and the individuals she was interacting with best. This approach helped the person she was talking to relax and feel connected to her, which could help her obtain needed information. "She didn't have to sound like a local, just meet them halfway, so without realizing it they felt as if she were a friend and not a stranger" (*The Consequences of Fear*, Winspear, 2021, p. 75).

Maisie is a high self-monitor because she understands the "power of the situation" and how people's thoughts (including their acceptance or approval) will influence their behavior. She understands that blending into the environment will help her be accepted by those in the community she is interviewing, leading to more clues and information for her investigation. As of 2024, there are 18 Maisie Dobbs books published, with the first appearing in 2003. Although the series is written in contemporary times, it is set during the 1920s through the 1940s, and therefore, it has elements of both soft-boiled and hard-boiled detective fiction.

Today's hard-boiled detectives, especially the female ones, drink less and have fewer vices, but they act in ways that personify order, hope, resourcefulness, persistence, and determination (Grafton, 2013). Many theories found within cognitive psychology, especially the ideas of information processing, schemas, and the self, are fundamental in these more recent female hard-boiled detective series. Because they realize the power of the situation and engage more cooperatively with others, their cases reflect contemporary socially relevant issues and diversity in writers and characters (Grafton, 2013). They demonstrate cultural sensitivity, acknowledging the importance of environment and behavior in their investigations.

Overall, the female hard-boiled detectives in contemporary detective fiction exemplify the intersection of cognitive psychology and detective work, employing information processing, self-awareness, and adaptation to tackle complex cases and address relevant societal issues. The focus on the environment, diversity, and self-awareness are essential considerations in the next chapter when we look at how psychology and detective fiction embrace the idea of multicultural differences.

Suggested Detective Fiction/Literature to Accompany This Chapter

- Susan Glaspell's one-act play *Trifles* (perform it with your class or reading group)
- *A Is for Alibi* by Sue Grafton
- Marcia Muller's *Sharon McCone series*
- Sara Paretsky's *V.I. Warshawski series*
- *Dead Time: A Marti MacAlister Mystery* by Eleanor Taylor Bland
- Jacqueline Winspear's *Maisie Dobbs series*
- *Murder by Tradition: A Kate Delafield Mystery* by Katherine V. Forrest

End-of-Chapter Mind Puzzlers

1. How do the characters' actions in one of the stories you read reflect the skills or characteristics described in Piaget's stages of cognitive development? Provide at least one example for each stage and explain their significance.

2. How do the characters search for the truth in the play *Trifles*? Do the characters' methods align with those of a psychologist? Explain the connection. Analyze the moral development level of their decisions using Kohlberg's and Gilligan's stages. Do you agree or disagree with their decisions? Explain your reasoning.

3. Choose one example of a personal construct utilized by either the detective or another character in a story you read. Explore the range of convenience, focus of convenience, and permeability related to this personal construct. Provide specific instances from the text to illustrate your points.

4. Select one of the detectives you have read about so far. What are their schematic and aschematic characteristics? Evaluate how these traits impact their investigative actions and strategies.

5. Do any of the characters in the stories you have read so far display self-handicapping or defensive pessimism? If so, provide examples to back up your answer. Additionally, examine whether any characters display the fundamental attribution error or the actor-observer effect and discuss the potential factors contributing to these cognitive biases and errors.

6. Provide an example of a character's behaving like a cognitive miser using heuristics or making other attributional errors when judging others' behaviors.

7. Select one detective and assess whether this individual is primarily motivated by their private or public self. Cite examples from the text to support your answer. Do any of the characters engage in self-monitoring behavior? How so? Provide relevant examples to back up your answer.

8. The novels of Marcia Muller and Sue Grafton are considered "hard-boiled" detective fiction. Connect their actions to the psychological elements discussed in the course so far, providing illustrative examples. Moreover, identify the psychological paradigm that best aligns with Kinsey Millhone or Sharon McCone, supporting your choice with at least three quotes and page numbers from the novels.

Key Terms and People

- **cognitive psychology**: the psychological paradigm that examines how people's thoughts, including memories, and the way they process information, influence their behavior and personality
- **Jean Piaget**: a Swiss psychologist and pioneer in the field of children's cognitive development, whose theory focused on understanding how knowledge grows and changes systematically over time, from infancy to adulthood
- **scheme**: a cognitive structure that allows children to organize and make sense of the world and their experiences by representing information in their minds
- **organization**: the process of combining and integrating abilities or concepts in a coordinated manner
- **adaptation**: a cognitive tool for dealing with tasks and demands presented by the environment by trying to adjust to them
- **assimilation**: occurs when new information is incorporated into existing schemes
- **accommodation**: when new information is taken in and integrated into existing knowledge—but because it does not easily fit into previous ideas and concepts, the old scheme needs adjustment or modification
- **sensorimotor stage**: Piaget's first stage of cognitive development, lasting from birth to about age 2, during which babies learn about their environment through their senses and motor responses
- **object permanence**: when a child understands that an object continues to exist even when it is not visible
- **preoperational stage**: Piaget's second stage, from about age 2 to about age 7, in which children develop language and learn through pretend play but are still unable to perform mental operations that require more concrete logic
- **egocentrism**: a limitation of the preoperational stage in which children have difficulty imagining another person's point of view
- **concrete operational stage**: Piaget's third stage, occurring between ages 7 to about 11, when children gain the ability to think logically about concrete events and exhibit reversible thinking
- **conservation**: a skill that develops in the concrete operational stage, allowing a child to understand that the amount of an object does not change even if its appearance slightly changes

- **formal operational stage**: Piaget's final stage, beginning around age 11 or 12, when a child's reasoning ability expands from concrete thinking to abstract, logical, analytical, and hypothetical thinking
- **morality**: the rules or ideals that guide social and interpersonal behavior and help us distinguish between right and wrong
- **Lawrence Kohlberg**: an American psychologist who developed a theory and stages of moral development
- **Carol Gilligan**: a psychologist known for her research on the moral development of girls and women
- **information processing approach**: a psychological shift that likened human problem-solving to the operations of simple computers at the time, where input is processed to produce an output
- **George Kelly**: a cognitive theorist who believed that people behave like naive scientists, continually making and testing hypotheses
- **personal constructs**: cognitive structures used to interpret and predict events
- **range of convenience**: a set of events or topics to which a personal construct applies
- **focus of convenience**: a set of events to which a personal construct best applies
- **permeability**: the degree to which a personal construct can be applied to new events
- **Hazel Markus**: a social psychologist known for her research on the self
- **schema**: an active information processing structure that represents knowledge about a particular concept or domain
- **cross-situational consistency**: when individuals retain similar or consistent behaviors across different situations
- **working self-concept**: the part of an individual's self-knowledge that is active at a particular time
- **self-protective strategies**: actions taken to protect oneself from negative feelings by maintaining positive private self-image
- **self-presentational strategies**: actions aimed at preserving positive impressions others have of a person's public self-image
- **self-handicapping**: a strategy in which individuals (unconsciously) create obstacles to performance, allowing them

to blame the obstacle if they don't perform well and protect their positive self-image
- **defensive pessimism**: a cognitive strategy used by individuals to maintain self-esteem in uncertain or risky situations by strategically setting low expectations beforehand
- **fundamental attribution error**: when individuals ignore the situation to explain the behavior of others and instead assign behavioral blame to personal characteristics
- **actor-observer effect**: when people are more likely to explain their behavior with external causes in contrast to the internal causes they attribute to others' behavior
- **cognitive misers**: when individuals do not want to expend too much effort when trying to make inferences or attributions about a person or situation, preferring the quick and easy solution to the problem
- **heuristics**: mental shortcuts that help us make decisions quickly
- **availability heuristic**: when we make a judgment based on how quickly we can think of similar situations
- **representativeness heuristic**: when we make a judgment based on how similar it is to a typical example of that situation
- **confirmation bias**: when people only look for evidence that supports their beliefs
- **hindsight bias**: when people feel like they knew the answer all along after learning the solution
- **private self**: the part of the self that is hidden from the view of others
- **public self**: the part of the self that can be observed and evaluated by others
- **self-monitoring**: a person's ability to constantly monitor and change behavior when in a public setting
- **dynamic self-concept**: the characteristic of the self that is active, forceful, and capable of change

Chapter Notes

1. For a more comprehensive summary of "theory of mind" and "false-belief tasks," see Martin Doherty's (2008) book *Theory of Mind: How Children Understand Others' Thoughts and Feelings*, Psychology Press; or Henry Wellman's (1990) book *The Child's Theory of Mind*, MIT Press; or Wellman, Cross, & Watson (2001); Meta-analysis of theory-of-mind development: The truth about false belief. *Child Development, 72*, 655–684.

2. For a listing of some of the most influential cognitive psychologists of the current

time, see https://www.onlinepsychologydegree.info/30-most-influential-cognitive-psychologists-alive-today/.
3. To determine which aspect of the self you are more concerned with, or have a "trait" for, take the *Self-Consciousness Scale* (Fenigstein et al., 1975).
4. To determine if you are a high or low self-monitor, take *The Self-Monitoring Scale*, found in Snyder (1974) or Brown (1998) p. 167.

References

Anderson, J.R. (1983). A spreading activation theory of memory. *Journal of Verbal Learning and Verbal Behavior, 22*(3), 261–295. https://doi.org/10.1016/S0022-5371(83)90201-3.
Baldwin, M.W., & Holmes, J.G. (1987). Salient private audiences and awareness of the self. *Journal of Personality and Social Psychology, 52*, 1087–1098.
Baumeister, R.F., & Tice, D.M. (1986). Four selves, two motives, and a substitute process self-regulation model. In R. Baumeister (Ed.), *Public Self and Private Self* (pp. 63–74). Springer-Verlag.
Beal, M.F. (1977). *Angel Dance: A Thriller*. Daughters Publishing Co.
Berglas, S., & Jones, E.E. (1978). Drug choice as a self-handicapping strategy in response to noncontingent success. *Journal of Personality and Social Psychology, 36*, 405–417.
Brown, J. (1998). *The Self.* Mc-Graw Hill.
Burger, J. (2018). *Personality* (10th edition). Cengage Learning.
Cantor, N. (1990). From thought to behavior: "Having" and "doing" in the study of personality and cognition. *American Psychologist, 40*, 735–750.
Cantor, N., & Michel, W. (1979). Prototypes in person perception. In L.L. Berkowitz (Ed.), *Advances in Experimental Social Psychology* (vVol. 12, pp. 3–53). Academic Press.
Carver, C.S., & Scheier, M.F. (1981). *Attention and Self-regulation: A Control-theory Approach to Human Behavior.* Springer.
Chomsky, N. (2021). In *Encyclopædia Britannica*. Retrieved from https://academic-eb-com.proxy.bc.edu/levels/collegiate/article/Noam-Chomsky/82316.
Christianson, S. (1995). Talkin' trash and kickin' butt: Sue Grafton's hard-boiled feminism. In Irons, G. (Ed.), *Feminism in Women's Detective Fiction* (pp. 127–147). University of Toronto Press. Retrieved February 20, 2021, from http://www.jstor.org/stable/10.3138/j.ctt1287pdb.13.
Clark, J.L. (2012). *Mind Magic and Mentalism for Dummies.* For Dummies.
Colby, A., & Kohlberg, L. (1987). *The Measurement of Moral Judgment (Vol. 1): Theoretical*
Davidson, C.N., Wagner-Martin, L., Ammons, E., & Cairns Collection of American Women Writers. (1995). *The Oxford Companion to Women's Writing in the United States.* Oxford University Press.
Epstein, S. (1980). The self-concept: A review and the proposal of an integrated theory of personality. In E. Staub (Ed.), *Personality: Basic Aspects and Current Research* (pp. 82–132). Prentice-Hall.
Fenigstein, A., Scheier, M.F., & Buss, A.H. (1975). Public and private self-consciousness: Assessment and theory. *Journal of Consulting and Clinical Psychology, 43*, 522–527.
Fiske, S.T., & Taylor, S.E. (1991). *Social Cognition* (22nd. Ed.). McGraw-Hill, Inc.
Gilligan, C. (1982). *In a Different Voice: Psychological Theory and Women's Development.* Harvard University Press.
Glaspell, S. (1916). *Trifles.* Frank Shay.
Grafton, S. (1982). *A Is for Alibi.* Bantam Books.
Grafton, S. (1998). *N Is for Noose.* Henry Holt.
Grafton, S. (2013). *Kinsey and Me: Stories.* Marian Wood/G.P. Putnam's Sons.
Greenberg, J., Schmader, T., Arndt, J., & Landau, M. (2018). *Social Psychology: The Science of Everyday Life* (2nd Edition). Worth Publishers.
Greenwald, A.G. & Pratkanis, A.R. (1984). The self. In Wyer, R.S. & Srull, T.K. (Eds.), *Handbook of Social Cognition* (Vol. 3). Erlbaum.
Greenwald, A.G., & Banaji, M.R. (1989). The self as a memory system: Powerful but ordinary. *Journal of Personality and Social Psychology, 57*, 41–54.

Heckel, S., & Glaspell, S. (1980). *A Jury of Her Peers*. Susan Heckel.
Hergenhahn, B.R. (2009). *An Introduction to the History of Psychology* (6th Edition). Wadsworth.
Higgins, E.T., Van Hook, E., & Dorfman, D. (1988). Do self-attributes form a cognitive structure? *Social Cognition, 6,* 177–207.
Hughes, F.P., Noppe, L.D., & Noppe, I.C. (1996). *Child Development*. Prentice Hall.
Iowa Cold Cases. (n.d.). John Hossack homicide. Retrieved from https://iowacoldcases.org/case-summaries/john-hossack/.
Jackson, C. (2002). *Myth and Ritual in Women's Detective Fiction*. McFarland.
Jaffee, S., & Hyde, J.S. (2000). Gender differences in moral orientation: A meta-analysis. *Psychological Bulletin, 126,* 703–726.
James, W. (1890). *The Principles of Psychology* (Vol. 1). Macmillan.
Johnson, P.E. (2004, March). Sex and betrayal in the detective fiction of Sue Grafton and Sara Paretsky. *The Journal of Popular Culture, 27*(4), 97–106. https:// doi: 10.1111/j.0022-3840.1994.2704_97.x.
Jones, E.E., & Harris, V.A. (1967). The attribution of attitudes. *Journal of Experimental Social Psychology, 3*(1), 1–24. https://doi.org/10.1016/0022-1031(67)90034-0.
Jones, E.E., & Nisbett, R.E. (1971). *The Actor and the Observer: Divergent Perceptions of the Causes of Behavior*. General Learning Press.
Kalat, J.W. (1999). *Introduction to Psychology* (5th Edition). Brooks/Cole, Wadsworth.
Kaufman, N.H., & Kay, C.M. (1997). *"G" Is for Grafton: The World of Kinsey Millhone*. Henry Holt.
Kelly, G.A. (1955). *The Psychology of Personal Constructs*. Norton.
Kihlstrom, J.F., Cantor, N., Albright, J.S., Chew, B.R., Klein, S.B., & Niedenthal, P.M. (1988). Information processing and the study of the self. *Advances in Experimental Social Psychology, 21,* 145–178.
Kimble, C.E., Funk, S.C., & Da Polito, K.L. (1990). The effects of self-esteem certainty on behavioral self-handicapping. *Journal of Social Behavior and Personality, 5,* 137–149.
Klein, K.G. (1995). *The Woman Detective: Gender & Genre* (2nd ed.). University of Illinois Press.
Kohlberg, L. (1963). The development of children's orientation toward a moral order: Sequence in the development of moral thought. *Vita Humana, 6,* 11–33.
Kohlberg, L. (1981). *Essays on Moral Development: The Philosophy of Moral Development*. Harper & Row.
LaGrand, V., & Mattson, C.E. (2007). Peter Wimsey and Precious Ramotswe: Castaway detectives and companionate marriage. *Christianity and Literature, 56*(4), 633–664.
Lewandowski, G.W., Ciarocco, N.J., & Strohmetz, D.B. (2023). *Discovering the Scientist Within: Research Methods in Psychology*. Worth Publishers.
Linville, P.W. (1982). Affective consequences of complexity regarding the self and others. In M.S. Clark & S.T. Fiske (Eds.), *Affect and Cognition*. Erlbaum.
Markus, H. (1977). Self-schemata and processing information about the self. *Journal of Personality & Social Psychology, 35,* 63–78.
Markus, H. (1990). Unresolved issues of self-representation. *Cognitive Therapy and Research, 14,* 241–253.
Markus, H., & Nurius, P. (1986). Possible selves. *American Psychologist, 41*(9), 954–969.
Markus, H., & Wurf, E. (1987). The dynamic self-concept: A social psychological perspective. *Annual Review in Psychology, 38,* 314–337.
McKillop, K.J., Berzonsky, M.D., & Schlenker, B.R. (1992). The impact of self-presentations on self-beliefs: Effects of social identity and self-presentational context. *Journal of Personality, 60*(4), 789–808.
Mello-Goldner, D., & Wurf, E. (1997). The self in self-handicapping: Differential effects of public and private internal audiences. *Current Psychology, 15*(4), 319–331.
Miller, G.A. (1956). The magical number seven, plus or minus two: Some limits on our capacity for processing information. *Psychological Review, 63,* 81–97.
Muller, M. (1977). *Edwin of the Iron Shoes*. The Women's Press.
Muller, M. (1982). *Ask the Cards a Question*. St. Martin's Press.

Newell, A., Shaw, J.C., & Simon, H.A. (1958). Elements of a theory of human problem solving. *Psychological Review, 65*(3), 151–166. https://doi.org/10.1037/h0048495.
Norem, J.K. (1989). Cognitive strategies as personality: Effectiveness, specificity, flexibility and change. In D.M. Buss & N. Cantor (Eds.), *Personality Psychology: Recent Trends and Emerging Directions* (pp. 45–60). Springer-Verlag.
Paretsky, S. (2018). *Shell Game.* William Morrow.
Piaget, J. (1929). *The Child's Conception of the World.* Harcourt Brace.
Piaget, J. (1952). Autobiography. In E. Boring (Ed). *History of Psychology in Autobiography.* Vol. 4. Clark University Press.
Pinker, S. (1997). *How the Mind Works.* Norton.
Plotnik, R. (1999). *Introduction to Psychology* (5th Edition). Brooks/Cole/Wadsworth.
Priestman, M. (Ed.). (2003). *The Cambridge Companion to Crime Fiction.* Cambridge University Press.
Rhodewalt, F., Morf, C., Hazlett, S., & Fairfield, M. (1991). Self-handicapping: The role of discounting and augmentation in the preservation of self-esteem. *Journal of Personality and Social Psychology, 61*(1), 122–131. https://dx.doi.org/10.1037/0022-3514.61.1.122.
Santrock, J.W. (2018). *Children* (14th edition). Mc-Graw Hill Education.
Schlenker, B. (1986). Self-identification: Toward an integration of the private and public self. In R. Baumeister (Ed.), *Public Self and Private Self* (pp. 21–62). Springer-Verlag.
Schlenker, B.R., & Weigold, M.F. (1992). Interpersonal processes involving impression regulation and management. *Annual Review of Psychology, 43*, 133–168.
Schultz, D. (1986). *Theories of Personality* (3rd edition). Brooks/Cole Publishing Company.
Shaffer, D.R. (1996). *Developmental Psychology: Childhood and Adolescence* (4th Edition); Brooks/Cole Publishing Company.
Shaffer, D.R. (2008). *Social and Personality Development* (6th edition); Cengage Learning.
Showers, C. (1992a). Compartmentalization of positive and negative self-knowledge: Keeping bad apples out of the bunch. *Journal of Personality & Social Psychology, 62*, 1036–1049.
Showers, C. (1992b). The motivational and emotional consequences of considering positive or negative possibilities for an upcoming event. *Journal of Personality and Social Psychology, 63*, 474–484.
Shweder, R.A., Mahapatra, M., & Miller, J.G. (1987). Culture and moral development. In J. Kagan & S. Lamb (Eds.), *The Emergence of Morality in Young Children.* University of Chicago Press.
Snyder, M. (1974). Self-monitoring of expressive behavior. *Journal of Personality and Social Psychology, 30*, 526–537.
Susan Glaspell. (2021). In *Encyclopædia Britannica.* Retrieved from https://academic-eb-com.proxy.bc.edu/levels/collegiate/article/Susan-Glaspell/36987
Tedeschi, J.T. (1986). Private and public experiences of the self. In R. Baumeister (Ed.), *Public Self and Private Self* (pp. 1–20). Springer-Verlag.
Tice, D.M., & Baumeister, R.F. (1990). Self-esteem, self-handicapping, and self-presentation: The strategy of inadequate practice. *Journal of Personality, 58*, 443–464.
Wellman, H.M., & Wooley, J. (1990). From simple desires to ordinary beliefs: The early development of everyday psychology. *Cognition, 35*, 245–275.
Winspear, J. (2003). *Maisie Dobbs: A Novel.* Penguin Books.
Winspear, J. (2004). *Birds of a Feather.* Penguin Books.
Winspear, J. (2008). *An Incomplete Revenge.* Picador: Henry Holt and Company
Winspear, J. (2012). *Elegy for Eddie.* Harper Perennial.
Winspear, J. (2021). *The Consequences of Fear.* HarperCollins Publishers.

6

Focus on Culture

Recognizing the importance of others and social relationships in influencing behavior and thoughts is well-established (Harris & Orth, 2020). Individuals characterize each other into the various groups perceived as belonging to them, including categories or groups such as ethnicity, race, gender, and culture. Boas (1901) believed that to study the mind, researchers needed to adapt to the thinking and environment of those they were studying, freeing themselves from personal cultural biases. Cooley (1902), an American sociologist, argued that individuals' feelings toward themselves are socially determined. Cooley introduced the term **looking-glass self** to explain how self-perceptions are determined by how we see ourselves reflected in others' eyes, very much like how we see ourselves when looking in a mirror. Cooley believed that others socially influence the self, so we develop our self-concept by observing how others view us. We create our "self" as we think others see us (Tice & Wallace, 2005).

In 1932, psychologist Frederic Bartlett published a book detailing his research on memory, which included examples from different cultures. His most famous experiment involved participants reading a Native American story about ghosts, after which they had to recall as much detail as possible about the story. He found that his participants changed some of the details in the story that they could not understand to reflect their own cultural experiences better. Bartlett's (1932) research also compared memory differences between Swazi African culture and British culture in what may have been one of the first studies in cross-cultural psychology. Many early psychologists interested in culture would fall into the social psychology[1] area, although developmental psychologists like Vygotsky and Bruner also made significant contributions[2] (Kitayama & Cohen, 2007).

During the late 20th century, psychology acknowledged the importance of culture's influence on attitudes and behaviors. Tice (1992) clarified this influence on an individual's self-concept by stating that "the looking glass self (Cooley) may function as a magnifying glass during self-perception so that what one sees in oneself while others are present has an extra powerful impact on the self-concept" (Tice, 1992, pp. 449–450). Culture and race, in particular, can strongly influence values, beliefs, and behaviors by persuading its members to conform to established standards (Plotnik, 1999). The term culture can have several different meanings. For our purposes, **culture** is the set of behaviors, attitudes, beliefs, and values held and shared by a group of individuals that is passed on from generation to generation (Barnouw, 1985; Matsumoto, 1994). Culture includes information learned from others and the specific group of individuals providing or sharing that information (Heine, 2012). Each culture has its own **cultural beliefs**, commonly held norms, and moral standards, including the standards of "right and wrong" that set the expectations for behavior and activities such as dating, marriage, and sexuality (Arnett, 2013).

Culture influences how individuals evaluate others and themselves (Brown, 1998). It should enhance our understanding of each other and never be used as a label to explain divergent behavior (Lonner & Malpass, 1994). Culture is a type of cognitive schema (schemas were discussed in Chapter 5) because it organizes information and beliefs around a similar concept and can guide or direct behavior (Cross & Gore, 2012). When interpreting others' behaviors, many individuals will look to a person's culture as influencing that behavior, mainly positively. Still, sometimes the behaviors can be interpreted negatively by those outside of that particular group and can serve as an example of bias, **prejudice**, or **discrimination**. These negative beliefs and behaviors are errors in judgment (Brehm & Kassin, 1996) and are often the result of **stereotypes** (broad overgeneralizations) about the traits and behaviors of the members of a particular group (Brehm et al., 2007; Greenberg et al., 2018).

Individuals are socialized to believe that acting consistently with their specific cultural group is the "normal" or correct way to behave. If someone deviates from that behavior, they are considered problematic. This error in judgment, where individuals use the standards of their own culture to judge others, is called **ethnocentrism** (Heine, 2012). The concept of ethnocentrism was known even to the early Greek historians and philosophers, with Herodotus acknowledging that people tend to "see themselves as the centers of the world, and processes that are common in their locations are 'good,' whereas processes that are different are 'bad'" (Triandis, 2007, p. 59).

Cross-cultural interaction often results in discomfort and feeling unsettled in an unfamiliar setting, termed **culture shock** by researchers (Bochner, 2003). People who temporarily visit a new culture or location before returning to their home country (**sojourners**) or individuals who are interacting with a different culture in a multicultural society can experience culture shock. Culture shock can often occur in countries that are melting pots of cultures and ethnicities, such as the United States (Bochner, 2003; Sussman, 2002). However, these interactions need not always be negative. Engaging with other cultures can have positive consequences once we understand certain stumbling blocks and biases. Willingly exposing themselves to different cultures and new experiences helps these individuals avoid stress and tension, resulting in more positive interactions (Barna, 2013).

Cultural Versus Cross-Cultural Psychology

Cultural psychology focuses on how cultures reflect and shape their members' behavior and psychological processes (Heine, 2012). It is not necessarily considered a separate paradigm of psychology but rather an interdisciplinary approach to studying individuals that borrowed topics and techniques from anthropology, sociology, and social sciences. For the first 100 years of psychology, cultural influences did not receive much attention, even though many early psychologists were from different cultural groups and were interested in this topic. Wilhelm Wundt, the father of psychology, established the beginnings of experimental psychology and co-authored a 10-volume series titled *Elements of Folk Psychology* (Wundt & Schaub, 1921). This series focused on the connections and reciprocal relationships among different "folk" or social groups.

The more recent focus on cultural psychology began in the early 1990s. This focus recognized the importance of culture as one type of context that influences how individuals process information (Heine, 2012). It provided a "powerful way to operationalize the influence of nurture" in developmental research (Luszcz, 2006, p. 290). Cultural psychology continues to look into the relationship between culture and people's behavior (Fiske et al., 1998).

Culture and psychology reciprocally influence each other (Vaughn, 2019). This reciprocal relationship is especially important because multiculturalism is growing, especially in the United States. The U.S. Census Bureau projects that the U.S. will become "minority white" around 2045. During that year, people identifying as white will make up approximately 49.7 percent of the U.S. population, in contrast to 24.6 percent Latino/Hispanic (some prefer the new term Latinx), 13.1 percent Black, 7.9 percent Asian, and 3.8 percent for biracial or multiracial individuals (Frey, 2018). (Frey, 2018). For this reason, we should embrace diversity across cultural, racial, and ethnic groups, not dismiss or fear it. It should focus on not only the differences across these groups but the similarities as well. When teaching a *Group Dynamics* course or other courses that involve groups, leadership, or the interpretation of behavior (which is almost every psychology course), I always advise my students never to say that they are "color-blind" to differences in people based on skin color, race, ethnicity, or culture. Ignoring a person's race, ethnicity, or culture diminishes their experiences that would otherwise help strengthen the group and help people learn from one another.

These various groups (and others such as gender, religion, gender identity, or sexual orientation) should never be ignored but should be acknowledged. Recent psychology (and detective fiction) has attempted to challenge the previously accepted "deficit perspective" when writing about various racial or cultural groups. This perspective change is important for research and literature focusing on Black or African American people.[3] While acknowledging that challenges remain, recent research focuses more on strengths and characteristics that have led to resilience, ego strength, and success across various areas (DeFreitas, 2019).

The two approaches combining culture and psychology are called cultural psychology and cross-cultural psychology. Cultural psychology is the more "micro" approach, focusing on individual differences within specific cultures. Typical research may include **ethnographic research**, naturalistic observations, or field studies of a particular cultural group studied in their real-life environment, such as American anthropologist Margaret Mead's study of American Samoan adolescents during the 1920s (Heine, 2012; Mead, 1928). Ethnographic studies attempt to understand the culture from its context (Biswas-Diener & Thin, 2021). **Cross-cultural psychology** is a more "macro" approach, focusing on how culture influences behavior *across* cultural groups (Lonner, 2015; Vaughn, 2019). Cross-cultural research broadens the typical introduction to psychology course content by including research involving participants from different cultures (Matsumoto, 1994), thus providing those students with the knowledge to apply the information in many situations and with many different kinds of people.

One distinction applied to researchers who study culture deals with the perceived differences between cultures. Some focus on culture's **"etic"** aspects, the universal principles or behaviors consistent across cultures. Other researchers study culture's **"emic"** aspects, which are culture-specific principles or behaviors that differ across cultures (Vaughn, 2019). Researchers interested in either approach will make comparisons across cultures, but those who emphasize the emic approach believe there are more than just a few ways to evaluate cultures. Those emphasizing the etic approach collect data from many cultures.

Because there are many different cultures worldwide, there must be numerous methods of observing and studying their distinctiveness. Data collection will vary based on the approach, with the etic approach favoring quantitative methods that involve administering surveys and questionnaires that result in larger sample sizes. Researchers who emphasize the emic aspects of culture opt to collect data from only a few cultures at a time and use methods (often qualitative methods such as the open-ended questions common in interviews) that result in smaller sample sizes (Cohen, 2011). Many researchers are interested in both approaches, as they complement each other and are not dichotomous or mutually exclusive (Fischer & Poortinga, 2018; Vaughn, 2019).

Culture is an essential social construct that teaches us what behaviors and emotions are appropriate in different situations. It is a "social" construct because culture is socially determined, meaning others influence it to a large degree. We learn behaviors and emotions chiefly by watching the behaviors of others—a type of learning called observational learning, discussed in Chapter 3 (Biswas-Diener & Thin, 2021). Within the last 20 years, researchers have recognized the importance of being aware of cultural differences. Earley and Ang (2003) defined **cultural intelligence** as the ability and willingness to apply cultural awareness to practical uses and adapt to new cultural settings. According to Earley and Ang, people with high cultural intelligence (or have high C.Q., rather than I.Q.) interact effectively with people from different cultures because they are good at making judgments about behavior based on their understanding of various groups of people. They also would understand how characteristics and traits are often reciprocally related to the situation. Cultural intelligence is similar to **cultural awareness**, or being conscious of cultural similarities and differences (Vaughn, 2019).

One final term that is important when considering cultural differences in psychology is the idea of **cultural competence**. Cultural competence involves three components: being aware of one's assumptions, values, and biases; understanding the worldview of culturally diverse others; and developing appropriate strategies and techniques to best work effectively with diverse or multicultural others (Sue & Sue, 2016; Vaughn, 2019). The goal of a therapist is to help any client seeking their counsel, so today's therapists must be trained to recognize how individuals from different cultures may approach therapy. Many graduate counseling and clinical psychology programs now offer specific mental health training for working with Latino (Latinx), Black, African, Caribbean, and Asian populations.[4] Fictional (and real-life) detectives would benefit from having high C.Q. so that they could effectively interact with suspects who may come from a different culture than their own. High cultural intelligence would allow the detective to eliminate any suspicious behavior resulting from cultural differences rather than guilt. Readers also would benefit from reading stories set in different cultures to understand how people approach situations and problems from different yet effective perspectives.

Independent vs. Interdependent Construals of the Self

One of the earliest and most extensive research examples in cross-cultural psychology involves looking at differences in how people perceive themselves, especially regarding self-concept and self-esteem differences. As defined in Chapter 5, the **self-concept** is the part of a person's self that includes *thoughts* about themselves, while **self-esteem** is how people *feel* about themselves. An easy way to remember the difference is that self-concept involves cognitions or thoughts about the self, and self-esteem involves emotions or feelings about the self. Culture and the self are not mutually exclusive (Osborne, 1996).

An early example of research explicitly looking at self-perceptions in different cultures occurred in 1950 when anthropologist Dorothy Lee found differences in self-concept across cultures. Lee (1950) found that individuals from the Wintu Native American community of Northern California defined themselves through stories relating to other family members rather than individual experiences or characteristics (Westen, 1991). This study supported the idea that cultural differences influence how others see themselves and thus are likely to influence how others perceive us. In the early 1990s, social psychologist Hazel Markus and other researchers focused on the relationship between self, culture, and behavior. Markus and Kitayama (1991) were likely the first to define a difference in self-perceptions based on the type of culture a person was raised in and called the two distinct selves, the **independent self,** and the **interdependent self**.

The independent self is more of a Western self-view, where individuals do things more for themselves than others. Individuals with an independent self view their characteristics as distinctive of others—they focus on individualism and are socialized to focus on their uniqueness (Kunda, 2000). These individuals have a "me" mindset or approach, and their behavior is often motivated by a preference to stand apart from others, personifying the American saying, "the squeaky wheel gets the grease" (Markus & Kitayama, 1991). The motivation guiding their behavior is more internal and self-serving. People with an independent self want to be noticed and describe their self-concept (such as when answering the "Who am I?" question) in terms that are related to their inner characteristics

(Kunda, 2000). They also prefer personal freedom and making their own decisions (Biswas-Diener & Thin, 2021; Triandis, 2018). When someone with an independent self achieves success, they believe their actions caused the success; any influence from others was secondary to the success. Because of this focus, overly optimistic self-views are more common in Western, individualistic cultures and less common in Eastern and some Latin American cultures that are more interdependent or collectivist (Falbo et al., 1997; Heine & Lehman, 1995).

People with an independent self will also engage in strategies that protect the private self or are more self-enhancing. Individuals in collectivistic cultures are likelier to use other-enhancing strategies (Triandis, 2018). A final research finding comes from Markus and Kitayama (1991), who found that because people from individualistic cultures believe they are unique, they develop self-esteem through personal accomplishment. Those with an independent self may focus less on social relationships when explaining behavior. Those from a more collectivist culture will recognize that social relationships influence behaviors, self-concept, and self-esteem, with meta-analytic studies supporting this finding (Harris & Orth, 2020).

In contrast, the interdependent self (sometimes called a collective self) is more of an Eastern view. Individuals do things for others or their groups, especially their families. The interdependent self is more other-directed than internally-directed (Osborne, 1996). It involves a "we" mindset and is personified by the Japanese saying, "The nail that stands out gets pounded down" because being distinctive or making yourself stand out is frowned upon (Markus & Kitayama, 1991). Because people with an interdependent self acknowledge the value of others, they are more likely to seek help from others and the broader community. They have a strong sense of family connection, which is important to their self-concept and identity. The interdependent self is more situationally described than individually because people from collectivist cultures realize that the situation, including others, influences decision-making and motivation.

Markus and Kitayama (1991) found that collectivistic cultures place the greater good above individual happiness, resulting in less inequity. Individuals from a collectivist culture emphasize their connectedness to others and are more likely to sacrifice their personal preferences for those of the larger group (Triandis, 2018). They are also more likely to conform (Markus & Kitayama, 1994). Collectivist/interdependent individuals value others' opinions more and seek help from others to solve a problem. It does not matter if they are the specific individuals who solve the problem; as long as the group solves it successfully, that is most important.

Individuals from collectivistic/interdependent cultures also are more committed to their family or clan, seeing themselves as part of the bigger family picture (Osborne, 1996). These individuals develop a sense of self from that larger family unit's values, beliefs, and characteristics—their individual needs become less important. As an example, individuals in many Asian cultures develop their sense of self from their family's reputation; people from the Indian culture from their community (or in the past, perhaps more from the caste system), and in Japan from their occupational or work communities (Roland, 1991). The interdependent self "embraces its assigned role, focuses on social roles and obligations, and tries to figure out what others are thinking and feeling so as to best meet their expectations" (Kunda, 2000, p. 519), which contrasts with the more individualized self-serving independent self in many Western cultures.

In summary, individuals with a more Western self-view are more independent and describe the self as possessing distinct characteristics that differ from others—think of two circles of attributes for self and other that are near each other but do not overlap. Those with an Eastern self-view see the connection between self and others, with attributes of others influencing their personality and behavior—think of two circles of attributes for self and others that overlap (Markus & Kitayama, 1991; Nisbett, 2021). While independent and interdependent selves are sometimes referred to as Western or Eastern self-views, one should not limit their application purely based on a geographical standpoint. Many individuals live in Western hemisphere countries and possess more of an interdependent or collectivist self than an independent self. Social factors such as culture, family, and personal experiences are more influential than geographical location in determining how a person sees themselves. It is also important to note that no correct view of the self exists. Both have advantages and disadvantages and are two possible ways individuals socially construe themselves (Biswas-Diener & Thin, 2021).

Culture and Cognition

Besides differences in how individuals from varying cultures view themselves, disparities also exist within thinking processes. In the previous chapter, you learned about the fundamental attribution error, when people ignore the situation and attribute others' behaviors to internal causes rather than external causes. Individuals from Eastern countries are less likely to be guilty of the fundamental attribution error, although they still use it. A possible explanation for this comes from the research of Richard Nisbett. Over several decades, Nisbett and his colleagues collected empirical evidence that individuals from Eastern and Western cultures think differently (Nisbett, 2003). As an example, Nisbett et al. (2001)

found that East Asians pay more attention to their environment and assign causality. Individuals from Eastern cultures are less likely to use categories and formal logic in their thinking and believe that contradictions are common and that reality can often change (Peng & Nisbett, 1999). Easterners pay more attention to the relationships between objects.

On the other hand, Westerners are more analytic in their thinking and pay more attention to the object and the categories to which it belongs rather than the environment surrounding the object. Individuals from Western cultures use more logical rules to understand behavior. Nisbett (2021) hypothesized that these developed because of differences in social systems, the development of science in the West, the reliance on contradictions in Eastern folk stories, and even differences in geography and occupations (i.e., farmers vs. herders). These factors explain cognitive differences and may help explain disparities in how individuals from Eastern and Western cultures define their identities.

Culture and Identity

As defined earlier in this chapter, we can break down a person's sense of self into two elements: the self-concept (thoughts about the self) and self-esteem (feelings about the self). So, where does identity fit into this? First of all, identity is not a singular concept. **Identity**, or more accurately our identities, contain the traits, relationships, and groups that we belong to and define us as individuals (Oyserman et al., 2012). Whereas some psychologists use the terms self and identity to mean the same thing, the two concepts are distinct cognitive structures, and both direct our behavior. Identities can be considered structures within a person's self-concept, as they are part of how a person would answer the question "Who am I?" (Oyserman et al., 2012).

In Chapter 2, we discussed identity in terms of Erikson's psychosocial theory. Erikson felt that during adolescence, individuals undergo a redefinition of the self as they attempt to figure out who and what they are. Erikson believed adolescents must decide their values or ideology, career, and relationships (Arnett, 2013). Adolescents start developing their thoughts, beliefs, interests, and values and thus slowly begin to define themselves differently. That new identity may coincide or may differ from the identities of their parents and other family members. Adolescents begin developing ideological thoughts by considering ethnicity, race, or other cultural factors (Arnett, 2013). Phinney (1991) defines **ethnic identity** as individuals' sense of pride in their ethnicity, involvement in ethnic events or practices, and cultural commitment to the ethnic group.

Berry was among the first researchers to identify four strategies individuals use to navigate two distinctive cultural groups (Arnett, 2013; Berry, 1990; cited in Cross & Gore, 2012; Berry et al., 1986). In **assimilation,** there is a strong identification with the new/majority culture and weak identification with the original ethnic group (similar to the American melting pot). **Separation** involves weak or low identification with the new/majority culture but a strong identification with the original ethnic group (individuals using this strategy or viewpoint may only associate with other members of their own ethnic group). **Marginality** includes weak identification with both the new/majority culture and the original ethnic group (in this case, the person may feel rejected by both cultures). Finally, an **integrated or bicultural** approach involves strong identification with both the new/majority culture and the original ethnic group (here, the person would have a well-defined dual identity). Evidence suggests that individuals with a more integrated or bicultural approach experience higher self-esteem (Phinney, 1991, 1992).

> *Investigative thinking challenge:*
> *Are ethnic identity and racial identity synonymous?*
> *How would you describe your ethnic and racial identities?*
> *Which approach do you feel aligns most with your beliefs?*
> *Which individuals or communities shaped your identity the most?*

Researcher Jean Phinney has continued to look into how adolescents, in particular, respond to their ethnicity (Arnett, 2013). Phinney (1990, 1993) developed an identity model rooted in the theories of Erik Erikson and James Marcia. Phinney's model includes three stages: **unexamined ethnic identity**, when race or ethnicity is not salient or defined; **ethnic identity search**, when adolescents are exploring and trying to understand the meaning of their ethnicity/race/culture; and **achieved ethnic identity**, when they have developed a clear and positive sense of their own ethnicity/race/culture. Developing a solid sense of identity with a particular ethnic, racial, or cultural group protects self-esteem and can defend against the concept of **stereotype threat** (Tatum, 2017). Stereotype threat is the feeling that one is at risk for confirming a negative stereotype about a group, e.g., one's ethnic, racial, religious, gender, sexual orientation, or cultural group (Steele & Aronson, 1995).

Much of the research on ethnic identity development has attempted to incorporate as many adolescents and adults of color as possible; however, it would be impossible to include every group. It is also essential to remember that there is much diversity within these groups, especially when discussing Black, Latinx (Latino), Native American, Asian, or Middle Eastern and North African (MENA) individuals (Tatum, 2017). There are shared similarities (such as a focus on families, traditions, and culture) and differences. Identity development is vital for individuals from any ethnicity, race, or culture, and similarities and discrepancies should be embraced so that all individuals can find a voice and feel valued and connected to others, both in and outside their own group.

Culture and Emotions

Emotions regulate social behaviors (Markus & Kitayama, 1994) and can be experienced differently by individuals across cultures. Markus and Kitayama (1991) found that people from individualistic cultures express more self-focused emotions like jealousy and pride. Those brought up in collectivistic cultures express other-focused emotions like indebtedness and love more often. Some emotions may connect more with an independent or interdependent self. For example, Mesquita et al. (2005; cited in Kitayama et al., 2007) conducted a study with American and Japanese adults (both college students and adults from local communities) and their experiences of three emotions: pride, anger, and humiliation.

When looking at the emotion of pride, 80 percent of American participants took responsibility for a positive event, in contrast to only 37 percent of Japanese participants. To make this difference even more striking, 61 percent of the Japanese participants were self-critical of their positive performance, indicating they could still improve. Because pride stresses individual achievement, it makes sense that those from an individualistic culture would express it more often. In the anger condition, American participants were likelier to justify their anger, while Japanese participants were likelier to express sympathy toward the offending other.

This finding demonstrates how individuals from interdependent or collectivist cultures consider others more when making attributions for behaviors and consider the "common good" rather than only self-interest. When looking at the final emotion, humiliation, Japanese participants were more likely to take responsibility for the humiliating incident and indicate they would try to improve; American participants became aggressive and reaffirmed the self rather than indicate that they could improve in the future. As stated earlier in this chapter, those from an individualistic culture, who have an independent self, are more likely to take credit for their success and either disregard the influence of others in their success or may actually blame others for failure.

People also can interpret certain emotions differently along a positive and negative scale. In a study involving Japanese and American undergraduate students, Kitayama et al. (1993; cited in Matsumoto, 1994) asked participants to indicate how often they experienced certain emotions. Some emotions were considered "fillers" or not socially connected, such as relaxed, joyful, and calm. The researchers then categorized other emotions as either socially engaged (such as friendly and respect) or socially disengaged (such as pride or superiority). They found that the American participants felt more positive when experiencing socially disengaged emotions, and the Japanese participants felt more positive when experiencing socially engaged emotions. The cultural differences in participants' sense of self influenced how they experienced happy or positive feelings—those with an independent self felt more positive when experiencing emotions reflecting independence and personal achievement.

In contrast, the participants with an interdependent self felt more positive when experiencing emotions reflecting their interaction and success with the larger community. Cultural differences also exist in preference for ideal emotions. European-American and Chinese-American participants prefer high-arousal positive emotions (such as excited, strong, and enthusiastic—emotions associated with joy) more than Chinese participants, who preferred low-arousal positive emotions (such as calm, relaxed, and peaceful—emotions associated with a sense of sereneness) more than European-American participants (Mesquita & Leu, 2007; Tsai et al., 2006).

Facial Expression Research

In the late 1960s and early 1970s, **Paul Ekman** published several ground-breaking studies providing evidence that certain key or basic emotions are expressed through similar facial configurations regardless of culture (Ekman, 1972, 1973; Ekman & Friesen, 1969, 1971, 1975, 2003; Ekman et al., 1969). The **facial feedback theory** is an alternative and controversial theory of emotion that states that the actual formation of emotional expressions by using specific facial muscles is interpreted by the brain as corresponding to certain emotions (Coon & Mitterer, 2014; Plotnik, 1999). Followers of this theory believe that facial expressions contribute to the feeling of certain emotions; they are not merely the end product of them. Many people are skeptical of this approach as a theory that explains the creation of emotions; however, there is much agreement regarding the belief that the interpretation of facial expressions is universal (Ekman et al., 1987) or innate since even infants make similar facial expressions as adults (Izard, 1994).

Ekman and Friesen (1971) conducted one study with participants from five countries: the United States, Argentina, Brazil, Chile, and

Japan. They picked which of the six basic emotions common in most literate cultures (anger, disgust, fear, happiness, sadness, and surprise) were expressed in a particular photograph. The participants in all five cultures did an excellent job matching the photo with the correct emotion, typically with an accuracy of 80 to 90 percent (Heine, 2012).

In a second study, they recruited participants from an isolated cultural group called The Fore from New Guinea, presenting adults and children with 40 photographs of individuals expressing emotions. Participants were read a story and asked to pick the photograph matching the emotion described in the story. The results for the adults and children supported the hypothesis that individuals from different cultures could match facial behaviors with specific emotions. The New Guinean participants guessed the correct emotion expressed by people in photographs from a different culture at comparable rates to individuals from a more Western/literature-focused culture.

Another study by Ekman and Friesen (1971) videotaped New Guineans expressing emotions and asked American college students to guess the emotions. The participants accurately identified the emotion, even when expressed by individuals from a culture they likely had never interacted with previously. A later study by Ekman et al. (1987) expanded the number of cultures used. Participants from 10 cultures completed a task where they were presented with photographic slides and had to identify multiple emotions and the intensity of each emotion. Ekman et al. (1987) also found high agreement in identifying which emotion was the most intense and the second most intense. Overall, Ekman's research presented evidence for cross-cultural agreement in the judgment of facial expression but acknowledged several limitations—such as using photographs rather than real-time socialization (Ekman et al., 1987).

Some variability in the accuracy exists, with Elfenbein and Ambady (2002) conducting a meta-analysis that found participants were about 9 percent more accurate in judging the correct facial expression in photos of people from their own culture compared to photos with people from another culture. Even if emotions are universal, some minor cultural differences exist in recognizing facial expressions. There also are differences in the rules for the appropriateness of displaying certain emotions in particular social situations (Matusmoto, 1994). Ekman (1972) called these **cultural display rules**, which may lead to differences in how and when individuals across cultures express emotions. For example, sticking out your tongue in the U.S. would be considered rude or insulting, whereas, in China, it is considered an expression of surprise (Coon & Mitterer, 2014).

One final area of Ekman's facial expression research may benefit fictional and real-life detectives. Ekman showed that people good at detecting lies pay careful attention to nonverbal cues, especially facial expressions. Ekman believes that the "face often contains two messages—what the liar wants to show and what the liar wants to conceal" (Ekman, 1985, p. 123). Based on years of research, Ekman developed a classification for human facial expressions that can help distinguish between true and false emotional expressions by labeling which muscles of the face are active in each emotion. Ekman specifically found **micro-expressions**, or quick changes in a person's facial expression, especially revealing (Ekman & Friesen, 2003; Lying, 2021). These micro-expressions can reveal the genuine emotions behind those that an individual or suspect is deceptively displaying. Ekman also showed that people could be taught to recognize and interpret micro-expressions, a skill that helps them detect lies. When investigating a crime, you cannot assume everyone is always telling the truth; therefore, identifying deception can be very advantageous to a detective.

> *Investigative thinking challenge:*
> *At what times do you believe individuals are most inclined to be untruthful? In which circumstances is it acceptable to deceive, and in which should lying always be avoided?*

Cross-Cultural Influences in Self-Reflection and Detective Fiction

Edmund Wilson (1944, 1945) famously criticized the detective fiction genre in several essays published in *The New Yorker*. He claimed that detective fiction or mystery novels could be better written; they contain characters with little substance, involve stories with little interest to most people, and describe settings with an uninteresting atmosphere. Wilson was especially critical of Agatha Christie, a writer who is outsold only by the Bible and Shakespeare and whose books are published in more than 100 languages, making Dame Agatha the most translated writer of all time (AgathaChristie.com, 2020). While many people undoubtedly agreed with Wilson at the time, and likely even today, even more would contradict his assertions. Goldman (2011) expounds on the appeal of detective fiction and mystery stories claiming they, in fact, are worthy of our time and intellectual effort because they do challenge and engage our intellectual abilities and allow the reader to broaden their thinking. Detective fiction and mystery stories are akin to an intellectual puzzle or mind game, with the solving of the puzzle producing relaxation and enjoyment in the reader (Goldman, 2011), not the frustration and distaste Wilson felt.

Their popularity has endured even as the genre itself has changed over the years.

Introducing new detectives from different backgrounds has only added to the appeal of the mystery, as more readers can now identify with the detectives and other characters. Many of these more recent diverse stories include storylines that address social issues and inequities and can serve as starters in conversations to address these issues. Readers and students alike can learn from these diverse detectives of color. Detective fiction allows readers to embrace the similarities and differences between the characters within the stories, and between the characters and themselves.

Since the 1990s, when cultural and cross-cultural psychology were expanding, the number of culturally diverse detectives also increased. It would be impossible to include all of these detectives. The writers and detectives discussed in the remainder of this chapter were selected because they fit well with the cultural research discussed. They also engage in similar techniques to detectives addressed in previous chapters. There are many other excellent options, and I suggest instructors and readers use my examples as a starting point for the discussion.

Black Female Sleuths

Barbara Neely (who often rendered her name as BarbaraNeely) wrote four books in the *Blanche White* series from 1992 to 2000. Blanche is described as a dark-skinned, overweight African American woman in her 40s who works as a domestic servant/maid in North Carolina (Witt, 2001). In the first book in the series, *Blanche on the Lam* (Neely, 1992), we are introduced to Blanche during her court hearing for bouncing a check (for a fourth time), resulting in her being sentenced to jail for 30 days. Blanche takes morality into her own hands and decides to run for it while using the bathroom. After she leaves the courthouse, a white woman mistakenly identifies Blanche as the temp from a maid servicing agency. This error leads to Blanche hiding from the law while serving as a maid for a wealthy white family in the country, serving as one plot within the book. Soon after she arrives at the house, a dead body is discovered. Blanche becomes a suspect, necessitating her taking on the role of a sleuth to save herself and get to the bottom of things, which becomes a second plot.

Neely wrote the Blanche series to add to the prototypical female detective's image and especially appeal to female African American readers (Witt, 2001). Blanche White may be a Black housemaid, but her sleuthing abilities parallel Agatha Christie's Miss Marple. Like Miss Marple, Blanche uses her past relationships and intuition to solve crimes. She equates the behaviors of some potential suspects and witnesses in the novel to people in her family and community with similar characteristics. This strategy allows Blanche to deduce the motivation behind their behavior, or alternately when a given behavior seems wrong or out of place. More strikingly, the two share the similar characteristic of "invisibility." Miss Marple is invisible because she is an older woman; Blanche is invisible because she is a Black domestic servant. Blanche explains how she uses her invisibility and "false self" to confront the prejudice and discrimination often experienced by Black workers, especially those working in the households of wealthy white employers. In *Blanche on the Lam* (Neely, 1992), Blanche describes how she adopts an almost blank expression that hides her actual intelligence. Blanche states that she has learned from her experiences that playing "dumb" made her interactions with her employers easier, and they trusted her more. She further explains that she is not unique in this understanding and behavior because many of her Black friends and colleagues do the same. They also enjoyed fooling these clueless and prejudiced employees who just assumed they were more intelligent and worthier than her solely based on the difference in their appearances and occupations.

> Blanche had learned long ago that signs of pleasant stupidity in household help made some employers feel more comfortable.... Putting on a dumb act was something many black people considered unacceptable, but she sometimes found it a useful place to hide. She also got a lot of secret pleasure from fooling people who assumed they were smarter than she was by virtue of the way she looked and made her living [*Blanche on the Lam*, Neely, 1992, p. 16].

This passage provides a powerful opportunity for readers to address white privilege and the prejudices, stereotypes, and discriminations it brings. Rather than see her race and culture as an obstacle, Blanche recognizes the advantages it provides her, especially in gathering information to help her solve her case. Blanche describes how her employers remain clueless about the information she can learn about them from simple things like emptying their trash and cleaning their rooms. Blanche, and other domestic servants, are disregarded by the people whose homes they enter because they consider them invisible. Blanche even states that she and her fellow domestic help laugh or even pity their employers behind their backs (Neely, 1992).

In a short time of about one week, Blanche uses her community connections and problem-solving skills to solve the case. When she confronts the killer at the end of the novel, she proves that her skill for processing the relevant information related to the case is just as effective as the skills of Sherlock Holmes or Hercule Poirot. By doing so, she triumphs over the negative racial and social class stereotypes she often experienced, which came from how her employers thought of her. Explaining how her employers thought of her, Blanche says they often believe that women like her are incapable of complex thinking. In contrast, Blanche is highly observant and solves the case because she can draw conclusions that her more privileged white employers cannot complete (Neely, 1992). Blanche's invisibility may have helped her solve the case, but invisibility is typically not a positive characteristic and is often equated with inferiority. The *Blanche White* series (along with the *Miss Marple* series) can help readers address why some groups (most notably women and people of color) are perceived as invisible and what can be done to make them more visible in the real world.

The *No. 1 Ladies' Detective Agency*[5] series by Alexander McCall Smith currently includes 24 novels published between 1998 and 2023. At first, you might be skeptical that a white Scottish man could convey the feelings and thoughts of a Black female detective from Botswana. Nevertheless, McCall Smith describes the country vividly using his experience living and working in Botswana. The stories in this series exude a sense of pride in the country and the Tswana language and customs. Each book provides more information about the history and traditions of Botswana or its previous name Bechuanaland Protectorate. The main character, Precious (Mma) Ramotswe, decides to open up the first and only female detective agency in Botswana after receiving some money upon her father Obed's death. She feels she can do this because she has an abundance of intelligence and intuition and is an accurate observer of human nature (McCall Smith, 1998).

Mma Ramotswe learned many things from her father, or her "Daddy," as she calls him, an African word that refers to an honored parent (LaGrand & Mattson, 2007). Her father taught her the observational skills of a good detective, an interest in solving mysteries, and a love for her country of Botswana. Family is essential to her, even if her family now is a "family of choice," mainly consisting of friends and colleagues rather than blood relatives. She uses all of these skills in her detection. While Mma Ramotswe wants to become a successful detective, her primary aim is not for personal success but for more collective success, exemplifying an interdependent self. She uses her community and family network to help her solve her cases (LaGrand & Mattson, 2007). Mma Ramotswe is who she is because of her experiences and the knowledge and history passed on from others, especially individuals from her family and community. In the first chapter of *The No. 1 Ladies Detective Agency* (McCall Smith, 1998), she explains how much she loves Botswana and its people. She feels she owes them her detective skills out of love and duty to the country.

> She was a good detective, and a good woman.... She loves her country, Botswana, ... and she loved Africa.... I especially know how to love the people who live in this place. They are my people, by brothers and sisters. It is my duty to help them solve the mysteries in their lives. That is what I am called to do [*The No. 1 Ladies Detective Agency*, McCall Smith, 1998, p. 4].

The goal of Mma Ramotswe's detective agency is to solve people's problems while also maintaining the beauty and customs of her country. Despite the early doubters, she is successful, explaining in *The Minor Adjustment Beauty Salon* (McCall Smith, 2013) how people laughed at her and expected her to fail when she first started her detective agency.

Mma Ramotswe is assisted in her detective work by her secretary/assistant Grace Makutsi, a character who provides both comic relief and shrewd insight into human nature. They work together as a team and utilize their knowledge of the Tswana culture to their advantage. Understanding the culture of the setting of a crime is very important for a detective, and Mma Ramotswe and Mma Makutsi are as successful as they are in solving their cases because of their understanding. As LaGrand and Mattson (2007) explain, Mma Ramotswe solves her cases by trying to:

> ...figure out the cultural assumptions and patterns—the "language" of the crime. She must translate the assumptions and relevant motivations that make the crime clear. Sometimes it is the language of traditional Botswana culture that explains the crime; sometimes the explanation comes from the colonial system of education and certification. Other times the explanatory cues are cross-cultural... [LaGrand & Mattson, 2007, p. 649].

Mma Ramotswe is not considered invisible like Blanche White or Miss Marple but shares similar characteristics. Mma Ramotswe is like Miss Marple (and Blanche White) in that she uses her understanding of human nature to solve her cases. She trusts her instincts and intuition and judges human nature well. Mma Makutsi also possesses these skills. In Chapter 15 of *The Minor Adjustment Beauty Salon* (McCall Smith, 2013), Mma Ramotswe comments that Mma Makutsi has utilized effective detective skills. Mma Makutsi is uncharacteristically modest, claiming that she merely used good observational skills and that Mma Ramotswe would eventually have reached the same conclusion.

> Mma Ramotswe saw what she meant. "That is amazing, Mma," she said. "That is detective work of the highest order." Mma Makutsi gave a modest shrug. "It is knowing what to look for," she said. "That is all. I'm sure you would have seen the same thing when you started to look for it" [*The Minor Adjustment Beauty Salon*, McCall Smith, 2013, p. 204].

Mma Ramotswe also recognizes that women notice things more than men (McCall Smith, 1998). She uses her understanding of traditions, superstitions, and people to solve her cases, and like Miss Marple, she is a good judge of human nature. Mma Ramotswe believes that her ancestors watch over her, a belief also found in the writings of Native American and Asian cultures, discussed later in this chapter.

The *Marti MacAlister* series by Eleanor Taylor Bland is a final series featuring a strong female Black detective. This series includes 14 books published from 1992 to 2007. Marti is a Black female police officer, widowed with two children, who moves from Chicago to the fictional town of Lincoln Prairie, Illinois. Her investigative technique demonstrates less similarity to Miss Marple and more like her fellow hard-boiled female detective, Kinsey Millhone. Like Kinsey, Marti pays close attention to details and writes them down on a pad of paper so that she can process them later, as she explains in *Dead Time* (Taylor Bland, 1992).

> She took out a legal-sized yellow pad. She preferred to write down her impressions with elaborate detail but in a less formal way... [*Dead Time*, Taylor Bland, 1992, p. 33].

The cultural implications of the Marti MacAlister series differ from those in the other books discussed in this chapter. However, they allow the reader to explore some of the other invisible groups found within American society—e.g., older individuals, those suffering from mental health issues, and homeless children—groups all located within the novel *Dead Time* (Taylor Bland, 1992). Marti engages in the familiar self-talk of the female hard-boiled detective and uses her gun when needed. She provides another example of a positive Black female sleuth that can complement other female detectives discussed within this book.

Investigative thinking challenge:
Marti MacAlister is described as "at five-ten and a hundred and sixty pounds she was what her mother had called healthy. Her size pleased her, and most people tended to move out of her way"
(Dead Time, Taylor Bland, 1992, p. 10).
Blanche White and Precious Ramotswe are both described as overweight or "traditionally-built" women. Why do you think these three female Black sleuths are portrayed this way?

Literary choices in character description can vary widely across different authors or literary genres. The portrayal of these female Black sleuths should be interpreted within the specific context of each story and the author's intentions. While their descriptions may seem negative, diverse representation in literature is crucial for promoting inclusivity and breaking away from harmful stereotypes. In these stories, the female detectives are successful and well-liked by those around them, providing positive role models.

Chinese Detectives

Western detective novels do sometimes include characters from different cultures. Examples include the Chinese detective Charlie Chan, a Chinese-American detective on the Honolulu police force created by Earl Derr Biggers, who appeared in six novels from 1925 to 1932 (Earl Derr Biggers, 2021); and Fu Manchu, the hero-villain who appeared in a series of 20th-century novels and short stories by British author Sax Rohmer (Fu Manchu, 2021). However, these Chinese detectives and characters are often misrepresented within the detective stories related to Western culture. Chinese detective fiction originated in China centuries before Sherlock Holmes ever appeared in print. Short stories and plays that revolved around solving crimes, identified as gong'an and translated to "court-case fiction" in English, may have originated in the 6th century AD, with longer novels beginning in the 17th century (Benedetti, 2014; van Gulik, 1976). Not many of those novels have been translated into English because they would require extensive explanations of Chinese cultural traditions and policies. The other reason is that there are some significant differences in Chinese detective fiction's writing style and plotlines compared to Western detective fiction. The five main differences include:

1. The element of "whodunit" suspense, which characterizes the process of discovering the culprit, is conspicuously absent in Chinese detective narratives, where the guilty party is typically introduced early in the story. An example of a Western detective fiction novel that uses this technique is James Patterson's first novel in the *Women's Murder Club* series, *1st to Die* (Patterson, 2001). In Patterson's novel, the reader learns the killer's identity in the second chapter, although not without a twist (no spoilers included here).

2. Chinese culture's mysticism and supernatural aspects are intricately woven into the fabric of these tales. During their investigations, the detective may encounter ghosts and spirits, conversing animals, and voyages into the netherworld, all contributing to the mystery's resolution.

3. Traditional Western detective novels range in chapter count and overall length, typically falling below 500 pages and encompassing fewer than 50 chapters unless the chapters are short in length. They are considered a relatively quick or good beach read. In contrast, traditional Chinese detective novels are much longer and may include 100 or more chapters.

4. Because oral history is important in Chinese culture, the stories can sometimes include an expansive cast of hundreds of characters. This length could challenge readers accustomed to comparatively concise character rosters featured in Western detective fiction, which usually entail at most 10 to 15 characters.
5. Western detective novels typically end with the climactic "big reveal," wherein the identity of the guilty person is disclosed alongside the motive for the crime. Punishment may be mentioned briefly, but there are typically few details about that punishment. In many Agatha Christie novels, for example, the guilty person's fate is either ambiguous or self-determined (as when they take their own life). Conversely, traditional Chinese detective novels extensively detail the punishment, often describing gory details of torture or execution (van Gulik, 1976).

An example of one of these early Chinese detective stories is *The Celebrated Cases of Judge Dee: An Authentic Eighteenth-Century Chinese Detective Novel* (Dee Goong An) translated by Robert van Gulik (Van Gulik, 1976) and written by an unknown original author. In this series of stories, the detective is called a magistrate (typical of Chinese detective novels) and simultaneously serves as the detective, prosecutor, jury, and judge. The original short stories were likely written around 663 AD, and van Gulik then wrote his own detective novels with Judge Dee as the main character during the 1950s and 1960s. The translated Judge Dee novel contains several stories that are more similar to a Western detective novel than other examples of Chinese detective fiction: the impossible crime; the guilty person is not exposed at the very beginning; there are not too many supernatural elements; there are a manageable number of characters; and there are few moral digressions (Benedetti, 2014; van Gulik, 1976). The stories also present the Western reader with a snapshot of the Chinese class system from a previous century.

Judge Dee solves the crimes in three independent cases by psychological insight and deductive reason, each related to a person of a different social class (van Gulik, 1976). Judge Dee has helpers (lieutenants) who sometimes function like a foil similar to Sherlock Holmes and Watson, but the judge always solves the crime. The detective is also in danger (like Nancy Drew always getting locked in places). The stories explicitly discuss torture, and the cover photo of the most common English translation of the book depicts the graphic torture of a woman (Klineberg, 1938). Van Gulik's translation presents a modernized and interesting look at the Judge Dee stories and early Chinese culture.

A more contemporary look at Chinese culture is presented in the *Mei*

Wang series by Diane Wei Liang, which includes three novels, with the first, *The Eye of Jade*, published in 2007. Mei Wang has been described as a Chinese version of Maisie Dobbs, and her assistant, Gupin, is similar to Maisie's assistant, Billy Beale. We learn in the first chapter that private detectives were prohibited in China. Mei Wang, like other similar business persons in China, must secretly register her business with the government as what she calls an "information consultancy" (Liang, 2008, p. 3).

The matriarchal culture is very apparent in the stories, along with the importance of ancestors and spiritualism. In *The Eye of Jade* (Liang, 2008), after speaking with Uncle Chen, Mei remarks that she feels cold air touching her and wonders if a ghost is present and trying to tell her something important.

> A strange sensation came over her. She felt as if cold air had risen from nowhere and, like a ghost, had tapped her with its invisible hand [*The Eye of Jade*, Liang, 2008, p. 103].

Mei Wang also personifies the interdependent self because of her focus on others and the family. Even as an adult, she is concerned with bringing shame to her family. She tells the reader that she loves her mother and wants to obey her, but she may also have caused her mother emotional distress because of Mei's failings, including those related to her stubbornness (Liang, 2008).

Mei Wang shares other similarities with other female sleuths in that she is methodical and rational in processing information related to the crime. She uses her connections to her advantage to solve the case in the first novel. The series provides an entertaining mystery to solve and introduces Western readers to some aspects of the more current Chinese government and societal regulations. *The Eye of Jade* also presents the reader with a moral dilemma to consider at the novel's end that is very much related to the cultural differences between Western and Eastern cultures.

Investigative thinking challenge:
Mei Wang, Maisie Dobbs, Nancy Drew, and Mma Ramotswe all own and drive their own vehicles. Why is this important in their stories and for them as detectives?

The Skull Mantra by Eliot Pattison (1999) is a compelling mystery that explores a case and detective work but also delves into the intricate relationship between culture, psychology, and human behavior. The story's setting in Tibet allows it to depict the cultural struggles and clashes between Tibet and neighboring China, shedding light on the complexities of their histories and beliefs. As an example of the conflict between the Tibetan and Chinese cultures, early in the book, one of the imprisoned monks comments,

And that was just the beginning, just giving them the time they needed for the real fight. Now they take our souls. They put their people in our cities, in our valleys, in our mountains. Even in our prisons. To poison us. To make us like them. Our souls shrivel up. Our faces disappear. We become nobody [*The Skull Mantra*, Pattison, 1999, p. 9].

The protagonist, former Chinese police detective Shan Tao Yin, must solve the murder of an American on a Tibetan mountain where he is also a prisoner because he offended someone influential in the Chinese government. The first chapter introduces readers to several tenets of Tibetan Buddhism, such as a Khata scarf, described as a "makeshift prayer scarf" and "taking four" when a prisoner committed suicide. Suicide is a severe negative act in Buddhism that leads to the person being reborn in a lesser form, like an animal walking on four legs, which the prisoners may have preferred rather than continuing to live in the harsh Chinese labor camp (Pattison, 1999, pp. 1–2). These examples illustrate the importance of religion on an individual's thoughts and behaviors, emphasizing the consequences of certain behaviors. The influence of self versus others also runs throughout this novel, allowing for the exploration of personal and social identities and their influences on human behavior. Overall, by examining the clash of cultural values along with the mystery, the novel prompts readers to reflect on the complexities of human behavior, self-identification, and the influence of culture on individual lives in a fictional (i.e., safer) setting.

Latinx/Latino Detectives

There are many examples of Latin American detective fiction and stories geared toward teenagers in Sarah Cortez's collection, *You Don't Have a Clue: Latino Mystery Stories for Teens* (Cortez, 2011). Each author introduces the readers to detectives from various geographical locations and Latinx or Hispanic cultures. One of these authors, Suzanne Chazin, created the Jimmy Vega series, which includes six published books through 2021. Jimmy Vega is a police detective of Puerto Rican descent who lives and works in the fictional town of Lake Holly in upstate New York. In the first book in the series, *Land of Careful Shadows* (Chazin, 2014), Jimmy must unravel the circumstances of a suspicious death tied to the community of undocumented immigrants within the town. The novel intricately details the prejudice directed at the immigrants and the loneliness, fear, and obstacles the immigrants constantly experience, with the fear of deportation being their primary concern.

Even Jimmy experiences that prejudice at the beginning of the novel when he is mistaken for a suspect rather than a detective because he is wearing clothes related to being undercover. In the first chapter of *Land of Careful Shadows* (Chazin, 2014), readers can feel and possibly connect to Jimmy's anger as he describes being frisked by his fellow police officers because of his skin color and appearance. He realizes that prejudice is a problem in all professions and all towns.

> Something burned slow and deep. He thought he was past the stage where people judged him by the color of his skin or the cast of his features. He thought his line of work insulated him from that. But now, spread-eagled across the Escalade, he wondered if all he'd really done was get better at navigating people's prejudices [*Land of Careful Shadows*, Chazin, 2014, p. 3].

The novel abundantly includes examples of prejudices and discrimination directed at the immigrant community, including discrepancies in police and court business. Vega observes that the immigrants in Lake Holly do not choose to come forward as witnesses to crimes because they fear deportation. Likewise, the police seem to ignore crimes involving the Lake Holly Latino/Latinx community unless the victims are legal residents or if their crimes could lead to deportation (Chazin, 2014). These fictional descriptions parallel many of the recent and current issues involving undocumented individuals in the country and could lead to a robust discussion of xenophobia and related topics. For example, in the fourth book in the series, *A Place in the Wind* (Chazin, 2017), Jimmy talks to a Guatemalan deli owner the day after a white teenage girl disappeared. Jimmy and Oscar, the deli owner, discuss the consequences if someone from the Latinx community hurt the girl. Oscar laments that the white town residents may shun any stores owned by someone from the Latinx community. Jimmy reminisces about how people from groups treated with prejudice and discrimination by other groups display their biases towards other ethnic groups. He remembers how when he was a boy in the Bronx, individuals from his Puerto Rican community would get upset when some Jewish community members looked down on them. Still, Puerto Rican individuals from his youth would do the same when looking down on those from the Dominican Republic. Again, the literary dialogue would allow a class or group to engage in real-world discussions.

Along with the mystery, Chazin introduces many of the customs and traditions of the Latinx/Hispanic community, including the food, dance, and La Fiesta de Quinceañera. In *Land of Careful Shadows* (Chazin, 2014), Jimmy also experiences a reconnection to his heritage that many readers would likely share. Jimmy grew up in the area as one of the few non–white residents, and the prejudice he experienced as a younger teen and adult has followed him throughout his life. He is finally learning to embrace his bicultural or integrated approach to his cultural heritage. White readers can learn from the descriptions made by Jimmy and others to understand how individuals from other cultures perceive their cultural and racial ingroup. Jimmy describes Anglo parties as devoid of dancing, food that has little taste due to lack of spices, and women who do not necessarily dress like Latina women. He describes living in the predominantly white community as "...like living with a coffee filter over your senses" (Chazin, 2014, p. 129).

Rudolfo Anaya's *Sonny Baca series* provides an alternative view of the Latinx/Hispanic culture from the one described in Chazin's series. The *Sonny Baca series* includes four novels published between 1995 and 2005. The main character is Sonny Baca, a Chicano private investigator who lives and works in Albuquerque, New Mexico. These novels provide the reader with an exciting and engaging mystery to solve and provide insight into the Southwest Chicano and Pueblo Native American culture, including a focus on spirituality, mysticism, and symbolism. In *Zia Summer* (Anaya, 1995), Sonny must solve the murder of his cousin Gloria, which involves a symbol[6] tied to the Pueblo culture (Munoz et al., 2015). Readers are introduced to the beliefs of this culture that persist today. Sonny talks about the old traditions that involved witches and rituals such as dancing with the devil. He explains that these ideas were still believed by those in his Chicano community, even though they are highly religious in a more traditional sense (Anaya, 1995).

The themes of the spirit world and evil are intertwined in the story. There is a possibility that witches, or brujas, are involved in the killing. Sonny is plagued by images, dreams, and nightmares that he does not fully understand and seeks help interpreting them from his girlfriend, Rita. He feels connected to his great-grandfather, El Bisabuelo, a famous lawman in New Mexico. Sonny carries his great-grandfather's pistol with him for protection but also because it allows him to embrace his family's heritage. Sonny feels compelled to find Gloria's killer partly because of his sense of duty to his family (an example of a belief from someone with an interdependent self) but also perhaps because he, and others, feel that Gloria's spirit may be urging him to action. Sonny describes how Rita uses traditional healing techniques and that along with physical healing, she also is in touch with the spiritual world and could provide some psychic and psychological healing like the Chicano healers, or "curanderas" (*Zia Summer*, Anaya, 1995, p. 63) from the olden days.

> Rita knew the old traditional world of the Nuevo Mexicanos.... She didn't need Freud, she knew the symbols in dreams, and she knew how the people of the valley had used folk psychiatry for centuries. She had grown up in the tradition of the last curanderas who practiced in the valley. She had learned not only the remedies, she also had the gift of seeing into the soul. But this was too

much, suggesting something of Gloria's soul had gotten into him [*Zia Summer,* Anaya, 1995, pp. 62–63].

The spirits of his ancestors help Sonny in his quest to find the killer in *Zia Summer.* Other books in the *Sonny Baca* series also include elements of spiritualism along with old and new Southwestern culture. The series provides readers with an introduction to Southwestern and Chicano cultures. The series contains numerous examples of how Sonny embraces culture to assist in the detective process.

Many of the culturally diverse novels discussed in this chapter will introduce readers to traditions and scenery from different cultures, which may entice them to learn more about them and perhaps visit their locations one day. More importantly, though, these stories present a powerful platform for individuals to discuss social issues that people might otherwise find uncomfortable. Talking about them by applying them to the characters in the novels can provide a safer alternative to start the discussions. We all have some degree of impact on those we interact with; in other words, we exist within a sphere of social influence (Massey & Brodmann, 2014). These spheres influence who we are, who we will become, and our private and public selves.

Human beings need spheres of social influence that promote positive and healthy social and emotional development. Family, friends, and peers can play pivotal roles in fostering positive connections, leading to more balanced interactions between different class, racial, economic, religious, sexual orientation, and gender groups. The Black Lives Movement (Black Lives Matter, n.d.), which began in 2020, exemplifies the power of collective knowledge-sharing and learning from others' experiences. Prejudice against individuals leads to the misperception that those "others" are inferior (Aronson, 1972). By working together, people can bond to become allies and effect change by working against systemic racism and other examples of prejudice and discrimination that continue to linger within the United States.

Detective fiction, as discussed in this chapter, is a crucial stepping stone for these discussions. These mysteries and detective stories also include abundant evidence that refutes Wilson's (1944, 1945) assertion of their frivolity and lack of intellectual depth. They serve as an entry point for dialogue surrounding social justice and the psychological factors underpinning prejudice and discrimination. Through an open and honest exchange of ideas facilitated by these stories, we can forge a path toward a more inclusive and understanding society, free from the constraints of prejudice and discrimination. By acknowledging and confronting these issues, we empower ourselves to be agents of positive change in our interconnected world.

Investigative thinking challenge:
Which tradition, experience, or location from a culture different from your own, mentioned in this chapter, entices you to visit or experience it? What motivated your choice of this particular cultural aspect?

Suggested Detective Fiction/Literature to Accompany This Chapter

- *Blanche on the Lam* by Barbara Neely—features a Black female detective set in North Carolina, USA
- *The #1 Ladies' Detective Agency* series by Alexander McCall Smith—features a Black female detective and is set in Botswana
- *Dead Time: A Marti MacAlister Mystery* by Eleanor Taylor Bland—features a Black female detective set in a fictitious city of Lincoln Prairie, supposedly near Chicago, Illinois, USA
- *The Eye of Jade* by Diane Wei Liang—features a Chinese female detective set in Beijing, China
- *The Skull Mantra* by Eliot Pattison—features a Chinese male detective set in Tibet
- *Land of Careful Shadows: Jimmy Vega Mystery #1* by Suzanne Chazin—features a Latino male detective set in New York, USA
- *Zia Summer: The Sonny Baca Novels Book 1* by Rudolfo Anaya—features a Chicano male detective set in Albuquerque, New Mexico, USA

End-of-Chapter Mind Puzzlers

1. Analyze the influence of community and culture on the main characters in one of the novels you read. Assess whether the detective's self-view aligns more with an independent or interdependent self and explore its impact on their general behaviors and detective techniques. Additionally, identify other psychological characteristics or techniques the detective(s) exhibited, providing specific examples with corresponding page numbers to support your analysis.

2. Choose one of the detectives from the following options: Mma Ramotswe, Blanche White, Jimmy Vega, Sonny Braca, or Mei Wang. Evaluate the detective's cultural intelligence (CQ) level and ability to interact effectively with individuals from different cultures or groups. Explain how this skill aids in their detection process and present at least three instances demonstrating their CQ.

6. Focus on Culture

3. Select one of the detectives you have read to accompany this chapter. What types of emotions do they express? Would you describe them as primarily engaged or disengaged emotions? Assess whether these emotional expressions align with the type of self the detective best exemplifies, providing relevant examples to support your assessment.
4. Select one detective and evaluate their proficiency in detecting lies in their suspects. Share your perspective on whether you consider them skilled at this aspect of their detective work, providing examples from the text.
5. Select one of the detectives you have read to accompany this chapter. Analyze which strategy associated with ethnic identity (assimilation, separation, marginality, or integration/bicultural) best explains your chosen detective's behavior and mindset. Use specific examples from the text to support your explanation.
6. Do any of the characters in the novel(s) you read experience any stereotype threat? If yes, what was the stereotype and group associated with the threat? How did they deal with it? Provide examples from the text to support your answer.
7. Compare and contrast Precious Ramotswe to Blanche White. Additionally, compare and contrast them with Miss Marple and Nancy Drew. Offer at least two examples that demonstrate how they are similar or different in their actions and detective techniques.
8. Compare and contrast Mei Wang with Maisie Dobbs. Provide at least two examples illustrating how they are similar or different in their actions and detective techniques.
9. Identify the similarities and differences between Mei and other female detectives encountered in your readings so far. Provide explanations to support your findings.
10. Compare and contrast Marti MacAlister with Kinsey Millhone. Use at least two examples to demonstrate their similar or different actions and detective techniques.
11. Examine the roles of children and family in the lives of female detectives such as Marti MacAlister, Mma Ramotswe, and Blanche White. Analyze how including these elements enhances the storylines and character development, which are often absent from male detective stories. Provide specific examples to support your analysis.

Key Terms and People
- **looking-glass self**: the concept of perceiving ourselves through the reflection of how others see us, much like gazing at our own image in a mirror
- **culture**: the set of behaviors, attitudes, beliefs, and values held and shared by a group of individuals, passed down from one generation to another
- **cultural beliefs**: the commonly accepted norms and moral standards within a culture, including the ideas of "right and wrong" that dictate behaviors and activities like dating, marriage, and sexuality
- **prejudice**: negative attitudes and beliefs about people because of their membership in a certain group
- **discrimination**: negative behaviors directed at others because of their membership in a certain group
- **stereotypes**: broad generalizations about the characteristics and behaviors of the members of a particular group
- **ethnocentrism**: an error in judgment where individuals use the standards of their own culture to evaluate and judge others
- **culture shock**: the feeling of discomfort and unsettlement experienced when in an unfamiliar cultural setting
- **sojourners**: people who temporarily visit a new culture or location before returning to their home country
- **cultural psychology**: the branch of psychology that studies how cultures reflect and influence the behavior and psychological processes of their members
- **ethnographic research**: a naturalistic observation or field study of a specific cultural group studied in their real-life environment to gain insights into their way of life
- **cross-cultural psychology**: a "macro" or broader approach to psychology, focusing on how culture influences behavior across multiple cultural groups
- **etic**: refers to aspects of culture thought to be universal principles or behaviors that are consistent across cultures
- **emic**: refers to aspects of culture that are culture-specific principles or behaviors that differ across cultures
- **cultural intelligence**: the ability and willingness to apply cultural awareness to practical uses and to adapt to new cultural settings

- **cultural awareness**: being conscious of cultural similarities and differences
- **self-concept**: the part of the self that includes people's thoughts and perceptions about themselves
- **self-esteem**: the part of the self that reflects how people feel about themselves
- **independent self**: a Western self-view or "me" mindset, where individuals emphasize their distinctiveness and focus on individualism and uniqueness
- **interdependent self**: an Eastern view or "we" mindset, where individuals prioritize the needs of others or their groups, especially family, over individual desires
- **identity**: the traits, relationships, and group affiliations that define individuals and influence their behavior
- **ethnic identity**: a sense of pride in one's ethnicity, involvement in ethnic events or practices, and cultural commitment to the ethnic group
- **assimilation**: strong identification with the new or majority culture while weakly identifying with the original ethnic group
- **separation**: when an individual weakly identifies with the new or majority culture but strongly identifies with their original ethnic group
- **marginality**: when an individual has weak identification with both the new or majority culture and the original ethnic group
- **integrated or bicultural**: strong identification with both the new or majority culture and the original ethnic group
- **unexamined ethnic identity**: when race or ethnicity is not salient or clearly defined for individuals
- **ethnic identity search**: when individuals are actively exploring and trying to understand the meaning of their ethnicity, race, or culture
- **achieved ethnic identity**: when individuals have developed a clear and positive sense of their own ethnicity, race, or culture
- **stereotype threat**: the feeling that one is at risk for confirming a negative stereotype about one's own group
- **Paul Ekman**: an American psychologist known for his groundbreaking studies providing evidence that certain key or basic emotions are expressed through similar facial configurations across different cultures

- **facial feedback theory**: an alternative and controversial theory of emotion that proposes that facial expressions contribute to the experience of specific emotions rather than being mere consequences of those emotions
- **cultural display rules**: cultural differences in the rules establishing the appropriateness of displaying certain emotions in particular social situations
- **micro-expressions**: quick changes in a person's facial expression that may reveal a hidden emotion

Chapter Notes

1. Social psychology became a separate recognized field within American psychology around 1924 with the publication of F.H. Allport's book *Social Psychology* (Allport, 1924). Other books soon followed, each presenting quantitative research about the influence of social situations on human behavior.

2. For a good summary detailing the history of the relationship between psychology and culture, see *Crossroads Between Culture and Mind* by Jahoda (1993) or *History of Cross-Cultural and Cultural Psychology* by Jahoda and Krewer (1997).

3. Below is a list of many influential Black psychologists from the past century. These individuals challenged the racial myths and inequities in mainstream psychology and society and inspired future generations to help bring about needed changes.

Dr. Solomon Carter Fuller (1872–1953). Renowned as the first African American psychiatrist, Solomon Carter Fuller, M.D., made significant contributions to the field. In 1974, the Black Psychiatrists of America established the Solomon Carter Fuller Program to support aspiring black psychiatrists in completing their residency. Additionally, the Fuller Mental Health Center in Boston, often referred to as "The Fuller," was named in his honor.

Dr. Inez Prosser (1891–1934). A trailblazer as America's first black female psychologist, Dr. Inez Prosser dedicated her research to examining segregation well before the landmark *Brown V. Board of Education* Supreme Court decision in 1954. Her dissertation focused on self-esteem and personality variables among African American middle-school children attending segregated schools, highlighting the imperative to enhance educational systems.

Dr. Francis Cecil Sumner (1895–1954). A student of G. Stanley Hall of Clark University, Sumner is sometimes called the "Father of Black Psychology" because he was the first African American to receive a Ph.D. degree in psychology. Despite facing racial bias that denied him research funding, he became a respected professor at multiple universities, dedicating his work to understanding racial bias and advocating for educational justice.

Dr. Albert Sidney Beckham (1897–1964). Dr. Beckham is regarded as the first African American to hold the title of "school psychologist" and earned his bachelor's degree in psychology from Lincoln University under the mentorship of Francis Sumner. Dr. Beckham was the first professor to teach psychology at Howard University and established the institution's inaugural psychological laboratory, which offered counseling, intelligence testing, and consultations. Dr. Beckham's efforts fostered a groundbreaking church-neighborhood-school relationship that benefited African American youth.

Dr. Ruth Winifred Howard Beckham (1900–1997). Dr. Howard Beckham, a pioneering feminist psychologist and wife of Albert Beckham, was one of the earliest African American women to earn a Ph.D. in psychology from the University of Minnesota. She actively participated in various professional organizations, including the American Psychological Association and the Women's International League for Peace and Freedom.

Dr. Herman George Canady (1901–1970). Distinguished as a social psychologist, Dr. Herman George Canady gained fame for his work on "The Effect of 'Rapport' on the I.Q.: A New Approach to the Problem of Racial Psychology." His research was groundbreaking in investigating the role of the examiner's race as a potential bias in IQ testing.

Dr. Mamie Phipps Clark (1917–1983) and **Dr. Kenneth Clark (1914–2005).** The Clarks were the first African Americans to earn doctoral degrees in psychology from Columbia University. Dr. Kenneth Clark later became the first African American to serve as president of the American Psychological Association, while Mamie Clark's master's thesis centered on racial identity and self-esteem. Their research significantly contributed to understanding child development and racial biases in education.

Dr. Robert Lee Williams II (1930–2020). An influential founding member and second president of the National Association of Black Psychologists who devised the Black Intelligence Test of Cultural Homogeneity, utilizing African American vernacular and personal experiences. His research debunked the notion of intellectual inferiority in African Americans and revealed the impact of language and experiences on IQ scores. He also coined the term "Ebonics" to refer to African American Vernacular English.

Dr. Joseph L. White (1932–2017). A pioneering figure, Dr. Joseph L. White challenged the racist beliefs within the American Psychological Association that perpetuated stereotypes of Blacks as ignorant or deviant.

Dr. Claude Steele (1946–PRESENT). Distinguished as a professor of psychology at Stanford University, Dr. Claude Steele's groundbreaking research focused on stereotype threat and its impact on minority student academic performance. His book, *Whistling Vivaldi and Other Clues to How Stereotypes Affect Us* synthesizes years of research on this topic.

Dr. Beverly Daniel Tatum (1954–PRESENT). A highly esteemed figure in psychology, Dr. Beverly Daniel Tatum received the 2013 Carnegie Academic Leadership Award and the American Psychological Association Award for Outstanding Lifetime Contributions to Psychology in 2014. Formerly serving as President of Spelman College, she authored the best-selling book *Why Are All the Black Kids Sitting Together in the Cafeteria? and Other Conversations About Race.*

Sources: Coon & Mitterer, 2014; https://www.ciis.edu/ciis-news-and-events/newsroom/black-history-initiative; https://www.apa.org/pi/about/black-history; https://www.activeminds.org/blog/10-african-african-american-psychologists-you-should-know/; and https://www.apa.org/pi/oema/resources/ethnicity-health/psychologists/sumner-prosser.

4. One college focusing on multicultural mental health training is William James College (www.williamjames.edu) in Newton, Massachusetts.

5. The Home Box Office (HBO) network aired a captivating adaptation of the series (Bricknell, 2008–2009) starring Jill Scott as Precious Ramotswe and Anika Noni Rose as Grace Makutsi. For those yet to experience the seven episodes, it comes highly recommended due to the breathtaking depiction of Botswana's beauty and the authentic portrayal of its traditional language, songs, and dances. The mysteries woven into the storyline are engaging, and the characters leave a lasting impression.

6. The Zia Pueblos of New Mexico considers the Zia symbol sacred. It includes a circle in the center, which represents life and love. There are four groupings of four lines emanating from the circle. Four is a sacred number for the Zia and represents the four seasons, the four directions of a compass, the four periods of each day (morning, noon, evening, night), and the four stages or seasons in a person's life cycle (childhood, youth, middle age, and old age)—source: Munoz, et al., 2015.

References

AgathaChristie.com (2020, September 10). *100 Facts About Agatha Christie.* https://www.agathachristie.com/news/2020/100-facts-about-agatha-christie.
Allport, F.H. (1924). *Social Psychology.* Houghton Mifflin Company.
Anaya, R. (1995). *Zia Summer.* Warner Books.
Arnett, J.J. (2013). *Adolescence and Emerging Adulthood: A Cultural Approach* (5th Edition). Prentice Hall.
Aronson, E. (1972). *The Social Animal.* W.H. Freeman and Company.
Barna, L.M. (2013). Stumbling blocks in intercultural communication. In M.J. Bennett (Ed.) *Basic Concepts of Intercultural Communication; Paradigms, Principles & Practices* (2nd ed.)., pp. 235–257. Intercultural Press.

Barnouw, V. (1985). *Culture and Personality*. Dorsey Press.
Bartlett, F.C. (1932). *Remembering: An Experimental and Social Study*. Cambridge University Press.
Benedetti, L. (2014). Killing Di Gong: Rethinking Van Gulik's translation of late Qing dynasty novel Wu Zetian Si Da Qi'an. In P. Santangelo (Ed.), *Ming Qing Studies* (pp. 8–72).
Berry, J., Trimble, J., & Olmedo, E. (1986). Assessment of acculturation. In W. Lonner & J. Berry (Eds.), *Field Methods in Cross-cultural Research* (pp. 291–324). Sage.
Berry, J.W. (1990). Psychology of acculturation. In N.R. Goldberger & J.B. Veroff (Eds.), *The Culture and Psychology Reader* (pp. 457–488). New York University Press.
Biswas-Diener, R. & Thin, N. (2021). Culture. In R. Biswas-Diener & E. Diener (Eds), *Noba Textbook Series: Psychology*. DEF publishers. Retrieved from http://noba.to/y9xcptqw.
Black Lives Matter (n.d.). *Black Lives Matter*. Retrieved from https://https://blacklivesmatter.com/.
Boas, F. (1901). The mind of primitive man. *Journal of American Folklore*, 14(52), 1–11.
Bochner, S. (2003). Culture shock due to contact with unfamiliar cultures. *Online Readings in Psychology and Culture*, 8(1). https://doi.org/10.9707/2307-0919.1073.
Brehm, S., & Kassin, S.M. (1996). *Social Psychology* (3rd edition). Houghton Mifflin.
Brehm, S.S., Kassin, S.M., & Fein, S. (2007). *Social Psychology* (6th edition). Houghton Mifflin.
Bricknell, T. [Producer]. (2008–2009). *The No.1 Ladies' Detective Agency* [TV series]. Home Box Office (HBO).
Brown, J. (1998). *The Self*. Mc-Graw Hill.
Chazin, S. (2014). *Land of Careful Shadows*. Kensington Books.
Chazin, S. (2017). *A Place in the Wind*. Kensington Books.
Cohen, D. (2011). Cultural psychology. *Oxford Bibliographies*. https://doi: 10.1093/obo/9780199828340-0020.
Cooley, C. (1902). *Human Nature and the Social Order*. Schocken Books.
Coon, D., & Mitterer, J.O. (2014). *Psychology: A Journey* (5th Edition). Wadsworth Cengage Learning.
Cortez, S. (2011). *You Don't Have a Clue: Latino Mystery Stories for Teens*. Pinata Books.
Cross, S.E., & Gore, J.S. (2012). Cultural models of the self. In M.R. Leary & J.P. Tangney (Eds.), *Handbook of Self and Identity* (pp. 587–614). The Guilford Press.
DeFreitas, S. (2019). *African America Psychology: A Positive Psychology Perspective*. Springer Publishing Company.
Earl Derr Biggers. (2021). In *Encyclopædia Britannica*. Retrieved from https://academic-eb-com.eu1.proxy.openathens.net/levels/collegiate/article/Earl-Derr-Biggers/104118.
Earley, P.C., & Ang, S. (2003). *Cultural Intelligence: Individual Interactions Across Cultures*. Stanford Business Books.
Ekman, P. (1972). Universals and cultural differences in facial expressions of emotion. In J. Cole (Ed.), *Nebraska Symposium on Motivation, 1971* (Vol. 19, pp. 207–282). University of Nebraska Press.
Ekman, P. (1973). Cross-cultural studies of emotion. In P. Ekman (Ed.), *Darwin and Facial Expression: A Century of Research in Review* (pp. 169–222). Academic Press.
Ekman, P. (1985). *Telling Lies: Clues to Deceit in the Marketplace, Politics, and Marriage*. Berkley Books.
Ekman, P., & Friesen, W.V. (1969). The repertoire of nonverbal behavior: Categories, origins, usage, and coding. *Semicotica*, 1, 49–98.
Ekman, P., & Friesen, W.V. (1971). Constants across cultures in the face and emotion. *Journal of Personality and Social Psychology*, 17, 124–129.
Ekman, P., & Friesen, W.V. (1975, 2003). *Unmasking the Face: A Guide to Recognizing Emotions from Facial Clues*. Prentice-Hall.
Ekman, P., Friesen, W.V., O'Sullivan, M., Chan, A., Diacoyanni-Tarlatzis, I., Heider, K., Krause, R., LeCompte, W.A., Pitcairn, T., Ricci-Bitti, P.E., Scherer, K., Tomita, M., & Tzavaras, A. (1987). Universals and cultural differences in the judgments of facial expressions of emotion. *Journal of Personality and Social Psychology*, 53(4), 712–717. https://doi.org/10.1037/0022-3514.53.4.712.

Ekman, P., Sorenson, E.R., & Friesen, W.V. (1969). Pan-cultural elements in facial displays of emotions. *Science, 164(3875),* 86–88.
Elfenbein, H.A., & Ambady, N. (2002). On the universality and cultural specificity of emotion recognition: A meta-analysis. *Psychological Bulletin, 128,* 203–235.
Falbo, T., Poston, D.L., Triscari, R.S., & Zhang, X. (1997). Positive evaluations of the self and others among Chinese schoolchildren. *Journal of Cross-Cultural Psychology, 28,* 172–191.
Fischer, R., & Poortinga, Y.H. (2018). Addressing methodological challenges in culture-comparative research. *Journal of Cross-Cultural Psychology, 49*(5), 691–712.
Fiske, A., Kitayama, S., Markus, H.R., & Nisbett, R.E. (1998). The cultural matrix of social psychology. In D. Gilbert & S. Fiske & G. Lindzey (Eds.), *The Handbook of Social Psychology* (4th Ed., pp. 915–81). McGraw-Hill.
Frey, W.H. (2018). *Diversity Explosion: How New Racial Demographics Are Remaking America.* Brookings Institution Press.
Fu Manchu. (2021). In *Encyclopædia Britannica.* Retrieved from https://academic-eb-com.eu1.proxy.openathens.net/levels/collegiate/article/Fu-Manchu/484904.
Goldman, A.H. (2011). The appeal of the mystery. *The Journal of Aesthetics and Art Criticism, 69*(3), 261–271. https://doi.org/10.1111/j.1540-6245.2011.01470.x.
Greenberg, J., Schmader, T., Arndt, J., & Landau, M. (2018). *Social Psychology: The Science of Everyday Life* (2nd Edition). Worth Publishers.
Harris, M.A., & Orth, U. (2020). The link between self-esteem and social relationships: A meta-analysis of longitudinal studies. *Journal of Personality and Social Psychology, 119*(6), 1459–1477. http://dx.doi.org/10.1037/pspp0000265.
Heine, S.J. (2012). *Cultural Psychology* (2nd edition). W.W. Norton & Company.
Heine, S.J., & Lehman, D.R. (1995). Cultural variations in unrealistic optimism: Does the West feel more invulnerable than the East? *Journal of Personality and Social Psychology, 68,* 595–607. https://doi.org/10.1037/0022-3514.68.4.595.
Izard, C.E. (1994). Innate and universal facial expressions: Evidence from developmental and cross-cultural research. *Psychological Bulletin, 115,* 288–299.
Jahoda, G. (1993). *Crossroads Between Culture and Mind.* Harvard University Press.
Jahoda, G., & Krewer, R. (1997). History of cross-cultural and cultural psychology. In J.W. Berry, Y.H. Poortinga, & J. Pandey (Eds.), *Handbook of Cross-cultural Psychology* (2nd Ed., pp. 1–42). Allyn & Bacon.
Kitayama, S., & Cohen, D. (2007). *Handbook of Cultural Psychology.* The Guilford Press.
Kitayama, S., & Markus, H.R. (1994). *Emotion and Culture: Empirical Studies of Mutual Influence.* American Psychological Association.
Kitayama, S., Duffy, S., & Uchida, Y. (2007). Self as a cultural mode of being. In S. Kitayama, & D. Cohen (Eds.), *Handbook of Cultural Psychology* (pp. 136–174). The Guilford Press.
Kitayama, S., Markus, H.R., Kurokawa, M., & Negishi, K. (1993). Social orientation of emotions: Cross-cultural evidence and implications. Unpublished manuscript, University of Oregon.
Klineberg, O. (1938). Emotional expression in Chinese literature. *The Journal of Abnormal and Social Psychology, 33*(4), 517–520. http://dx.doi.org/10.1037/h0057105.
Kunda, Z. (2000). *Social Cognition: Making Sense of People.* Bradford Book/MIT Press.
LaGrand, V., & Mattson, C.E. (2007). Peter Wimsey and Precious Ramotswe: Castaway detectives and companionate marriage. *Christianity and Literature, 56*(4), 633–664.
Lee, D. (1950). *Freedom and Culture.* Prentice-Hall.
Liang, D.W. (2008). *The Eye of Jade: A Novel.* Simon & Schuster Paperbacks.
Lonner, W.J. (2015). Half a century of cross-cultural psychology: A grateful coda. *American Psychologist, 70* (8), 804–814. http://dx.doi.org/10.1037/a0039454.
Lonner, W.J., & Malpass, R.S. (1994). *Psychology and Culture.* Allyn and Bacon.
Luszcz, M. (2006). Introduction back to nurture: Cross-cultural research as a paradigm for understanding bio-cultural dynamics of cognitive ageing. *Gerontology, 52,* 290–294.
Lying. (2021). In *Encyclopædia Britannica.* Retrieved from https://academic-eb-com.eu1.proxy.openathens.net/levels/collegiate/article/lying/608546#323284.toc.

Markus, H., & Kitayama, S. (1991). Culture and the self: Implications for cognition, emotion, and motivation. *Psychological Review, 98*, 224–253.

Markus, H., & Kitayama, S. (1994). Cultural construction of self and emotion. In S. Kitayama, & H.R. Markus (Eds.), *Emotion and Culture: Empirical Studies of Mutual Influence*. American Psychological Association.

Massey, D.S., & Brodman, S. (2014). *Spheres of Influence: The Social Ecology of Racial and Class Inequality*. Russell Sage Foundation.

Matsumoto, D. (1994). *People: Psychology from a Cultural Perspective*. Waveland Press Inc.

McCall Smith, A. (1998). *The No. 1 Ladies' Detective Agency*. Polygon Books.

McCall Smith, A. (2013). *The Minor Adjustment Beauty Salon*. Pantheon Books.

Mead, M. (1928). *Coming of Age in Samoa: A Psychological Study of Primitive Youth for Western Civilization*. William Morrow and Co.

Mesquita, B., & Leu, J. (2007). The cultural psychology of emotion. In S. Kitayama, & D. Cohen (Eds.), *Handbook of Cultural Psychology* (pp. 136–174). The Guilford Press.

Mesquita, B., Karasawa, M., Haire, A., Izumi, K., Hayashi, Y., Idzelis, M., et al. (2005). *Emotions as Culture-specific Ways of Relating: A Comparison Between Japanese and American Groups*. Unpublished manuscript, Wake Forest University.

Munoz, V., McQuerry, M., Rimmer, M., & Vargas, D. (2015, March 25). What do the colors of the Zia symbol represent? New Mexico News Port. Retrieved from https://newmexiconewsport.com/what-do-the-colors-of-the-zia-symbol-represent/.

Neely, B. (1992). *Blanche on the Lam*. Penguin Books.

Nisbett, R.E. (2003). *The Geography of Thought. How Asians and Westerners Think Differently ...and Why*. Free Press.

Nisbett, R.E. (2021). *Thinking: A Memoir*. Agora Books.

Nisbett, R.E., Peng, K., Choi, I., & Norenzayan, A. (2001). Culture and systems of thought: Holistic versus analytic cognition. *Psychological Review, 108*(2), 291–310. http://dx.doi.org/10.1037/0033-295X.108.2.291.

Osborne, R.E. (1996). *Self: An Eclectic Approach* (Chapter 6). Allyn & Bacon.

Oyserman, D., Elmore, K., & Smith, G. (2012). Self, self-concept, and identity. In M.R. Leary & J.P. Tangney (Eds.), *Handbook of Self and Identity: Second Edition* (pp. 69–104). The Guilford Press.

Patterson, J. (2001). *1st to Die*. Little, Brown and Company.

Pattison, E. (1999). *The Skull Mantra*. St. Martin's Press.

Peng, K., & Nisbett, R.E. (1999). Culture, dialectics, and reasoning about contradiction. *American Psychologist, 54*(9), 741–754. http://dx.doi.org/10.1037/0003-066X.54.9.741.

Phinney, J. (1990). Ethnic identity in adolescents and adults: A review of research. *Psychological Bulletin, 108*, 499–514.

Phinney, J.S. (1991). Ethnic identity and self-esteem: A review and integration. *Hispanic Journal of Behavioral Sciences, 13*(2), 193- 208. https://doi.org/10.1177/07399863910132005.

Phinney, J.S. (1992). The multigroup ethnic identity measure: A new scale for use with diverse groups. *Journal of Adolescent Research, 7*(2), 156–176. https://doi.org/10.1177/074355489272003.

Phinney, J.S. (1993). A three-stage model of ethnic identity development in adolescence. In M.E. Bernal & G.P. Knight (Eds.), SUNY series, United States Hispanic studies. *Ethnic Identity: Formation and Transmission Among Hispanics and Other Minorities* (pp. 61–79). State University of New York Press.

Plotnik, R. (1999). *Introduction to Psychology* (5th Edition). Brooks/Cole/Wadsworth.

Roland, A. (1991). The self in cross-civilizational perspective: An Indian-Japanese-American comparison. In R.C. Curtis (Ed.), *The Relational Self: Theoretical Convergences in Psychoanalysis & Social Psychology* (pp. 160–180). Guilford Press.

Steele, C.M., & Aronson, J. (1995). Stereotype threat and the intellectual test performance of African Americans. *Journal of Personality and Social Psychology, 69*(5), 797–811. http://dx.doi.org/10.1037/0022-3514.69.5.797.

Sue, D.W., & Sue, D. (2016). *Counseling the Culturally Diverse: Theory and Practice* (7th Edition). Wiley.

Sussman, N.M. (2002). Sojourners to another country: The psychological roller-coaster of cultural transitions. *Online Readings in Psychology and Culture, 8*(1). https://doi.org/10.9707/ 2307-0919.1067.

Tatum, B.D. (2017). *Why Are All the Black Kids Siting Together in the Cafeteria* (3rd Ed.). Basic Books.

Taylor Bland, E. (1992). *Dead Time*. St. Martin's Press.

Tice D.M., & Wallace, H.M. (2005). The reflected self: Creating yourself as (you think) others see you. In M.R. Leary & J.P. Tangney (Eds.), *Handbook of Self and Identity* (pp. 91–105). Guilford Press.

Tice, D.M. (1992). Self-concept change and self-presentation: The looking glass self is also a magnifying glass. *Journal of Personality and Social Psychology, 63*, 435–451.

Triandis, H.C. (2007). Culture and psychology: A history of the study of their relationship. In S. Kitayama, & D. Cohen (Eds.), *Handbook of Cultural Psychology* (pp. 59–76). The Guilford Press.

Triandis, H.C. (2018). *Individualism and Collectivism*. Routledge.

Tsai, J.L., Knutson, B., & Fung, H.H. (2006). Cultural variation in affect valuation. *Journal of Personality and Social Psychology, 90*(2), 288–307. http://dx.doi.org/10.1037/0022-3514.90.2.288.

Van Gulik, R.H. (1976). *Celebrated Cases of Judge Dee: An Authentic Eighteenth-century Chinese Detective Novel*. Dover Publications.

Vaughn, L.M. (2019). *Psychology and Culture: Thinking, Feeling and Behaving in a Global Context* (2nd Ed.). Routledge.

Westen, D. (1991). Cultural, emotional, and unconscious aspects of self. In R.C. Curtis (Ed.), *The Relational Self: Theoretical Convergences in Psychoanalysis & Social Psychology* (pp. 181–210). Guilford Press.

Wilson, E. (1944, October 14). Why do people read detective novels? *The New Yorker*. https://www.newyorker.com/magazine/1944/10/14/why-do-people-read-detective-stories.

Wilson, E. (1945, January 20). Who cares who killed Roger Ackroyd? *The New Yorker*.

Witt, D. (2001). Detecting bodies: Barbara Neely's domestic sleuth and the trope of the (in)visible woman. In M. Bennett & V.D. Dickerson (Eds.), *Recovering the Black Female Body: Self-representations by African American Women*. Rutgers University Press.

Wundt, W.M., & Schaub, E.L. (1921). *Elements of Folk Psychology: Outlines of a Psychological History of the Development of Mankind*. G. Allen and Unwin.

7

Neuropsychology and Forensic Psychology

From its beginning, psychology looked to explain behavior and the mind from various perspectives, which became its psychological paradigms. The final paradigm recognizes the importance of biological influences, particularly those involving the brain. While mainly focused on the brain and the nervous system, this biological perspective also acknowledges the influence of other concepts, such as **natural selection**. Charles Darwin developed his theory of evolution by natural selection after spending several years in the 1830s observing different animal species while traveling on the HMS *Beagle* to South America (Darwin/Encyclopædia Britannica, 2021). In *The Origin of Species* (Darwin, 1859), Darwin defined natural selection as the process by which species adapt to their environment by selectively reproducing genetic changes that will help them survive, in a survival of the fittest process of evolution.

> *Investigative thinking challenge:*
> *How do you believe evolution and the process of natural selection impact the selection of human behaviors based on their capacity to aid in adapting to the environment?*

Evolution and natural selection explain the continuation or discontinuation of certain genetic features in animals. They also can explain how human behaviors and characteristics evolved as well. Natural selection explains how animals adapt and change to their environments. Early humans also needed to adapt to their environment to solve potential survival issues and produce to allow them to continue. According to Sedikides et al. (2006), those behaviors and traits leading to higher reproductive success likely continue. While behaviors or physical changes are what most people think about when considering natural selection, psychological concepts can be adaptive and, therefore, have developed and been maintained for an evolutionary rather than a purely psychological reason. Sedikides et al. (2006) argue that psychological concepts like the self and self-esteem are adaptive and therefore have an evolutionary benefit for humans.

The notion of a self-concept likely emerged in Homo Erectus about 5–10,000 years ago due to the advanced brain structure of Homo Erectus and their increased social interactions. Homo Erectus were social beings and engaged in cooperative hunting. As these early humans began living in larger groups, they needed to develop better social skills. Therefore, the self became more relevant. Even early humans needed some degree of self-understanding to interact with others effectively. Engaging in self-evaluation helped these early humans choose tasks that would more likely lead to success, thus solidifying their value to the group, who would want them to remain with them.

It would be nearly impossible for a single Homo Erectus individual to survive unless they were in a larger group. Individuals with high self-esteem, including early Homo Erectus, are perceived as more competent, resourceful, and trusted. Because of how others would perceive them (again, a necessary skill with evolutionary advantages), they would be less likely to be excluded from the group and likely have greater reproductive success. This example provides evidence that both the "I" (self-regulatory, executive function) and "Me" (self-referent, object) components of William James' self (James, 1890) are adaptive.

One of the earliest **case studies** supporting the brain-behavior relationship occurred in 1848 in Cavendish, Vermont, when a young 25-year-old railroad foreman named **Phineas Gage**[1] was impaled by a 13-pound iron rod (Harlow, 1868; cited in Coon & Mitterer, 2014). Gage was clearing rocks for a new railway. He would drill a hole into the rocks, fill the hole with gunpowder, and then tamp it down with an iron rod before lighting a fuse. On September 13, 1848, when Gage used the tamping rod in one of his holes, the rod produced a spark that ignited the rod and caused it to fly up with great force and go through Gage's head, entering below his left eye and coming out at the top of his head (Gage, Encyclopædia Britannica, 2021). He miraculously survived the accident and was conscious and able to speak directly after it happened.

However, Phineas Gage was never the same man after the accident. Because the rod damaged his **frontal lobe**, the part of the brain related to emotions, behavior regulation, and social skills, Gage's personality changed drastically. The frontal lobe also is vital in decision-making and planning a response to a stimulus or new experience (Purves et al., 2008). Before the accident, Gage was well-liked, friendly, and a competent foreman. After the accident, he became argumentative, prone to outbursts, and had difficulty making decisions (Plotnik, 1999). Gage regained some skills but remained in poor health for the remainder of his life, dying in

1860 in California when he was 36 (Encyclopædia Britannica, 2021). Even though this accident occurred before the birth of psychology in 1879, when Wilhelm Wundt set up the first psychology lab, it provided an example of how the brain directly relates to individuals' personality and behavior. The field of psychology would continue to look to biological explanations for behavior over the following century.

Beginning around 1990, technology and methodological breakthroughs led to the development of new and improved treatments for many psychological illnesses. The main target of this new focus was the brain and nervous system, with **neuropsychology** becoming a popular new field of study. Neuropsychologists study behavior and the mind through neurological observations of the brain and the nervous system (Merriam-Webster, n.d.). Researchers from the many areas of psychology discussed in this book so far (e.g., behaviorism, cognitive psychology, developmental psychology, personality psychology, and social psychology) have worked to identify biological bases for personality and behavior (Canli, 2006a). Because of these technological advancements, psychologists from all subdisciplines can now explore biological links to the brain as potential causes of normal and abnormal behavior.

Neuropsychologists use various assessment techniques to evaluate impairment and determine damage in either behavior or thinking—the body and the mind studied by psychologists (Friedenberg, 1995). Doctors and researchers perform neuropsychological testing on adults and children, with some tests geared for specific age ranges. Some assessment techniques involve more low-tech cognitive tests that attempt to identify impairment or damage in some brain regions (Purves et al., 2008). These tests include the Draw-a-Clock task, intelligence tests (such as the Wechsler tests), and the Bender Visual-Motor Gestalt. **Test batteries**, a series of tests that measure different brain functions (such as the Halstead-Reitan Battery and the Luria-Nebraska Battery), are sometimes used rather than a single test (Friedenberg, 1995; Kaplan & Saccuzzo, 2013).

Besides the traditional paper tests, more recent tests can directly observe brain activity to determine impairment and damage. These include three well-known tests. **Computerized axial tomography (CAT)** is a diagnostic imaging method that uses a low-dose beam of X-rays that crosses the body at many different angles and provides a detailed image of the brain or other parts of the body (Computed Tomography/Encyclopædia Britannica, 2021; Kalat, 1999; Siegel & Sapru, 2015). **Positron emission tomography (PET)**, or PET scans, involves injecting a positron-emitting isotope into the body, entering the bloodstream. A detector placed around the head measures blood flow activity in the brain. PET scans can show people's brain activity while engaging in various cognitive, memory, or other tasks (Bear et al., 2016; Kalat, 1999; Positron emission tomography/ Encyclopædia Britannica, 2021; Siegel & Sapru, 2015). **Functional magnetic resonance imaging (fMRI)** is a neuroimaging technique that uses magnetic detectors to identify changes in oxygenated blood flow in various brain areas while participants are engaging in cognitive and mental tasks and can help look for effects of brain injuries or stroke (Bear et al., 2016; Functional magnetic resonance imaging/Encyclopædia Britannica, 2021; Kalat, 1999; Siegel & Sapru, 2015).

These techniques help researchers identify potential biochemical or anatomical causes or correlates of neurological and mental disorders. Recently, Boston University researchers and colleagues studied trauma-exposed U.S. Veterans and identified two brain areas, the right amygdala and right middle temporal gyrus, that are potential markers for suicide risk (Jagger-Rickels et al., 2023). Identifying specific brain areas associated with suicide risk could potentially help identify those most at risk for suicide before an attempt. Ultimately, these neuroimaging techniques could help determine the effectiveness of various therapeutic interventions.

Investigative thinking challenge:
Is there a singular region within the brain that can be considered the location of the "self"? What leads you to hold this perspective?

Heatherton et al. (2007) summarize several studies that used neuroimaging technology such as positron emission tomography (PET) and functional magnetic resonance imaging (fMRI) to demonstrate a biological basis for the sense of self. Heatherton et al. (2007) claim this research provides evidence for brain activity related to the cognitive self (self-knowledge), affective self (self-esteem), and executive self (self-regulation). They also acknowledge that no single spot in the brain contains the self—activity is distributed throughout the brain. However, the activity is mainly focused in the prefrontal cortex. Specifically, when participants were asked to identify self-relevant traits and information (cognitive self) correctly, the medial prefrontal cortex (MPFC) displayed activity. The ventral anterior cingulate cortex (vACC) was more active when participants judged questions about emotions and feelings. This significant finding supported that depression (affective self) is sometimes associated with decreased activity in the vACC. Finally, when participants were presented with a self-regulation task (executive self) and asked to suppress the thought of a white bear (Mitchell et al., 2006), parts of the prefrontal cortex (PFC) and anterior cingulate cortex (ACC) were active (Heatherton et al., 2007). Remember that Phineas Gage damaged his prefrontal cortex in his accident.

Investigative thinking challenge:
B.F. Skinner, renowned for his stimulus-reinforcement theory of behaviorism, asserted that the concept of the self lacks direct observability, leading psychologists to concentrate on studying observable behavior. However, with today's technological advancements enabling direct observation of specific brain regions functioning during self-related tasks, does this challenge Skinner's claim? In simpler terms, can we now observe the self in action, providing evidence for its existence?

In addition to the brain, researchers use other biological methods to identify physiological relationships to behaviors. One of these areas includes genetics. In the year 2000, the Human Genome Project[2] announced that a consortium of public research institutions around the world completed a working draft of the sequence of the **genome**, the genetic code or blueprint for humans that could then go on to provide an understanding of the development of certain diseases (Genome.gov, 2000). Gene therapy can treat various illnesses and works by targeting specific brain areas. For example, University of California San Diego researchers are assessing a gene therapy for patients with Alzheimer's disease by injecting brain areas with genetically altered cells that produce a protein (brain-derived neurotrophic factor, BDNF) and help neurons survive and grow (LaFee, 2021). We have already seen how neuroimaging research identified activity within some brain regions related to various traits and the self. Canli (2006b) also identified preliminary evidence for studying the trait of extraversion from a genomic imaging approach. Doctors and medical researchers can now use neuroimaging, genetics, and other techniques to investigate unknown illnesses and find clues related to their cause—similar to a detective's methods when investigating a case.

Genes and DNA became essential investigative techniques for forensic scientists and medical examiners in real life, as well as the detective fiction of the late 20th and 21st centuries. There is often a reciprocal relationship between literature and real-world discoveries and historical events. While detective fiction did not necessarily inspire the development of neuroimaging techniques, the increased use by forensic investigators and doctors who were characters within detective fiction likely led to an increased interest in understanding and studying them. By the late 20th century, individuals with no scientific or medical background were familiar with many types of medical technology and information. Detective fiction began to mirror this increased knowledge and interest in medicine and science (Anderson, 2002).

The Popularity of Forensic Science and Psychology

The technology described in this chapter and examples from detective fiction and the entertainment industry likely influenced the renewed and increased popularity of an already established area of psychology—**forensic psychology**. Forensic psychology comes from the Latin word *forens*, which means forum, a meeting place similar to a court in ancient Rome (Canter, 2012). Forensic psychology is defined as "the use of psychological knowledge or research methods to advise, evaluate, or reform the legal system" (Costanzo & Krauss, 2015, p. 10). Forensic psychology is a relatively new but growing specialization within psychology, with many post-graduate programs now available worldwide. It was not until 2001 that the American Psychological Association (APA) recognized forensic psychology as a separate specialty and created APA Division 41 (American Psychological Association, 2011).

Often, people confuse forensic psychologists with forensic investigators. Forensic psychologists do not go to crime scenes to collect or analyze the evidence collected by others. Forensic psychologists work with lawyers and the court system on behalf of their clients, often testifying in court. Forensic psychologists also conduct research on topics such as false confessions, how juries reach their verdicts, eyewitness memory, and effective interviewing techniques, to name a few areas (Bartol & Bartol, 2012; Costanzo & Krauss, 2015; Greene & Heilbrun, 2011). Another area of study for forensic psychologists involves studying serial killers through criminal profiling techniques. While not as popular or commonly used as in movies like *The Silence of the Lambs* (Demme, 1991) or television series such as *Criminal Minds* (Davis, 2005–2020), this area is quite popular in numerous detective fiction stories.

Forensic Evidence

Was Sherlock Holmes the first forensic investigator? Characters like Sherlock Holmes, Maisie Dobbs, and Kay Scarpetta use the forensic techniques and devices available in the time period their stories are written to collect the truth by investigating the victim's body or crime scene (Thomas, 1999). These investigators collect many types of forensic evidence at a crime scene and later analyze it. Forensic evidence examples include the following (Bartol & Bartol, 2012; Canter, 2012; Costanzo & Krauss, 2015; Greene & Heilbrun, 2011; McDermid, 2014): fingerprints[3]; DNA; blood pattern analysis; pathology information (such as body temperature and body decomposition); bullet matching; tool signature patterns; bite marks or dental records; and textile fibers (from clothing, rugs, or other textiles).

These types of forensic evidence provide fictional and real-life investigators with clues to solve their cases. However, finding, collecting, and analyzing the evidence often takes a reasonable amount of time. The amount of evidence found at any crime scene is typically limited and is often minute, partial, or fragmented. Crime scene investigators gather **trace evidence**, or fragments of physical or forensic evidence, and try to match it with one or more suspects (Costanzo & Krauss, 2015). Four possible results come from this matching:

- **exclusion**—when the two samples are substantially different so that the investigator concludes that they came from different sources
- **inconclusive**—when you are unsure whether the two samples match because one or both samples are incomplete or contaminated, which requires some additional analysis
- **inclusion**—when the samples do match on some features and appear similar, meaning the samples could have come from the same source, but the results are not conclusive
- **individuation**—when the samples match so that they exclude all other possibilities or suspects, meaning the samples could only have come from the same suspect (Costanzo & Krauss, 2015).

When reading detective fiction or watching a popular television series involving forensic evidence, you will notice that the investigators are almost always correct when matching evidence with suspects—if not immediately, at least by the end of the book or episode/movie. Unfortunately, the real world is inaccurate, and mistakes happen. For the most part, errors are unintentional. However, in 2012, Massachusetts State drug lab chemist Annie Dookhan was accused (and later convicted) of tampering with evidence and not correctly testing drug samples over a nearly 10-year period that affected thousands of cases (Lazar, 2012; Levitz, 2013). Dookhan served three years in prison and was released in 2016. This case clarified the need for more than one person to review lab results. When evaluating the accuracy of forensic evidence matching, four outcomes may result: a **hit,** which occurs with a correct match of the trace evidence with the correct suspected owner; a **miss,** considered a failure to match the trace evidence with the correct suspected owner; a **false alarm**, or an incorrect match of the trace evidence with the suspect; and a **correct rejection**, which occurs with a correct conclusion that the trace evidence does not match the suspect.

Investigative thinking challenge:
How might these four potential scenarios (hit, miss, false alarm, correct rejection) unfold when considering cheating on an exam?

Criminal Profiling

Collecting and evaluating forensic evidence is the job of a forensic or crime scene investigator, not a forensic psychologist. Forensic psychologists focus more on behavior and motive, much like the parallel thinking found in detective fiction. Anyone could be a criminal, so determining when a person was deceitful became important. In the 19th century, detective novels began to imagine a new technology to identify deceitfulness and introduced early versions of lie-detecting techniques before they even existed—a case of when fiction led to reality (Thomas, 1999). In addition to detecting deceitful behavior, forensic psychologists can assist in criminal (or crime scene) profiling. **Criminal profiling**[4] attempts to identify a criminal's behavioral, demographic, physical, and emotional characteristics, sometimes so that the profile can help catch the criminal (Bartol & Bartol, 2012). Profiles can help identify certain criminals who exhibit extremely deceitful and abhorrent behavior—namely serial killers.

Serial killers have killed two or more victims across two or more events. These killers often demonstrate similar characteristics, such as a lack of empathy, lack of guilt, poor relationship skills, and impulsivity (Burgess, 2021). A few of them lived relatively normal yet secretive lives in their communities (Egger, 1998). In 2005 the FBI revised the number of victims from the previously required number of three victims (Aamodt, 2016). Profilers aim to help apprehend these serial killers or understand what led to their grossly deviant behavior (Burgess, 2021; Canter, 2004). Good profilers need to have excellent observational and analytical skills. They also need to understand human nature and abnormal behavior, which will help them identify the characteristics of serial killers. A profile can provide psychologists and law enforcement with information about the personality and motivation of a serial killer. Profilers also can help identify two key aspects of a serial killer's behavior: their **modus operandi** (MO) and **signature**.

The MO is the criminal's distinct pattern or manner of committing the crime (e.g., the weapon or method they use to kill their victims or commit the crime). Criminals may slightly alter their MO with each successive act (Bartol & Bartol, 2012; Modus Operandi/Encyclopædia Britannica, 2021). The signature includes the unique or personal aspects of the killing and goes beyond what is needed to commit the crime (e.g., leaving a playing card at the scene or taking a "trophy" from the victim). The choice of the signature corresponds to the serial killer's personality (Bartol & Bartol, 2012; Costanzo & Krauss, 2015). An example of a criminal's MO would be a thief who robs a bank with a gun while wearing a clown mask. Their signature could be asking everyone in the bank to undress and taking a picture before the thief leaves. The signature is not necessarily needed to accomplish the crime but is something the criminal performs for personal or emotional satisfaction (Douglas & Olshaker, 1998).

In the most basic approach, serial killers are classified into one of two types: **organized** versus **disorganized killers**. **Organized serial killers** operate in precisely the way you might think—they plan the abduction and killing of their victims. They are willing to wait for the perfect opportunity and plan the selection of their victim, often stalking them beforehand to ensure they will be successful. Organized killers also are more likely to torture and even dismember their victims. **Disorganized** killers are much more impulsive in their actions. They do not necessarily plan out the abduction, nor do they typically have a weapon selected beforehand and may use any tool or weapon handily available. Disorganized killers are also likelier to leave the victim's body out in the open, whereas a more organized killer will take the time to hide the body (Costanzo & Krauss, 2015; Ressler et al., 1988, 1986). While categorizing serial killers into organized and disorganized categories can provide some information about personality differences, the two categories are limited; therefore, experts developed another classification system to understand these individuals even more.

Holmes and Holmes (2010) further differentiated the motives of serial killers by placing them into four different types:

- **hedonistic**—serial killers who kill people for the fun of it or sometimes for profit; they are sadists and receive pleasure from torturing their victims
- **mission-oriented**—serial killers who kill people they believe are evil or deserve to die for some reason; they kill to make the "world a better place"
- **power-oriented**—serial killers who like to capture and control their victims and exert power over them, often keeping them for some time before killing them
- **visionary**—serial killers who are psychotic, often hearing voices or seeing visions that urge them to kill others

Most killers cannot be neatly classified into a single category, as with most classification systems (Costanzo & Krauss, 2015). But can profiles help law enforcement catch criminals? The effectiveness of criminal profiles in helping law enforcement catch criminals is inconclusive due to limited research in this area. In 1992, Radford University in Virginia established a serial killer database, later updated with the assistance of Florida Gulf Coast University in 2012. By 2016, the Radford/FGCU Serial Killer Database contained data on 4,743 U.S. and international serial killers (Aamodt, 2016).

Mokros and Alison (2002) analyzed 100 British male stranger rape cases. They coded the crimes for specific behaviors based on witness statements and examined police records to identify similarities in the features and criminal histories of the apprehended rapists. However, their study found no significant correlation between the behaviors of the rapists who committed the crimes. Their results indicate that the offenders were diverse, exhibited distinct behaviors, and came from various backgrounds. Criminal profiles, also called offender profiles, may be exciting and valuable when depicted in crime shows and detective fiction, contributing to the fame of such techniques and the FBI. However, their real-world effectiveness remains uncertain (Costanzo & Krauss, 2015).

Eyewitness Memory

A final forensic psychology research topic that is a critical component of both real-life and fictional crime involves the work of American social psychologist **Elizabeth Loftus** (Memory/Encyclopædia Britannica, 2021). Loftus (1984, 1997) and her colleagues study eyewitness memory and its unreliability. According to the Innocence Project[5] (2013), about 76 percent of wrongful convictions are due to eyewitness misidentification. These individuals were released from prisons after DNA evidence later proved their innocence, sometimes decades after they were initially sent to prison.

How can eyewitness memory be so inaccurate? Some memories are incorrect because they are too vivid for the person. These examples of episodic or **autobiographical memory** (the part of episodic memory in our long-term memory that includes personal memories and information; Coon & Mitterer, 2014) are called **flashbulb memories.** Flashbulb memories are memories created during high emotion or arousal that seem particularly vivid and elaborate for the individual (Coon & Mitterer, 2014). Individuals are confident about their flashbulb memories which begin as snapshots of a person or event in their minds because they are connected to a strong emotion or arousal. Many people have these memories of when they learned that President Kennedy was assassinated or heard about the 9/11 terrorist attack (Hirst & Phelps, 2016). Individuals often believe they will never forget those memories. Law enforcement or lawyers will ask eyewitnesses to recount accurate descriptions that occur in a state of arousal or distress. Although highly detailed, memory can still be incorrect because instead of the actual details of the event getting stored, only the emotion associated with the memory is stored (Hirst & Phelps, 2016). Confidence alone does not equate with accuracy in memories.

Eyewitness recall also can be influenced by the way the interrogator asks questions to the witness. In other words, suggestive or leading wording can influence how a witness remembers events. In a famous experiment by Loftus and Palmer (1974), participants viewed videos of a car crash. Some participants were asked to estimate how fast the cars were going when they "contacted" each other, and other participants were asked to estimate how fast the cars were going when they "smashed" into each other. When the word *contacted* was used, the mean (average) estimate for the speed of the vehicles was 31 mph, but when the word *smashed* was used, the mean speed was about 41 mph. Only one word was different in the questions, yet it yielded significant differences in memory (Costanzo & Krauss, 2015).

How can memory be so prone to errors? It is likely because several stages are involved in memory information processing, and errors can occur in any or multiple stages. Those three stages include **encoding**, when information is gathered and modified into a form held in memory; **storage**, holding or containing the information in the brain over time; and **retrieval**, the final stage of information processing, when the stored information is accessed and pulled out into consciousness for use (Rathus, 2013).

Many factors can impact the accuracy of information processing, including inattention, stress, suggestive questioning, and partial or selective memory retrieval. A real-world example of retrieval errors occurred in the UK, where a ticket clerk was robbed at gunpoint in a railway station. During a lineup to identify the suspect, the clerk confidently pointed out a sailor as the perpetrator. However, it turned out that the sailor had a solid alibi—being at sea on a ship with numerous other sailors who could vouch for his presence. A forensic psychologist involved in the case analyzed the situation and concluded that the sailor was misidentified due to a retrieval error stemming from previous encounters with him on other days. The sailor lived near the railway station that was robbed and bought tickets from the same clerk several times before the robbery. The sailor's proximity to the robbed station and repeated interactions with the clerk created a sense of familiarity, leading to the erroneous identification (Canter, 2012).

Why did this happen? The underlying cause was **retrieval inhibition**, wherein individuals selectively remember certain aspects of a memory or crime scene while ignoring other potentially crucial details, especially if investigators fail to inquire about those aspects (MacLeod & Saunders, 2008). The questions asked and feedback provided to witnesses can influence their confidence level in their memories, potentially altering their recollections (Shaw, 2018). Such errors in eyewitness memory and other types of memory present considerable challenges for both real-life and fictional detectives alike. Understanding the intricacies of memory and the various factors at play can help improve eyewitness reliability and ensure the detective discovers "whodunit" in factual and literary crime-solving scenarios.

Investigative thinking challenge:
Can you think of a time when you misremembered an event or person? What factors contributed to this mistake, and at which stage of information processing do you think this error likely originated?

Forensic and Medical Influences in Detective Fiction

The Doctor Thorndyke detective fiction series set in England and written by R. Austin Freeman was among the very first, if not the first, to feature a medical doctor as a detective (Anderson, 2002). The first story in the series was *The Red Thumb Mark*[6] published in 1907. The story describes Dr. Thorndyke as a medical jurist who was a medical doctor and lawyer. He uses his vast scientific knowledge and the most up-to-date equipment of the time to solve mysterious deaths. As Anderson (2002) explains, Dr. Thorndyke:

> ... has a well-equipped laboratory in his home and an assistant who can perform miracles of chemical and microscopic analysis, photography, radiography, casting, fingerprinting, and even metal-working. He carries a miniature laboratory in a green case to crime scenes [Anderson, 2002, p. 1136].

This early series introduced readers to an appreciation for biological and forensic interpretations of behavior and death. Even before the Doctor Thorndyke series, Sherlock Holmes and Auguste Dupin described methods that became real forensic techniques—fingerprints, crime scene investigation, and even criminal profiling. The London police force and Scotland Yard first started using fingerprints in the mid–1890s, several years after the first Sherlock Holmes stories appeared in magazines (History.com, 2009). These stories also included examples of lie detection. Holmes also was known for his crime scene investigation techniques, where he would look for things like cigarette ash and other clues to the killer's identity (Thomas, 1999).

In the 1970s, a new television series debuted that introduced a broader population of American and international viewers to the investigative techniques of a medical examiner, also known as a coroner, called *Quincy, M.E.* (Larson & Shaw, 1976–1983). The show starred popular actor Jack Klugman as Dr. Quincy, a medical examiner or forensic pathologist who would gather clues and evidence to help solve suspicious deaths. The stories were similar to the style of a classic mystery story and introduced its viewers to elements of forensic science. Beginning in the 1990s, many female pathologists and forensic anthropologists appeared as detectives, using standard forensic techniques and science in detective fiction (Anderson, 2002). These television series include *Crossing Jordan* (Kring, 2001–2007) and *Bones* (Hanson, 2005–2017).

> *Investigative thinking challenge:*
> *Which detective TV series featuring forensic science*
> *or a medical examiner do you consider your favorite?*
> *What makes it stand out compared to others?*

Medical examiners' work, especially autopsies, continues to help detectives gather clues to help solve their cases. The body tells a story. Autopsies are especially important to those investigating a death; they can learn important facts about how a victim died by studying the body. In *The Consequences of Fear* (Winspear, 2021), Maisie Dobbs works with Dr. Jamieson, the medical examiner. She describes how the bruises and injury to the head and skull indicate that the victim may have suffered injuries before death. Her comments illustrate to the reader how the body provides clues allowing the investigators to create a story that will explain the most likely manner of death.

> You can see from here that the way the neck was broken, if that's what indeed happened, then this crushing of the skull would have happened on the other side of his head as he fell. And look at the bruises on his body—all on the right side, in line with the skull injury. The broken neck is telling a different story [*The Consequences of Fear*, Winspear, 2021, p. 134].

In 1988, the novel *The Silence of the Lambs* by Thomas Harris caused an explosion in the popularity of forensic science in books, television series, and movies. The novel was widely successful and won several literary awards. However, the movie adaptation starring Jodie Foster (Demme, 1991) led to forensic science's stronghold on scripted series that continues today. The novel and movie introduced readers to many elements of forensic science and forensic psychology: serial killers, criminal profiling, crime scene investigation, and **forensic entomology** (the study of insects at a crime scene; Joseph et al., 2011; McDermid, 2014).

Detective fiction not only entertains its readers but can educate them as well. Meeks (2020) believes that detective fiction is not only connected to neuroscience, it can help readers explore and challenge ethical dilemmas associated with current advancements in science and technology. As we saw in the previous chapter, today's detective fiction exposes readers to social, racial, and political topics. Detective fiction also can excite its readers about science and technology.

In 1990, Patricia Cornwell published *Postmortem* (Cornwell, 1990), the first in the Kay Scarpetta series. Cornwell's Kay Scarpetta is a complex character who presents a positive example of a strong female doctor and scientist (Robinson, 2006). Cornwell emphasizes the usefulness of forensic techniques and science in detection: Scarpetta engages in detailed scientific methodology, and Cornwell writes with much detail about the bodies she examines, the scientific instruments, and the lab equipment (Priestman, 2009). While the novels depict real techniques, the stories are still fiction, and Scarpetta does not exemplify how actual medical examiners work. For example, she engages more in on-the-scene work and interaction with suspects than an actual medical examiner. The forensic investigation of the body and crime scene often leads to the mystery or case resolution.

In *The Body Farm* (Cornwell, 1995), Scarpetta discovers Emily Steiner's killer by getting help from colleagues at a research laboratory called a **body farm**, a real-life research center for studying body decomposition at the University of Tennessee.[7] The *Kay Scarpetta* series also involves criminal profiling, although, in *The Body Farm* (Cornwell, 1995), profiling does not help Scarpetta solve the case (Priestman, 2009). More than one serial killer or psychopath taunts Kay Scarpetta and other characters throughout many of the novels in the series.

Kathy Reichs' novels follow forensic anthropologist Dr. Temperance (Tempe) Brennan in the Montreal, Quebec, area.[8] In the first novel of the Tempe Brennan series, *Déjà Dead* (Reichs, 1997), readers are introduced to the work of a forensic anthropologist in the first few pages. Brennan goes to a scene where skeletal remains are discovered, and she must determine if they are recent or have been there for some time. Like Cornwell, Reichs details the insects that swarm around the body. Forensic entomology can help determine the time of death as there is a predictable order to when insects turn up at a "corpse buffet" (Byrd & Castner, 2010; Costandi, 2015). Brennan encounters blowflies, maggots, and the smell of a decomposing body—all part of the process of **putrefaction**, the enzymatic decomposition or rotting of a body, resulting in a foul odor (Putrefaction, 2003). The presence of maggots with the body helps her determine the season and likely timeframe for the death.

In *Death Du Jour* (Reichs, 1999), Brennan explains the postmortem interval (length of time a person has been dead) and the presence of bugs to her college-aged daughter. Her description of the cycle (flies arrive first, followed by the maggots, which develop from fly larvae, followed by the pupa, which comes from the larvae/maggots, and finally, the flies that develop from the pupa and start the process anew) is vivid enough to disgust her daughter and likely many readers. The details are graphic indeed, but they also are accurate and informative.

In the second chapter of *Déjà Dead* (Reichs, 1997), Brennan describes how she prepares the bones for her forensic examination. By the end of the second chapter, in only about 35 pages, Reichs introduces the reader to many steps related to an **autopsy**, a postmortem examination to determine the time and cause of death (Autopsy/Encyclopædia Britannica, 2021). As a **forensic anthropologist**, her job is to use archaeological techniques and skeletal analysis to examine the bones during an autopsy to gather information about the cause of death or the identity of the victim (Forensic Anthropology, n.d.). Like Cornwell's Kay Scarpetta, Brennan describes using a Stryker saw to cut into the skull to inspect the brain during an autopsy (Reichs, 1997). Tempe also explains to a colleague how to identify the type of cutting tool used to dismember a victim based on the cuts to the bones.

Her colleague is a **forensic odontologist.** Forensic odontologists use techniques to help them identify unidentified human remains since teeth are among the last parts of the body to decay because of their structure (Krishan et al., 2015). The end of the second chapter of *Déjà Dead* also foreshadows the introduction of another focus of forensic psychology and a popular character typically found in detective fiction featuring medical examiners/doctors as investigators—a serial killer.

James Patterson's *Women's Murder Club* series (James Patterson, n.d.) follows a group of friends who discuss clues and solve crimes in San Francisco. Two characters, Lindsay Boxer, a homicide detective, and Claire Washburn, the chief medical examiner, often work together professionally. In the first book of the series, *1st to Die* (Patterson, 2001), Claire describes how a murder victim died by examining the stab wounds during the autopsy. She can identify the type of knife based on the wounds, estimate the killer's height, and the fact that he was right-handed based on the angle of the stab incision. The explanation is informative and provides the reader with a literary application of these forensic techniques.

A final example of a series that details the close relationship between a medical examiner and the police is the *Rizzoli & Isles series*[9] by Tess Gerritsen. The first novel in the series, *The Surgeon* (Gerritsen, 2001), involves a serial killer who uses his medical training as a surgeon to torture and kill women around Boston, Massachusetts. Gerritsen earned an M.D. degree from the University of California, San Francisco (Gerritsen, 2017) and used her medical expertise in her storylines. Medical examiner Maura Isles is not introduced until the second book in the series, *The Apprentice* (Gerritsen, 2002). However, *The Surgeon* (Gerritsen, 2016) still contains information related to forensic psychology and medicine. When Detective Jane Rizzoli is about to reach the killer at the novel's end, she finds containers with trophies from his victims, reinforcing this common characteristic of a serial killer for the readers.

Before this, as Rizzoli begins to gather evidence about the killer's identity, she discovers he may have a genetic defect called "Netherton's Syndrome" (Gerritsen, 2016, p. 51). Gerritsen writes about the disorder's characteristics along with other accompanying symptoms, like skin rashes, which might be an important clue. The abundance of medical knowledge and techniques within the medical examiner type of detective fiction can be informative, generate interest in new topics for readers, and parallel the increase in knowledge known by the general public. However, this increase in medical jargon and biological/forensic detail also may be related to an unintended consequence—an increase in violence and distrust. Anderson (2002) says

> I think the association of science with torture and serial killers is not an accident ... it does reflect widespread hostility toward medicine and science. Dr. John Thorndyke's scientific reasoning would not prevail in a court today [Anderson, 2002, p. 1138–1139].

Overall, the sub-genre of medical examiner detective fiction delves into death and the examination of deceased bodies in a highly graphic manner. Often, the victims are killed in a horrifyingly violent manner, with intricate details shared openly with the reader. A prime example of this graphic style occurs in *Death Du Jour* (Reichs, 1999). Author Kathy Reichs describes a body's condition in great detail when her protagonist, Tempe Brennan, investigates a fire scene, describing the victim's body in a chillingly vivid manner. Brennan explains how the fire's intense heat can cause a fire victim's brain to boil and expand within the skull, leading to a gruesome outcome. Unlike traditional mysteries like Agatha Christie's Miss Marple series, these medical examiner detective stories paint detailed pictures of the victim's torture and death. What makes them compelling is that many authors writing such tales have direct experience in the professions and activities they portray, lending an air of authenticity to the gruesome depictions.

However, despite the potentially disturbing nature of these narratives, they have gained immense popularity. This popularity mirrors the contemporary surge in the use and appreciation of neuropsychological, medical, forensic science, and forensic psychology techniques. The connection is evident; just as readers are drawn to the gripping realism of medical examiner detective fiction, the fascination with real-life psychological and forensic sciences has grown substantially. Anderson may question Dr. Thorndyke's scientific reasoning, but the present-day medical examiner characters and series are built on more solid ground, making them highly believable and resonating with readers. The success of these best-selling stories parallels the increasing acceptance and demand for credible applications of forensic science and psychology in solving real-life mysteries and crimes. As a result, this sub-genre not only entertains but also reflects society's growing interest in the intriguing intersection of psychology and forensic science.

Investigative thinking challenge:
In your opinion, does Kay Scarpetta (or any medical examiner or investigator from a novel you read for this chapter) demonstrate the traits of a hard-boiled or soft-boiled detective? Explain the reasoning behind your choice.

Suggested Detective Fiction/Literature to Accompany This Chapter
- *The Body Farm (Kay Scarpetta series)* by Patricia Cornwell
- *The Rizzoli & Isles series* by Tess Gerritsen
- *1st to Die (Women's Murder Club Book 1)* by James Patterson
- *The Crossing Places: Ruth Galloway Book 1* by Elly Griffiths
- *Déjà Dead: A Novel (Temperance Brennan Book 1)* by Kathy Reichs
- *The Secret History of Las Vegas: A Novel* by Chris Abani
- *The Face of Deception: The first Eve Duncan novel* by Iris Johansen
- *The Bone Collector (Lincoln Rhyme Book 1)* by Jeffery Deaver
- *One Grave Too Many (Diane Fallon Book 1)* by Beverly Connor

End-of-Chapter Mind Puzzlers
1. Analyze the traits or behaviors of the detective and at least one other character displayed in one of the novels you read for this chapter. Would they be considered beneficial from an evolutionary standpoint? Explain your reasoning using relevant examples.
2. Forensic science has been integral to several detective fiction series since 1990. Select five examples of forensic technology or techniques mentioned in *The Body Farm, The Surgeon,* or another novel you read. How do the police and investigators use this

7. Neuropsychology and Forensic Psychology

information to catch the suspect? Is the evidence mentioned in the book you read similar to how it is used in real life? Why or why not?

3. Both *The Body Farm* and *The Surgeon* involve killers who would be classified as serial killers. Select one of these or another similar novel, identifying whether the serial killer in your chosen novel is organized or disorganized. Next, identify the type (hedonistic, mission-oriented, power-oriented, or visionary) that best describes them. Analyze their modus operandi (MO) and signature, supporting your analysis with specific examples.

4. Evaluate whether errors in eyewitness memory or misidentification occurred in the novel(s) you read for this chapter. Identify the stage of information processing that you believe is primarily responsible for the error and support your explanation with examples.

5. Describe Kay Scarpetta's relationships with Pete Marino, her niece Lucy, and Benton Wesley in the Patricia Cornwell novel you read. Assess how these relationships influence her detective or investigative skills and how they impact her as a woman. Analyze how these relationships contribute to Kay's motivation, self-reflection, and personal growth. Determine the level of Maslow's hierarchy of needs that best represents Kay, providing two examples with corresponding chapter/page numbers to support your assessment.

6. Examine the rise in popularity of stories featuring medical examiners as detectives over the past one to two decades. What explains their popularity? How does the text of *The Body Farm* or *The Surgeon* differ from other detective novels we have read? What features do you feel define the medical examiner as a detective subgenre?

7. Select one of the novels you read for this chapter and compare it to popular television programs featuring forensic science and crime scene investigation. Analyze the potential influence of psychology on the popularity of both the novel and television series.

8. Characterize the personality traits of Kay Scarpetta, Jane Rizzoli, Maura Isles, or another female character from a book you read. Evaluate how their character contributes (positively or negatively) to the world of female detectives and detective fiction as a whole.

Key Terms and People

- **natural selection**: the process by which species adapt to their environment by selectively reproducing genetic changes that will help them survive
- **case study**: a psychological research method that involves a detailed descriptive study of one person or, at times, one specific group
- **Phineas Gage**: In 1848, Phineas Gage, a young railway worker, survived an accident where a 13-pound iron rod impaled his skull, resulting in brain damage that led to significant alterations in his personality and behavior
- **frontal lobe**: the part of the brain responsible for regulating emotions, social skills, behavior, and decision-making
- **neuropsychology**: a field of psychology that studies the behavior and the mind through neurological observations of the brain and the nervous system
- **test batteries**: a set of tests designed to assess various brain functions, with each test focusing on different aspects
- **computerized axial tomography (CAT)**: a diagnostic imaging method that uses a low-dose beam of X-rays that crosses the body at many different angles and provides a detailed image of the brain or other body parts
- **positron emission tomography (PET)**: PET scans involve injecting a chemical compound into the body to observe brain activity while individuals engage in a variety of cognitive, memory, or other tasks
- **functional magnetic resonance imaging (fMRI)**: a neuroimaging technique that uses magnetic detectors to identify changes in blood flow, identifying brain activity as participants perform cognitive and mental tasks
- **genome**: the genetic code or blueprint specific to humans
- **forensic psychology**: the use of psychological knowledge or research methods to advise, evaluate, or reform the legal system
- **trace evidence**: fragments of physical or forensic evidence left behind at a crime scene
- **exclusion**: when the two samples are substantially different so that the investigator concludes they came from different sources

7. Neuropsychology and Forensic Psychology 185

- **inconclusive**: when you are unsure whether two samples match because one or both samples are incomplete or contaminated, necessitating additional analysis
- **inclusion**: when the samples match on some features and appear similar, meaning the samples could have come from the same source, but the results are not conclusive
- **individuation**: when the samples match so that they exclude all other possibilities or suspects, meaning the samples could only have come from the same suspect
- **hit**: a correct match of the trace evidence with the correct suspected owner
- **miss**: a failure to match the trace evidence with the correct suspected owner
- **false alarm**: an incorrect match of the trace evidence with the suspect
- **correct rejection**: a correct conclusion that the trace evidence does not match the suspect
- **criminal profiling**: an attempt to identify the behavioral, demographic, physical, and emotional characteristics of a criminal
- **serial killers**: individuals who have killed two or more victims across two or more events (as revised by the FBI from the previously required number of three deaths)
- **modus operandi (MO)**: the criminal's distinct pattern or manner of committing the crime, such as the weapon or method used to commit the crime
- **signature**: the unique or personal aspects of the killing that go beyond what is needed to commit the crime, such as leaving a playing card at the scene or taking an item from the victim
- **organized serial killers**: serial killers who plan the abduction and killing of their victims, often stalking them beforehand to make sure they will be successful
- **disorganized serial killers**: serial killers who act impulsively, without detailed planning, and may use any readily available tool or weapon
- **hedonistic serial killers**: serial killers who derive pleasure and thrill from torturing their victims; they are sadistic
- **mission-oriented serial killers**: serial killers who believe their victims are evil or deserving of death for some reason

- **power-oriented serial killers**: killers who like to capture and control their victims, often keeping them alive for some time before killing them
- **visionary serial killers**: killers who are psychotic, often hearing voices or seeing visions that urge them to kill others
- **Elizabeth Loftus**: an American psychologist well-known for her studies on eyewitness testimony and false memories
- **autobiographical memory**: the part of episodic memory in our long-term memory that includes personal memories and information
- **flashbulb memories:** vivid and detailed memories connected to strong emotions or arousal, often originating as snapshots of a person or event in the mind
- **encoding**: the first stage of information processing, when information is gathered and modified into a form that can be held in memory
- **storage**: the second stage of information processing, which involves holding the information in the brain over time
- **retrieval**: the final stage of information processing, when the stored information is accessed and pulled out into consciousness for use
- **retrieval inhibition**: selectively recalling some parts of a memory while inhibiting or preventing the recall of other aspects
- **forensic entomology**: the study of insects in the context of a crime scene or criminal investigation
- **body farm:** a real-life research center for studying body decomposition at the University of Tennessee, Knoxville's Anthropology Research Facility
- **putrefaction:** the enzymatic decomposition, or rotting, of a body, resulting in a foul smell and other bodily changes
- **autopsy:** a postmortem examination conducted by a coroner or medical examiner to determine the time and cause of death
- **forensic anthropologist:** researchers who use archaeological techniques and skeletal analysis to gather information about the cause of death or identity of the victim from bones
- **forensic odontologist**: a professional with dental training who uses dental techniques to identify teeth from unidentified human remains or to match bite marks on a victim

7. Neuropsychology and Forensic Psychology

Chapter Notes

1. To learn more about Phineas Gage, go to https://www.npr.org/sections/health-shots/2017/05/21/528966102/why-brain-scientists-are-still-obsessed-with-the-curious-case-of-phineas-gage or read John Fleischman's book, *Phineas Gage: A Gruesome but True Story About Brain Science* (2002). Gage's skull resides at Harvard Medical School's Warren Anatomical Museum in Cambridge, MA.

2. To learn more about the Human Genome Project, go to https://www.genome.gov/human-genome-project.

3. For a quick and easy way to get your own (and family and friends') fingerprints, gather a few items: a blank piece of paper, a pencil, and some scotch tape. You could use an ink pad rather than a pencil, but the pencil is easier to find and works just as well, if not better. Use the pencil to color a 6-inch circle on the blank paper. Rub a finger from your non-dominant hand across the penciled-in circle until the finger is covered (it is easiest to start with your thumb). Grab the tape dispenser, tear off a piece of clean scotch tape, and press the sticky side onto your pencil lead-covered finger. Push it against your finger for a few seconds, then pull it off. Stick the tape onto a non-colored section of your paper. Write which finger it was, and then repeat the procedure for your other fingers on the same hand. When you are done, you should see similarities in the fingerprints of each finger, but they will differ from your family members. Try to identify if your fingerprints are mostly circular (whorls), oval (loops), or triangular (arches) and if you have any spaces or missing sections of your prints. Sources: https://www.youtube.com/watch?v=DHlqBNahOU8 and http://www.forensicsciencesimplified.org/prints/principles.html.

4. The FBI's Behavioral Science Unit (BSU) developed the method of criminal profiling. The BSU is part of the FBI's National Center for the Analysis of Violent Crime (NCAVC) and was the inspiration for the Behavioral Analysis Unit (BAU) in the CBS series *Criminal Minds* (Davis, 2005–2020). John E. Douglas and Robert Ressler began interviewing serial killers during the 1970s to understand serial killers' motivation, helping build a database of information called the Violent Criminal Apprehension Program (ViCAP). To read more about NCAVC's actual work, go to https://www.fbi.gov/file-repository/serialmurder-pathwaysforinvestigations.pdf/view. To watch a fictionalized version of the early days of the BSU, watch Netflix's *Mindhunter* series (Penhall, 2017–2019).

5. The Innocence Project was started in 1992 by Peter Neufeld and Barry Scheck at Cardozo School of Law. It has helped exonerate hundreds of wrongly convicted individuals and helped create reforms to the criminal justice system. To learn more about the program and read through the cases, go to https://innocenceproject.org.

6. To read *The Red Thumb Mark* (1907) by R. Austin Freeman; you can access a free eBook [EBook #11128] through Project Gutenberg at https://www.gutenberg.org/1/1/1/2/11128/.

7. To learn about the University of Tennessee–Knoxville's Anthropology Research Facility, go to https://fac.utk.edu/.

8. Quebec is the location of another successful mystery series, the *Armand Gamache* mystery series by Canadian author Louise Penny (Louise Penny, n.d.).

9. While not wholly faithful to the book series, the television series *Rizzoli & Isles* (Tamaro, 2010–2016), starring Angie Harmon and Sasha Alexander as the two main characters, is entertaining and worth viewing.

References

Aamodt, M.G. (2016, September 4). *Serial Killer Statistics*. Retrieved from http://maamodt.asp.radford.edu/serial killer information center/project description.htm

American Psychological Association. (2011, January 1). *Specialty Guidelines for Forensic Psychology*. http://www.apa.org/practice/guidelines/forensic-psychology.

Anderson, D. (2002). Physicians as detectives in detective fiction of the 20th century. *Southern Medical Journal*, 95(10), 1134–1139.

Autopsy. (2021). In *Encyclopædia Britannica*. Retrieved from https://academic-eb-com.eu1.proxy.openathens.net/levels/collegiate/article/autopsy/11380.

Bartol, C.R., & Bartol, A.M. (2012). *Introduction to Forensic Psychology: Research and Application* (3rd Ed.). Sage.
Bear, M.F., Connors, B.W., & Paradiso, M.A. (2016). *Neuroscience: Exploring the Brain.* Wolters Kluwer.
Burgess, A.W. (2021). *A Killer by Design: Murders, Mindhunters, and My Quest to Decipher the Criminal Mind.* Nachette Books.
Byrd, J.H., & Castner, J.L. (2010). *Forensic Entomology: The Utility of Arthropods in Legal Investigations* (second Edition). CRC Press/Taylor & Francis Group.
Canli, T. (2006a). *Biology of Personality and Individual Differences.* Guilford Press.
Canli, T. (2006b). Genomic imaging of extraversion. In T. Canli (Ed.), *Biology of Personality and Individual Differences.* Guilford Press.
Canter, D. (2004). Offender profiling and investigative psychology. *Journal of Investigative Psychology & Offender Profiling, 1*: 1–15. https://doi.org/10.1002/jip.7
Canter, D. (2012). *Forensic Psychology for Dummies.* Wiley.
Charles Darwin. (2021). In *Encyclopædia Britannica.* Retrieved from https://academic-eb-com.eul.proxy.openathens.net/levels/collegiate/article/Charles-Darwin/109642.
Computed tomography (CT). (2021). In *Encyclopædia Britannica.* Retrieved from https://academic-eb-com.eul.proxy.openathens.net/levels/collegiate/article/computed-tomography/25056.
Coon, D., & Mitterer, J.O. (2014). *Psychology: A Journey* (5th Edition). Wadsworth Cengage Learning.
Cornwell, P. (1990). *Postmortem.* Pocket Books.
Cornwell, P. (1995). *The Body Farm.* Berkley Books.
Costandi, M. (2015). Life after death: The science of human decomposition. *The Guardian.* Retrieved from https://www.theguardian.com/science/neurophilosophy/2015/may/05/life-after-death.
Costanzo, M., & Krauss, D. (2015). *Forensic and Legal Psychology: Psychological Science Applied to Law.* Worth Publishers.
Darwin, C. (1859). *On the Origin of Species by Means of Natural Selection, Or, the Preservation of Favoured Races in the Struggle for Life.* J. Murray.
Davis, D. [Creator]. (2005–2020). *Criminal Minds* [TV series]. CBS Television Studios.
Demme, J. (Director). (1991). *The Silence of the Lambs* [Film]. Strong Heart Productions.
Douglas, J., & Olshaker, M. (1998). *Obsession.* Scribner.
Egger, S.S. (1998). *The Killers Among Us: An Examination of Serial Murder and Its Investigation.* Prentice Hall.
Forensic Anthropology (n.d.) *What Do Forensic Anthropologists and Detectives Have in Common*? Smithsonian National Museum of National History. Retrieved from https://naturalhistory.si.edu/education/teaching-resources/social-studies/forensic-anthropology.
Freeman, R.A. (1907/2004). *The Red Thumb Mark.* D.W. Newton.
Friedenberg, L. (1995). *Psychological Testing: Design, Analysis, and Use.* Allyn & Bacon.
Functional magnetic resonance imaging (fMRI). (2021). In Encyclopædia Britannica. Retrieved from https://academic-eb-com.eul.proxy.openathens.net/levels/collegiate/article/functional-magnetic-resonance-imaging/444125.
Genome.gov. (2000, June). International human genome sequencing consortium announces "working Draft" of human genome. https://www.genome.gov/10001457/2000-release-working-draft-of-human-genome-sequence.
Gerritsen, T. (2001/2016). *The Surgeon: A Rizzoli & Isles Novel.* Ballantine Books.
Gerritsen, T. (2002/2008). *The Apprentice: A Rizzoli & Isles Novel.* Ballantine Books.
Gerritsen, T. (2017). *Tess Gerritsen.* Retrieved from https://tessgerritsen.com/about-tess-gerritsen/.
Greene, E., & Heilbrun, K. (2011). *Wrightsman's Psychology and the Legal System* (7th Edition). Wadsworth Cengage Learning.
Hanson, H. [Creator]. (2005–2017). *Bones* [TV series]. 20th Television.
Harlow, J.M. (1868). Recovery from the passage of an iron bar through the head. *Publication of the Massachusetts Medical Society, 2*, 327–347.

7. Neuropsychology and Forensic Psychology 189

Harris, T. (1988). *The Silence of the Lambs*. St. Martin's Press.
Heatherton, T.F., Krendl, A.C., Macrae, C.N., & Kelley, W.M. (2007). A social brain sciences approach to understanding self. In C. Sedikides, & S. Spencer (Eds.), *Frontiers in Social Psychology: The Self* (pp. 3–20). Psychology Press.
Hirst, W., & Phelps, E.A. (2016). Flashbulb memories. *Current Directions in Psychological Science, 25*(1), 36–41. https://doi.org/10.1177/0963721415622487.
History.com (Editors). (2009). "The Adventures of Sherlock Holmes" published. *History*. Retrieved from https://www.history.com/this-day-in-history/the-adventures-of-sherlock-holmes-published.
Holmes, R.M., & Holmes, S.T. (2010). *Serial Murder* (4th Edition). Sage.
Innocence Project (2013). Retrieved from http://www.innocenceproject.org.
Jagger-Rickels, A., Stumps, A., Rothlein, D., Evans, T., Lee, D., McGlinchey, R., DeGutis, J., & Esterman, M. (2023). Aberrant connectivity in the right amygdala and right middle temporal gyrus before and after a suicide attempt: Examining markers of suicide risk. *Journal of Affective Disorders, 335*, 24–35.
James Patterson. (n.d.) *Women's Murder Club*. Retrieved from https://www.jamespatterson.com/landing-page/james-patterson-books-womens-murder-club/.
James, W. (1890). *The Principles of Psychology* (Vol. 1). Macmillan.
Joseph, I., Mathew, D.G., Sathyan, P., & Vargheese, G. (2011). The use of insects in forensic investigations: An overview on the scope of forensic entomology. *Journal of Forensic Dental Sciences, 3*(2), 89–91. https://doi.org/10.4103/0975-1475.92154.
Kalat, J.W. (1999). *Introduction to Psychology* (5th edition). Brooks/Cole, Wadsworth.
Kaplan, R.M., & Saccuzzo, D.P. (2013). *Psychological Testing: Principles, Applications, & Issues* (8th edition). Wadsworth Cengage Learning.
Kring, T. (2001–2007). *Crossing Jordan* [TV series]. NBC Studios.
Krishan, K., Kanchan, T., & Garg, A.K. (2015). Dental evidence in forensic identification—An overview, methodology and present status. *The Open Dentistry Journal, 9*, 250–256. https://doi.org/10.2174/1874210601509010250.
LaFee, S. (2021, February 18). First-in-human clinical trial to assess gene therapy for Alzheimer's disease. https://health.ucsd.edu/news/releases/Pages/2021-02-18-first-in-human-clinical-trial-to-assess-gene-therapy-for-alzheimers-disease.aspx.
Larson, G.A., & Shaw, L. [Creators]. (1976–1983). *Quincy, M.E.* [TV series]. MCA TV & NBC Universal Television.
Lazar, K. (2012, September 30). How chemist in drug lab scandal circumvented safeguards. https://www.bostoncom/local-news/2012/09/30/how-chemist-in-drug-lab-scandal-circumvented-safeguards.
Levitz, J. (2013, November 22). Massachusetts crime lab ex-chemist Annie Dookhan gets 3-5 years: Scandal involving falsified records has thrown state's criminal justice system into turmoil. *The Wall Street Journal*.
Louise Penny (n.d.) *Louise Penny*. Retrieved from https://www.louisepenny.com.
Loftus, E.F. (1984). Expert testimony on the eyewitness. In G.L. Wells & E.F. Loftus (Eds.), *Eyewitness Testimony: Psychological Perspectives* (pp. 273–283). Cambridge University Press.
Loftus, E.F. (1997). Memory for a past that never was. *Current Directions in Psychological Science, 6*, 60–65. https://doi.org/10.1111/1467-8721.ep11512654.
Loftus, E.F., & Palmer, J.C. (1974). Reconstruction of automobile destruction: AN example of the interaction between language and memory. *Journal of Verbal Learning and Verbal Behavior, 13*, 585–589. https://doi.org/10.1016/S0022-5371(74)80011-3
MacLeod, M.D., & Saunders, J. (2008). Retrieval inhibition and memory distortion: Negative consequences of an adaptive process. *Current Directions in Psychological Science, 17*, 26–30. https://doi.org/10.1111/j.1467-8721.2008.00542.x.
McDermid, V. (2014). *Forensics: What Bugs, Burns, Prints, DNA, and More Tell Us About Crime*. Grove Press.
Meeks, S. (2020, March). Neuro-crime fiction: Detecting cognitive difference. *Crime Fiction Studies, 1*(1), 79–95.
Memory. (2021). In *Encyclopædia Britannica*. Retrieved from https://academic-eb-com.eu1.proxy.openathens.net/levels/collegiate/article/memory/109427.

Merriam-Webster. (n.d.). Neuropsychology. In *Merriam-Webster.com Dictionary*. Retrieved March 27, 2021, from https://www.merriam-webster.com/dictionary/neuropsychology.

Mitchell, J.P., Heatherton, T.F., Kelley, W.M., Wyland, C.L., Wegner, D.M., & Macrae, C.N. (2006). Separating sustained from transient aspects of cognitive control during though suppression. *Psychological Science, 18*(4), 292–297.

Modus operandi. (2021). In *Encyclopædia Britannica*. Retrieved from https://academic-eb-com.eu1.proxy.openathens.net/levels/collegiate/article/modus-operandi/53168.

Mokros, A., & Alison, L.J. (2002). Is offender profiling possible? Testing the predicted homology of crime scene actions and background characteristics in a sample of rapists. *Legal and Criminological Psychology, 7*(1), 25–43. https://doi.org/10.1348/135532502168360.

Patterson, J. (2001). *1st to Die*. Little, Brown and Company.

Penhall, J. [Creator]. (2017–2019). *Mindhunter* [TV series]. Netflix.

Phineas Gage. (2021). In *Encyclopædia Britannica*. Retrieved from https://academic-eb-com.eu1.proxy.openathens.net/levels/collegiate/article/Phineas-Gage/604924.

Plotnik, R. (1999). *Introduction to Psychology* (5th Edition). Brooks/Cole/Wadsworth.

Positron emission tomography (PET). (2021). In *Encyclopædia Britannica*. Retrieved from https://academic-eb-com.eu1.proxy.openathens.net/levels/collegiate/article/positron-emission-tomography/61026.

Priestman, M. (Ed.). (2003). *The Cambridge Companion to Crime Fiction*. Cambridge University Press.

Purves, D., Augustine, G.J., Fitzpatrick, D., Hall, W.C., LaMantia, A., McNamara, J.O., & White, L.E. (2008). *Neuroscience* (4th Edition). Sinauer Associates.

Putrefaction. (2003.) *Miller-Keane Encyclopedia and Dictionary of Medicine, Nursing, and Allied Health* (7th Edition). Retrieved from https://medical-dictionary.thefreedictionary.com/putrefaction.

Rathus, S.A. (2013). *Psychology: Concepts and Connections* (9th Edition). Cengage Learning.

Reichs, K. (1997). *Déjà Dead*. Scribner.

Reichs, K. (1999). *Death Du Jour*. Pocket Books.

Ressler, R.K., Burgess, A.W., & Douglas, J.E. (1988). *Sexual Homicide: Patterns and Motives*. Lexington Books.

Ressler, R.K., Burgess, A.W., Douglas, J.E., Hartman, C.R., & D'Agostino, R.B. (1986). Sexual killers and their victims: Identifying patterns through crime scene analysis. *Journal of Interpersonal Violence, 1*, 288–308. https://doi.org/10.1177/088626086001003003.

Robinson, B. (2006). Playing like the boys: Patricia Cornwell writes men. *The Journal of Popular Culture, 30*(1), 95–108.

Sedikides, C., Skowronski, J.J., & Dunbar, R.I.M. (2006). When and why did the human self evolve? In M. Schaller, J.A. Simpson, & D.T. Kenrick (eds.), *Frontiers in Social Psychology: Evolution and Social Psychology* (pp. 55–80). Psychology Press.

Shaw, J. (2018). How can researchers tell whether someone has a false memory? Coding strategies in autobiographical false-memory research: A reply to Wade, Garry, and Pezdek (2018). *Psychological Science, 29*(3), 477–480. https://doi.org/10.1177/0956797618759552.

Siegel, A., & Sapru, H.N. (2015). *Essential Neuroscience* (3rd ed.). Wolters Kluwer.

Tamaro, J. (2010–2016). *Rizzoli & Isles* [TV series]. TNT.

Thomas, R.R. (1999). *Detective Fiction and the Rise of Forensic Science*. Cambridge University Press.

Winspear, J. (2021). *The Consequences of Fear*. HarperCollins Publishers.

8

Putting It All Together

Throughout this book, we have discussed the historical development and progression of the field of psychology. However, rather than read several empirical articles or textbooks, you read several detective fiction short stories and novels to look for examples of the psychological concepts discussed. You used critical thinking to apply the psychological theories and information presented in the text to the fictional characters within the detective fiction examples you read. When reading the stories, you observed how the detectives in these stories employed deductive reasoning, analytical skills, and acute observation to unravel perplexing cases, reflecting the complexities of real-life psychological processes. In addition to making these connections, the fictional stories allowed you to discuss topics that may be uncomfortable or not as interesting.

Investigative thinking challenge:
Which detective portrayed in literary or cinematic
series would you most like to be? Why?

Integrating detective fiction into psychology courses can offer a fresh and engaging approach to teaching complex psychological concepts. It encourages individuals to think critically, apply their knowledge, and explore the interdisciplinary nature of literature and psychology. Through this combination, participants will likely develop a deeper understanding of psychological principles while cultivating an appreciation for detective fiction and its impact on popular culture.

This book could have addressed many other theories and approaches to psychology and its newer or future directions.[1] However, as mentioned earlier, this is a brief history of psychology and can be supplemented by additional readings and information. Each chapter provided examples and quotes from select detective fiction, which applied the psychological concepts discussed within that chapter. At the end of each chapter, a list of other suggested detective fiction, or in the case of Chapter 1, classic and gothic literature, was included to provide instructors, students, and readers with other possible reading choices. They are merely suggestions; you can substitute the suggested stories with the same effect.

Most of the recommended fiction involved early novels within a series. These early books were selected so that the reader could benefit from the detective's earliest description. However, this need not be the case, and you should make your accompanying literary selections based on preference, interest, and comfort level. Likewise, if you are worried about the number of required supplemental fiction, you could select one book to relate to concepts within multiple chapters. If you prefer to select only one author or series, I recommend Jacqueline Winspear's *Maisie Dobbs* series, as it applies most effectively to most, if not all, of the chapters in this textbook. However, multiple books in the *Maisie Dobbs* series likely need to be selected and read.

The most engaging and effective way of teaching a course that documents psychology's history using detective fiction would be to teach it as an interdisciplinary course,[2] co-taught by faculty from Psychology and English departments. Students would benefit from the additional literary analyses and critiques. A class (or reading group) could also focus on detective fiction's creative writing aspect, having participants create their own short stories or mini-mysteries. Following this chapter is a final story titled *Murder at the Manor*. The story was adapted from a murder-mystery event held during a student achievement day at Pine Manor College.[3] The course instructors and students developed the original storyline, and the students performed it at an end-of-year college achievement celebration. It serves as an example of an interdisciplinary activity or writing assignment. You can revise the plot or names to fit your community and its history. It also gives you a final opportunity to test your skills as a psychologist and detective.

Expanding on the theme of detective fiction and its potential use in teaching psychology, here are some additional points you could consider when structuring your course or group:

1. Interactive Classroom Activities: In addition to reading detective fiction, instructors and group leaders can organize interactive activities that involve role-playing, mock investigations, and problem-solving scenarios. Students or group members can take on the roles of detectives and apply psychological principles to solve fictional crimes. This hands-on approach can make the learning experience more engaging and memorable. Having students or group members read aloud and act out parts of novels or stories also can be an interactive and fun activity.

2. Psychological Profiling: Detective fiction often explores the art

of psychological profiling, where investigators analyze suspects' behavior to create a psychological profile. Instructors can use this concept to teach students about personality theories and how they relate to real-life scenarios, such as criminal investigations, or to understand the motives behind certain behaviors or criminals, such as serial killers.

3. Ethical Dilemmas in Crime Solving: Detective fiction frequently presents complex ethical dilemmas that investigators must navigate. These fictional dilemmas provide an excellent platform to discuss psychological ethics and how they apply in different situations, such as using deception to obtain information during an interrogation or the balance between individual rights and public safety.
4. Cultural and Social Context: Explore the cultural and social issues, different time periods, and settings in the stories you read. Instructors or group leaders can select stories highlighting societal norms, biases, and prejudices, prompting discussions about the role of psychology in understanding and addressing these issues.
5. Psychological Resilience: Many literary detectives face personal challenges and traumatic events while solving crimes. These fictional examples can be an opportunity to discuss the concepts of psychological resilience, coping strategies, and mental health in the face of adversity.
6. Group Discussions and Critical Analysis: Forming reading groups or class discussions around specific detective fiction books can encourage critical analysis of the psychological themes present in the stories. Students and readers can share their interpretations, insights, and connections to psychological theories.
7. Contemporary Detective Fiction: While classic detective fiction provides a valuable historical perspective, incorporating contemporary detective novels or series can showcase how the genre has evolved and adapted to modern societal changes and psychological insights.
8. Guest Speakers and Authors: Inviting authors of detective fiction or experts in criminal behavior or forensic psychology to speak to the class or group can offer unique perspectives and engage participants in discussions beyond the written text.

Detective fiction, with its compelling plots, intriguing mysteries, and fascinating characters, has long been an enjoyable and accessible genre of literature for readers of all ages. Its captivating nature and straightforward prose make it an easy-to-read choice that can be entertaining and thought-provoking. However, beyond its entertainment value, detective fiction can serve as a complementary tool for exploring psychological theories and concepts, delving into the human mind, and understanding the complexities of behavior.

Moreover, readers should consider the cultural significance of detective fiction. Beyond its literary merits, this genre impacts popular culture, shaping societal perceptions and initiating conversations about historical and social justice issues. Detective novels often delve into controversial or difficult topics, exposing injustices, highlighting societal inequalities, and offering insights into various aspects of human behavior that are not always apparent at first glance. Through these fictional (and therefore, somewhat safer) narratives, readers are encouraged to contemplate controversial societal issues, fostering empathy and promoting a greater understanding of diverse perspectives—all topics deeply rooted in psychology.

The ultimate goal of this book is to facilitate the active engagement of students and readers with the detective fiction genre, allowing them to immerse themselves in its enthralling and intellectually enlightening content. Ideally, a new group of lifelong learners will emerge, captivated by the genre's excitement and connection to psychological theory. This community of readers will undoubtedly contribute to the perpetuation of the genre, encouraging continued discussions, and ensuring that detective fiction remains a timeless and enduring aspect of literary and popular culture.

End-of-Chapter Mind Puzzlers

1. Assess the various psychological paradigms (structuralism, psychoanalytic, behaviorism, humanistic, cognitive, cultural, neuropsychological) and determine which best explains people's behavior and personality. Provide a comprehensive explanation of the chosen paradigm and illustrate how it explains people's behavior with relevant examples. Justify why you consider this paradigm to be the most suitable. Identify the detective(s) that best exhibit the characteristics of the chosen paradigm and analyze how this paradigm either assists or hinders their detective skills. Support your response with five examples (you may use multiple detectives in your answer).

2. Reflect on the characters or books you enjoyed reading the most during this course/group. Explain the reasons behind your preferences, considering factors such as plot, character

development, writing style, or any other aspects that contributed to your enjoyment. Similarly, discuss the character or book you did not enjoy reading or wished you could have skipped, and provide reasons for your feelings.
3. What book or series should have been included in this book or course/group discussion but was not? Explain your choice and explain how this book or series aligns with the psychological concepts discussed in this book.
4. Class/Group Activity: Use the one-act play that follows as a template to create your individualized version of "Murder at the [insert your school/group name here]." Adapt the names and descriptions to suit your school's or community's history or inside jokes. Present your modified play as a roughly 30-minute performance. At the end of the play, you may choose to explain the historical names or other information to your audience. Alternatively, if you prefer, you can use the following one-act play as it appears, making it an enjoyable experience for everyone involved.

Chapter Notes

1. How will psychology change in the next decade? Psychology is still evolving and expanding its areas of expertise and impact. The focus on biological influences and neuroscience will likely continue. Cultural differences and diversity, in particular, is critical not only for psychological research but for clinical work as well. The fluidity of gender will become an area of increased research over the next decade. More than a decade ago, Linstead and Brewis (2004) already recognized the lack of ethnographic research related to gender fluidity, and this gap has only increased since then. The recent COVID-19 pandemic will likely impact mental health research. Its long-term mental health and physical health issues need to be investigated. Mental health research should look into not only influences from culture and gender but on environmental features such as spacing, living conditions, climate change, and other community disparities (Rugel, 2019) that the pandemic brought to attention. Following individuals across their lifespan to monitor developmental changes will also be helpful. Late adulthood is the age group that will have the most growth in the coming decades. Concentrating on the "Miss Marples" of the world will help researchers identify the strengths and benefits that this age group can bring to its community. One area of psychology that is certain to grow is **industrial and organizational (I/O) psychology**, an applied area of psychology that focuses on using psychological theories and concepts in the workplace (Spector, 1996). I/O research and theorists can help shape the post-pandemic workplace by normalizing pandemic-created remote work. These researchers also can help clarify the intersection of work and family (O'Hara, 2020). Psychologists with leadership and crisis management expertise will become essential as the post-pandemic "new normal" takes shape. In the recent past and present, psychologists with these skills have increasingly assumed numerous academic administration positions (Abrams, 2021), and one can imagine the trend will continue. The need for leaders with emotional intelligence and leadership styles that stress **radical candor**, who can challenge others while also displaying empathy, care, and transparency, is essential to create a more effective work culture (Scott, 2017). Real-life and fictional detectives would benefit from the same approach.

2. If you are teaching an interdisciplinary course, you could require students to write a case study of Maisie Dobbs as depicted in one of the other books in the series that the class did not read together. The first novel, *Maisie Dobbs*, would be an excellent choice to read together as a class. The students, individually or in pairs/groups, would select one additional book to read over the course. At the end of the semester, they could complete the case study assignment below and present their findings (or a few key details) about the book to the class to illustrate how Maisie Dobbs changes and grows throughout the series. If the course is co-taught with an English faculty member, a fourth section related to literary analysis (that focuses on setting, narrative voice, imagery, and use of foils) could be added to this assignment.

Assignment Description: Write a five- to eight-page (double-spaced) case study of Maisie Dobbs, a female psychologist and investigator in the series by Jacqueline Winspear set in the 1920s–1940s around London (other series or novels can be substituted). A case study is an in-depth analysis of a single person. Read one additional book in the series from Books 2–18. Use these three headings in your paper. Address the following points and provide examples with chapter numbers to explain how you reached your conclusions.

- **Background/Contributing Events**: Which book did you read? What was the presenting problem or main plot of the story? What year does the story take place? Who are the main characters, and how do they influence Maisie's actions? What significant social, political, or historical events are portrayed in the book, and how do they contribute to the plot and character development? Can you provide specific examples with chapter and page numbers to support your answers? How does gender influence the main character's thoughts and behaviors? Explain your answers by providing several examples of passages with chapter and page numbers.

- **Diagnosis**: What type of detective is Maisie—soft-boiled or hard-boiled (give specific examples from the text to explain your choice)? What techniques does Maisie use to solve her cases? How does she use her psychological training during her investigations (provide specific examples from the text to explain your answer)? What psychological paradigm(s) best explains her techniques—structuralism, psychoanalytic, behavioral, humanistic, cognitive, or forensic? Please provide specific examples from the text and explain how the paradigm relates to her behavior.

- **Intervention/Therapy**: What other detectives from other stories or novels are similar to Maisie Dobbs? Provide examples from the text to support your answer. What is your final assessment of Maisie Dobbs as an investigator—is she an effective detective? How does Jacqueline Winspear portray Maisie Dobbs learning about herself while solving the mystery? What lessons or accomplishments do you think Maisie needs to pursue in future books to further develop as an investigator and a woman? Please share your suggestions to support Maisie's growth in the future.

3. Pine Manor College was established as a post-secondary school in 1911 by Helen Temple Cooke. Its mission was to educate women who might otherwise not have had the opportunity to attend college. Pine Manor became an independent junior college in 1969 and a four-year baccalaureate college in 1977. In 2014, the school became a co-educational college. However, its mission remained to "educate with purpose," serving a population of diverse and first-generation students. In 2020, due to financial strains from the Covid-19 pandemic, Pine Manor signed an agreement with Boston College, and following a two-year teach-out of its remaining students, the college permanently closed in 2022 (Pine Manor College, n.d.). The college may no longer exist as it once did, but its legacy and memories endure.

References

Abrams, Z. (2021, January). Psychologists are moving up in academia. *Monitor on Psychology, 52*(1). http://www.apa.org/monitor/2021/01/trends-psychologists-academia.

8. Putting It All Together 197

Kazan, E. (Director). (1947). *Gentleman's Agreement* [Film]. 20th Century Fox.

Linstead, A., & Brewis, J. (2004). Beyond boundaries: Towards fluidity in theorizing and practice [Editorial]. *Gender, Work and Organization, 11*(4), 355–362. https://doi.org/10.1111/j.1468-0432.2004.00237.x.

O'Hara, D. (2020, June 5). *Industrial and Organizational Psychologists Will Help Shape the Post-pandemic Workplace.* American Psychological Association. http://www.apa.org/members/content/post-pandemic-workplace.

Pine Manor College (n.d.). *Pine Manor College History.* Retrieved from https://www.pmc.edu/about/pmc-history/.

Rugel, E.J., Carpiano, R.M., Henderson, S.B., & Brauer, M. (2019). Exposure to natural space, sense of community belonging, and adverse mental health outcomes across an urban region. *Environmental Research, 171*, 365–377. https://doi.org/10.1016/j.envres.2019.01.034.

Scott, K. (2017). *Radical Candor: Be a Kick-ass Boss Without Losing Your Humanity.* St. Martin's Press.

Spector, P.E. (1996). *Industrial and Organizational Psychology: Research and Practice.* John Wiley & Sons.

Murder at the Manor: A Play in One Act

By
HANNAH BAKER-SIROTY *and*
DIANE MELLO-GOLDNER

Characters

TEMPERANCE COOK: President of the College. A born leader and an excellent fundraiser. She is working on accreditation approval to move the College from Junior-College status to a four-year college. She has a strict adherence to the rules and also a lack of transparency.

HELEN GAMIAN: The Head Librarian who spends most of her time trying to expand the library's collection. She has horrible allergies to just about all kinds of pollen and animals.

DR. ELIZA BULLICK: The College's Professor of English and Theater. She is a passionate Shakespeare scholar but is often impatient with students, feeling that they do not put as much effort into their academics as they should. She is up for tenure at the end of the next academic year. If she does not earn tenure, she will have to leave the College and look for another job.

DR. AGATHA MULLEN: A scholar of Classics. An excellent researcher who is helping move the College's special collections into the newly built Moncrief Library. President Cook brought Mullen to the College to move it into the future as a four-year research institution. Everyone thinks she would be a fantastic President one day.

DR. DAVID PRESCOTT: A scholar of Religion and Theology. A well-liked professor and colleague who is always ready to tell a story or drink some wine. He regularly wins the "Teacher of the Year" honor given by students. Prescott is dating Hermine Gold, whom he met in Rome last year.

DR. WILLOW SLEEPER: Professor of Psychology. She is a popular teacher with the students and is empathetic, a careful observer, understands human nature, a good listener, and discreet. She also becomes the number one suspect.

HERMINE GOLD: She is a visiting German scholar from Heidelberg University. She met David Prescott last summer in Rome and accepted a one-year visiting professorship at Pine Manor so that they could be together. She hopes to convince him to move to Germany when her year is over.

DR. MARIA POTTER: A long-serving and dedicated Professor of Biology and Chemistry. She has been increasingly frustrated by the President's refusal to increase funding for supplies and equipment or to repair some of the termite and mouse-damaged wood in her lab.

MARGARET SWAIN: The Assistant Librarian whose murdered body was found in the library area near the special collections.

GRACE CALDICOTT: She ran the Ellsworth Theater for the last 20 years but is missing. Many people think she left in a huff over some new rule changes the President has made. Recently, people noticed them arguing a lot.

NARRATOR

TIME
August 1, 1965
PLACE
Pine Manor Junior College, Chestnut Hill, Massachusetts.

ACT I
SCENE I

NARRATOR: "We find ourselves outside the faculty residences on the grounds of Pine Manor College. It is 4 a.m. Willow Sleeper, Psychology Professor, is unable to sleep. She decides to go for a walk on campus—usually, a quiet all-women's college located in Chestnut Hill, Massachusetts. Recently, Grace Caldicott has disappeared, which worries Sleeper. Fortunately, it is the summer, and no students are on campus, and only a few of the faculty and staff live on campus presently. But the date is August 1st, and the new term starts in only one month. So far, the President has been able to keep the news from the students and their families."

WILLOW SLEEPER: "Who on earth is awake at this hour?" (she says, looking into the lights coming from the library windows). "Perhaps Helen is up early, as well. Maybe we can have some coffee together?"

A Play in One Act

[SLEEPER enters the library only to discover Assistant Librarian MARGARET SWAIN motionless on the floor. SLEEPER starts shouting Margaret's name. The woman is clearly dead.]

WILLOW SLEEPER: "Margaret! Margaret! Maggie, are you awake?"

[The body was slumped over in a chair at the table. It looked like Margaret was writing down some notes, but there were no books nearby. SLEEPER notices a small teacup clenched in SWAIN'S fist and reaches for it. Sirens wail in the distance but are getting closer. She hears footsteps approaching and quickly slips the cup into her academic robe's pocket since she knew her fingerprints were on it.]

[ELIZA BULLICK enters the room] ELIZA BULLICK: "What are you doing, Willow! Was it you? What did you do to Maggie? Don't touch anything! The police are coming!"

WILLOW SLEEPER: "I just found Margaret here. I didn't do anything!"

ELIZA BULLICK: "I don't know why you are here right now, but the police should take over. You're just a psychology professor—stop pretending to be some sort of sleuth. Just because the students like you and think I'm too strict and boring doesn't mean you are the best at everything! The police will be here soon, I already called them. They are, after all, the ones with the appropriate credentials for this sort of thing. Fortunately, it was my turn to do the night rounds, and I saw the library lights were on."

NARRATOR: "Sleeper looks nervous as the police enter the campus. She thinks Margaret died within the last several hours because rigor mortis was already setting in. Sleeper knows things don't look good for her, so she decides to keep the teacup and will ask Professor Maria Potter (her friend who is Pine Manor's biology and chemistry professor, to run some tests on it later this morning). She needs to solve this case and clear her name." [The scene ends as the police enter the library.]

SCENE 2

[The faculty gather in the President's Dining room for breakfast at 7:00 a.m. The buffet meal is overflowing with the usual assortment of croissants, eggs, sausages, fruit, juice, and coffee, but no one appears hungry.]

PRESIDENT COOK: "I know we are all sad and nervous about what happened last night. I can assure you that the police are working hard to discover what happened, and I am sure things will be solved soon. Let's try to remain as calm as we can."

HERMINE GOLD: (nodding) "Yes, I agree, Madame President! It seems ever since I arrived earlier this summer, there have been strange things afoot. People 'disappearing' (she makes air quotes with her hands) and now dying. Is this what it is like in American colleges? If so, I might return to Germany before the year ends. Originally, I wanted to stay permanently in America, but maybe home is safer."

HELEN GAMIAN: "You think Grace Caldicott didn't run away?"
HERMINE GOLD: "Why would she? I barely knew the woman, but she didn't seem like the unreliable type."

[PRESIDENT COOK begins to fidget and her eyes tear up at the mention of CALDICOTT.]

AGATHA MULLEN: "I guess it is true that she seemed more upset lately than usual. I saw her crying near the pond the day before she disappeared. You know how much she enjoyed sitting by the pond and feeding the ducks and geese. Do you think she might have hurt herself?"
HELEN GAMIAN: "I knew Grace, and I don't think she would do anything to hurt herself. She would often come to talk to me when I was staying late at the library. She was helping me unpack the boxes of old books we found in storage. *Ahh choo*! Excuse me; the ragweed is really bothering my allergies this morning."
ELIZA BULLICK: "You and your allergies. Grace probably took off with her suitcases because she couldn't stand all of your sneezing! I, for one, think she's just gone because of allergy season!" [They all awkwardly laugh.]
WILLOW SLEEPER: "Helen, do you think Grace's disappearance has something to do with the books being moved into the library's new wing?"
HELEN GAMIAN: "I'm not sure, but how could my books be responsible for her disappearing?"
HERMINE GOLD (AGITATED): "Honestly, what's the big deal about books? There are too many in the library as it is." [HELEN GAMIAN gasps.]
ELIZA BULLICK: (getting up to grab some more breakfast) "Why doesn't someone ask Dr. Prescott and Fraulein Gold why they've been sneaking around the library. Maybe they saw something suspicious?"
DAVID PRESCOTT: "Oh, don't be ridiculous, Eliza! You already know why we were together. Hermine and I are going to be married." (He reaches for her hand, squeezes, then continues.) "We've been talking about me returning to Germany with her to teach at Heidelberg University. I didn't think any of you would like that kind of news. My research on the Heidelberg Catechism and Richard Rothe is much more popular in Europe. I could become famous there!"
AGATHA MULLEN: (with a look of contempt on her face, she looks towards BULLICK and says with hostility) "Leave David alone, Eliza. Why don't you worry about your writing? You know, a little birdy told me your tenure review hasn't been going so well. Maybe you're behind something…?"
ELIZA BULLICK: "How dare you, Agatha! I am a highly qualified scholar. I don't even know what you think you are accusing me of, but you should probably be looking at Willow. She's the one I found draped all over Margaret Swain's body this morning!" (She sits back down angrily.)
AGATHA MULLEN: "How do we know some maniac isn't entering our buildings at night and trying to kill all of us! Maybe Grace didn't run

away; maybe someone killed her too? You know the town has wanted this land for years. Maybe they hope they can buy it cheap if the College closes. I bet someone from the town is behind all of this. And what about the campus safety people? Maybe they are in on it too!"

PRESIDENT COOK: "Dr. Mullen, I think that's a bit far-fetched. Plus, you know the building doors are locked at 6:00 p.m. by campus safety. No one can enter the buildings without a key after hours."

[As she listens to the others, Professor SLEEPER considers all of the evidence.]

WILLOW SLEEPER: "I've already checked on the campus safety officers' alibis. They always go on their patrols in pairs, and everyone is accounted for last night. I do have a question for you, Dr. Bullick. You have spent a lot of time working in the Special Collections room lately. Did you ever notice any strange people in or around the building? And what is your new research about anyway?"

BULLICK: "No, I never saw anyone except for Pine Manor faculty in that building at night. Campus safety doesn't even come inside the building. I don't feel like I can talk about my new project in much detail, but you know I am a Shakespeare scholar." (She pauses and quickly changes the subject.) "President Cook, I'd hoped we could talk about this more privately, but I would like to talk to you about my tenure decision coming up. Things are getting too strange around here. How can I produce effective scholarship under all this stress?"

PRESIDENT COOK: (sighing) "Margaret Swain was only 38 years old. I don't know how she died, but I doubt she had a heart attack. If the parents find out, they won't be sending their daughters to us in a few weeks. I cannot be the person to cause this school to fail!"

[MARIA POTTER enters the room and goes over to SLEEPER. She hands her a piece of paper.]

MARIA POTTER: "Here's the analysis you asked me to run this morning, Willow. You were right to be suspicious about that teacup."

[WILLOW SLEEPER reads it and then looks up at everyone.]

WILLOW SLEEPER: "Thank you, Maria. The results from the chemical labs are in, and it seems that Margaret was poisoned with arsenic in her tea. And what is this other thing, fexofenadine HCL, what is that?"

MARIA POTTER: "It's an antihistamine found in many allergy tablets. There were only traces of the antihistamine in the teacup, so I couldn't tell if the arsenic was in the tea or the allergy tablet." (She goes over to the food table and grabs a croissant.)

PRESIDENT COOK: (rising from the table and walking over to Sleeper) "What, how could that happen? Arsenic? That's impossible? And how could it get into an allergy pill? You know what?!! I saw Margaret having a conversation with Helen in the library the night she was murdered. Helen, did you give her one of your allergy pills by any chance?"

HELEN GAMIAN: "I didn't! I was running low. My allergies are so severe this time of year, I even have asthma now from them. Margaret only had some slight congestion because of the dust in the library. I'm sure other people have allergies too. It's not just me. Margaret and I worked together and would frequently work late at night. Yesterday we talked about how the College has some interesting folios we didn't even realize were in the collection. And President Cook, I think the mice are now coming into the library. What if they damage my books!"

AGATHA MULLEN: "You know, Grace also asked me about valuable classics folios as well. Why was she so interested in folios all of a sudden? I don't remember her being interested in them before."

HELEN GAMIAN: (excitedly) "I don't know, but now that I think of it, I saw Dr. Bullick and Dr. Mullen in the library a few hours before Margaret's murder. It looked like they were arguing!"

ELIZA BULLICK: (angrily) "Agatha was trying to take out a reference book I needed, and I might have lost my temper with her. My research is vital to me, and I admit the stress has been getting to me recently. I apologized for yelling at her. Why don't you ask *Fraulein* Gold where she was?" (BULLICK emphasizes the word FRAULEIN to indicate GOLD is from elsewhere.) "She's always sneaking around the library and faculty offices."

HERMINE GOLD: "I was not sneaking around. I was merely curious about how things are done here in America. I will be sure never to bother you again, Dr. Bullick. If someone killed Margaret Swain with arsenic, why aren't you interrogating the President? She keeps a supply of arsenic in her office. I have seen it for myself."

PRESIDENT COOK: "That is true! I have some arsenic in my office, but it is a common remedy to get rid of mice and rats, and you know we have a huge mouse problem in the Dane science building. The grounds and maintenance crew keep arsenic in the facilities barn, and almost anyone on the staff could have easy access to it."

AGATHA MULLEN: (loudly) "Yes, but as you all know, the grounds and maintenance staff are all on vacation this week. They couldn't have put arsenic in anyone's tea or pills, so someone else did, and it's beginning to look like it was one of us!"

WILLOW SLEEPER: "Helen, are there any valuable folios in the library's special collection?"

HELEN GAMIAN: "I am not the special collections librarian and haven't looked at any of the books in years. But we did bring several boxes of additional books to add to the collection because the new Moncrief Library is much larger. The special collections room is twice the size we had before. I can't wait to buy more books for my library!"

DAVID PRESCOTT: "Now I remember that Grace Caldicott was researching Shakespeare shortly before she disappeared too." (He glances over at BULLICK.) "I just thought she was interested in performing one of his plays in the theatre next year. Her disappearance could be connected to Margaret's death, don't you think, Willow?"

WILLOW SLEEPER: "That's a good point, David. Selling a Shakespeare folio could bring in a lot of needed cash to this College and could help with the deferred maintenance."

[Everyone looks at PRESIDENT COOK.]

PRESIDENT COOK: "I did not kill anyone! I didn't mention this at first, but I was with Margaret last night before she was (pauses) killed. We were in my private rooms in the administration building. We talked, and then she left, and I went right to sleep. I felt terrible about Grace's disappearance. I told Margaret how worried I've been, but then we got distracted by the stupid geese honking at someone outside the building entrance. She decided to head back to the library when she left, going out the side door to avoid the geese. She left about 9:00 p.m., and I didn't leave the building until I heard the police sirens."

WILLOW SLEEPER: "I think we need to review a few things and check out the special collections room. Let's meet in the Moncrief Library in half an hour."

[As Helen GAMIAN was about to leave, SLEEPER pulls her over to talk privately.]

WILLOW SLEEPER: "Helen, can you find the inventory of all the special collections books and bring it to our meeting?"

HELEN GAMIAN: "I'll go get it right now. I will also find that unknown folio everyone has been talking about."

[GAMIAN leaves the dining room towards the library. SLEEPER looks up and smiles as she gets an idea. She leaves the dining room in the opposite direction, towards the west side of the campus.]

SCENE 3

[WILLOW SLEEPER is reviewing her notes in the Moncrief Library when the others start to arrive. As the others arrive, they sit on the couches and chairs of the new and spacious special collections room. PRESIDENT COOK, MARIA POTTER, and HELEN GAMIAN sit on two couches near the fireplace. ELIZA BULLICK and AGATHA MULLEN sit on separate chairs near the door. HERMINE GOLD sits on a chair near the window, with DAVID PRESCOTT seated on the chair's arm holding her hand.]

WILLOW SLEEPER: "I have a few additional questions for some of you that could help us solve our mystery."

ELIZA BULLICK: "Are you playing the detective again? You're only a psychology professor, you're not even a scientist let alone a detective! President Cook, why do we have to always listen to her? She was found WITH the body; the police likely consider Willow their number one suspect."

PRESIDENT COOK: "I don't think anyone is accusing Willow of murdering Margaret. Why don't we listen to what she has found so far?"

WILLOW SLEEPER: (ignoring Bullick and smiling at Cook before turning to Gamian) "Helen, before you said you didn't give Margaret an allergy pill because you were running low. But I remember walking over with you to the pharmacy a couple of weeks ago so you could refill your prescription. It was for a two-month supply. What happened?"

HELEN GAMIAN: (relaxing) "You're right, but I misplaced that bottle of allergy pills. I only had a few remaining from another bottle. I know I had the new bottle on my desk here in the library, but I can't find them. Do you think the killer took the bottle?"

WILLOW SLEEPER: "Interesting, Helen. Could be! In fact, it might be likely. Did you bring the special collections list and the folio with you?"

HELEN GAMIAN: "Yes. I have the list, and I noticed we do have something titled 'Early 17th century folio, author unknown.' Maybe it's actually a long-lost Shakespeare folio! But I couldn't find it anywhere in the special collections room. It's missing! It must have something to do with Maggie's death."

DAVID PRESCOTT: "That seems very suspicious to me."

HELEN GAMIAN: "Yes. We have to find Maggie's killer. We worked in the library for years, and she was the only person who shared my love of books. If you want my advice, I would start with Dr. Bullick. She's certainly been acting very strangely all summer long."

ELIZA BULLICK: "Helen, no one ever wants your advice. And if you want a suspect, why don't you ask Agatha why she was arguing with Margaret a few days ago?"

[Police sirens again are heard in the distance, getting louder as they approach the campus.]

AGATHA MULLEN: (looking directly at the group calmly) "We weren't arguing with each other; we were angry about you, Eliza, and your new research. You haven't been the same since you started working on this new project. You won't let anyone near your books or writing. Margaret said she saw you spending a lot of time in the special collections room with the door closed and coming out with ink-stained hands. I was going to complain to the President last night, but those stupid, aggressive nesting geese blocked me from entering the building."

DAVID PRESCOTT: "So, you were the one to make the geese honk last night. If you were near the administration building, you could have taken the arsenic from the President's office!"

AGATHA MULLEN: (excitedly) "I never went into the building. Why would I kill Margaret? She was a friend!"

DAVID PRESCOTT: "Maybe you were interested in stealing that missing folio—you are a classics expert after all."

AGATHA MULLEN: (shouting) "I did not steal anything!"

HERMINE GOLD: "I am new to this College, but David has told me a lot about you all, and I am only here for a year anyway. He told me he saw President Cook and that missing woman arguing quite a lot."

ELIZA BULLICK: "Yes, it could be the President. President Cook is always talking about money and raising the stakes to turn us into a four-year college. Selling a long-lost Shakespeare folio would be worth at least a million dollars, if not more. And if there was a real Shakespeare folio, don't you think I would be screaming from the roof-tops about it?"

PRESIDENT COOK: (shouting at the room, unable to restrain herself) "I told you I did not kill anyone! I don't need to steal and sell a manuscript to bring money into this College. I am an excellent fundraiser. I can get the money that way! I did not do anything to Grace. I could never hurt her. She and I, well, please promise to keep this between us." (She is very agitated.) "Grace and I have secretly been together for 15 years. We kept it quiet since we didn't know how others would react to our relationship. I know the theater is on hiatus for the summer, but she was refurbishing some of the seat cushions to get the theatre ready for the new academic year and was planning to be here all summer. She never even told me she was leaving." (She takes a deep breath.) "If anything has happened to her, I don't know what I will do!" (She begins sobbing uncontrollably.) "Please don't say anything about us. I love this college, and I love my job. I don't want to lose it over who I love!"

NARRATOR: "Sleeper sits and reviews her notes. She tries to fit the pieces together and connect the information she wrote down in her notebook. She starts to draw lines between some of the evidence to show how the clues and evidence fit together. While she works it out, does anyone in the audience want to guess whodunit????"

[Pause for guesses from the audience. The characters can improvise and interact with the audience if someone accuses them of being the killer.]

WILLOW SLEEPER: "I think I've got it now!" (She stands up before everyone.) "I know we all are worried and want things cleared up so we can begin our new academic year on time. I was confused by some of the clues, but I think it all comes down to the missing folio."

[Sounds of surprise come from the assembled faculty and staff.]

WILLOW SLEEPER: "Selling the folio could get someone a lot of money. Enough money to keep this College going for several more years."

PRESIDENT COOK: "How many times do I have to tell you I haven't done anything wrong. I would never taint my legacy to this College or hurt Grace!"

WILLOW SLEEPER: "Yes, I know that. I also know you like people to follow the rules, including yourself. You would never steal College property and try to sell it to raise money. But I think another person would be willing to forge a manuscript to raise money, get the chance to leave this College, and perhaps teaching in general. Isn't that right… Dr. Bullick?"

[Everyone turns to ELIZA BULLICK, who remains calm and seated.]

ELIZA BULLICK: "Preposterous, how do you think I committed these crimes? I work on my writing all day long."

WILLOW SLEEPER: "You did a good job trying to hide what you were doing, but you were a bit careless. People were getting suspicious about why you were spending so much time in the special collections room. Plus, you know there is a very good chance you won't be getting tenure next May and will have to find another job. Grace must have caught you forging the folio, and you killed her, probably confronting her at the pond. Before I came to the Moncrief Library, I quickly went over to the pond on campus because Grace spent a lot of her free time there. Because it's been so hot lately, the water level has gone down, and I could see two suitcases in the pond and something underneath them. Unfortunately, I think we will find Grace's body in the pond. I alerted the police to search there. I can hear them approaching the campus as we speak."

[Gasps of horrors came from everyone in the room except for BULLICK. PRESIDENT COOK begins sobbing again.]

HELEN GAMIAN: "I was so hopeful she just left because she and President Cook argued. Of course, we all knew you two were in a relationship; it was fairly obvious. Oh! This is terrible."

ELIZA BULLICK: "How do you know I killed her? She could have committed suicide."

WILLOW SLEEPER: "And took her suitcases with her? That seems unlikely. After Grace disappeared, Margaret became suspicious. She knew Grace started showing an interest in the new books, so she did her own investigating. Margaret knew you were interested in them as well. You knew you had to kill her, as it was only a matter of time before she put everything together. We all know you would love to write full-time and leave the teaching profession altogether. Last night you went to the library to finish your forgery and found Margaret in the special collections room. Margaret was very allergic to dust, and you probably offered her an allergy pill. One that you had already filled with arsenic. You must have panicked and taken the original folio so you could finish your forgery in your room before leaving the forged copy in the library. Why have you been carrying your briefcase around with you all day, Eliza? Can I look inside it?"

ELIZA BULLICK: (looking smug) "Feel free, look inside." (BULLICK gives SLEEPER the briefcase.)

[Sleeper opens it, but the compartment is empty except for a few papers.]

WILLOW SLEEPER: "The bag is empty, but it feels a lot heavier than it should if only a few papers are in it."

MARIA POTTER: "Let me take a look at it." (Potter grabs the bag and turns it upside down. She pulls a hairpin out of her hair bun and slips it into a hole in the briefcase's bottom. A compartment slides open inside the bag, and Potter pulls out two copies of a manuscript showing them to everyone.) "Looks like we found the original and forged copies!"

HELEN GAMIAN: (looking at the two copies) "This could be an original

Shakespeare folio! What a valuable addition for me, I mean, the College's library."

[BULLICK tries to grab her bag and run out of the room, but AGATHA MULLEN trips her as she is getting up. MULLEN takes the handbag, and DAVID PRESCOTT stands in front of the library door, preventing BULLICK from leaving. Defeated, BULLICK returns to her seat. PRESIDENT COOK lunges at BULLICK.]

PRESIDENT COOK: "How could you have killed Grace!" (POTTER and SLEEPER hold her back as the police enter the room and take away BULLICK in handcuffs.)

HERMINE GOLD: "Well done, Professor Sleeper. But why did you suspect Dr. Bullick?"

WILLOW SLEEPER: "I suspected her from the start. Eliza had spent a lot of time reviewing the manuscript and knew exactly how valuable it was. Plus, her comment about Grace taking suitcases was suspicious. I do know she hasn't left the campus all summer, so I thought the pond might be a good place to search for Grace or her suitcases. I'm very sorry for your loss President Cook."

PRESIDENT COOK: (making a slight effort to dry her tear-stained face) "I can't thank you enough, Willow, for all that you've done. I can let Maggie's family know what happened to her and know that Grace did not leave me willingly. The school can open on time in a few weeks. What can I do for you in return?"

WILLOW SLEEPER: (thinking) "Well, Maria was a big help in my investigation. You could increase her departmental funding and repair some of the termite and mouse-damaged wood in her lab. You might also want to solve the mouse problem in the building. Maybe we should try something besides arsenic."

PRESIDENT COOK: "Ha! Done! The increased funding will benefit the students too, and the students' well-being is always my number one priority. And I agree, no more arsenic on this campus. Maybe we just need to add some cats who are good mousers to all the buildings on campus. Maybe some dogs will help control the geese too. I'm sure the students will love to have pets on campus!"

HELEN GAMIAN: (her voice panicked) "What? But you know I'm very allergic to cats and dogs!" (Everyone starts laughing, including PRESIDENT COOK.)

NARRATOR: "The faculty and staff let out a sigh of relief and are glad that Professor Sleeper solved the case. Pine Manor College will continue to serve promising women for many more years."

CURTAIN

Author's Notes

The characters' names are based on Pine Manor faculty and staff who worked at the College when the campus was still in Wellesley or later when the campus moved to Chestnut Hill. Any characteristics or behaviors of the staff and faculty in this play are pure fiction and do not represent the actual Pine Manor staff or faculty in any way.

- Helen Temple Cooke was Pine Manor College's founder and was a pioneer dedicated to preparing women for successful lives and careers. Pine Manor College was initially established as a post-secondary division of Dana Hall School in Wellesley in 1911. In 1930, the College received a charter as an independent junior college and in 1959 could confer the degrees of Associate in Arts and Associate in Science. In 1965, Pine Manor Junior College moved from the Wellesley campus to Chestnut Hill. In 1977, the College expanded its mission and could begin conferring Bachelor of Arts degrees in the humanities and social sciences, and officially changed its name to Pine Manor College.
- Helen Paragamian was a librarian in 1965.
- Elizabeth Fullick was a teacher of art history, drawing, and painting in 1911.
- Alice Allen was a Greek and Latin scholar in 1911.
- Graham Prescott Teller was an Art Professor in 1965. There were no male teachers or staff in 1911.
- W.W. Sleeper was a Philosophy scholar in 1911. Margaret Sleeper's character was inspired by the novel *Maisie Dobbs* by Jacqueline Winspear (2003). Maisie Dobbs displays many of the characteristics of a good psychologist and detective throughout the series.
- Fraulein Hermine Heller was a German teacher in 1911.
- Marie Warren Potter also was a former President of Pine Manor from 1930 to 1952.

- Marjorie Swain Van Damme was the Assistant Librarian in 1965. [Margaret Swain was poisoned in an allergy pill because that is similar to the cause of death in one of the novels discussed in this book.]
- Mary Grace Caldwell was a Latin scholar in 1911.

Sources: https://www.pmc.edu/about/pmc-history/; and https://www.digitalcommonwealth.org/collections/commonwealth:vd66x090z

End-of-Book Assessment

Test your understanding of psychological concepts and detective fiction discussed in this text. The correct answers appear in the *Notes* section on page 217.[1]

1. True or False: Psychology is defined as the behavioral study of dreams and mental illnesses.

   True (T)   False (F)

2. A psychologist who researches the effects of self-esteem on college students asks students in her Introduction to Psychology class to fill out various surveys on self-esteem and other personality characteristics. This type of research is:

   a. basic   b. scientific   c. applied

3. What type of research is conducted when a sport psychologist studies the effects of self-esteem and goal-setting on college athletes, involving surveys and individual goal-setting with the teams?

   a. applied   b. basic   c. personality

4. In the scientific method, what is the second step where you form an educated guess about the research outcome?

   a. analysis   b. hypothesis   c. theory

5. True or False: Gothic novels often explore psychological issues, especially madness and mental illness, which contributes to the horror in the books.

   True (T)   False (F)

6. The detective in the short story "The Murders in the Rue Morgue" is named _____.

7. Who is considered the founder of psychology? _____.

Author's Notes 213

8. True or False: The first formal laboratory for psychological research was established at the University of Leipzig in Germany in the year 1897.

    True (T)   False (F)

9. True or False: Structuralism aimed to record thoughts and sensations and analyze them in the same way a chemist analyzes chemical compounds, with the goal of uncovering their underlying structure.

    True (T)   False (F)

10. True or False: Introspection involves similar steps as the scientific method.

    True (T)   False (F)

11. Sherlock Holmes often uses analytical and logical thinking to solve his cases. What is the type of logical thought where a conclusion is formed based on two presented truths?

    a. anagram   b. deductive reasoning   c. syllogism
    d. elementary thinking

12. Sherlock Holmes displays thinking beyond deduction that involves active observation and awareness. What did Ellen Langer call this type of thinking?

    a. syllogistic thinking   b. formal operational thinking
    c. mindfulness

13. Freud and his mentor, Jean Charcot, treated primarily female patients with problems that had no natural physical explanations. Freud referred to this as:

    a. free association   b. psychoanalysis   c. hypnosis
    d. hysteria

14. True or False: Freud believed that all human behavior is unconsciously motivated.

    True (T)   False (F)

15. True or False: According to Freud, the most significant part of our unconscious is the id.

    True (T)   False (F)

16. When you forget an embarrassing thing you said at work, you are likely using which defense mechanism?

    a. rationalization   b. projection   c. repression   d. denial

17. A man is angry with his wife, but instead of confronting her, takes out his anger by kicking his dog. This exemplifies:

   a. regression   b. reaction formation   c. repression
   d. displacement

18. True or False: In dreams, the hidden, symbolic meaning of objects and behaviors is referred to as the latent content.

   True (T)   False (F)

19. True or False: The collective unconscious is a part of Carl Jung's personality theory that has no parallel in Freud's theory.

   True (T)   False (F)

20. According to Jung, the archetype related to our unacceptable and hidden thoughts and feelings is the:

   a. self   b. anima   c. shadow   d. persona

21. True or False: Horney named a child's repressed sense of isolation, insecurity, and helplessness in a potentially hostile world basic anxiety.

   True (T)   False (F)

22. During the Covid-19 pandemic, Susan, aged 10, is anxious about socializing with the children in her classroom. She acts so stressed around them in class that they do not want to play with her anymore. Which neurotic trend does Samantha display, according to Horney?

   a. moving away from people   b. moving toward people
   c. moving against people

23. Older adults who feel satisfied when reflecting on their lives demonstrate what Erikson called a sense of:

   a. generativity   b. identity   c. attachment   d. ego integrity

24. True or False: Erikson's stage of identity vs. role confusion occurs during young adulthood.

   True (T)   False (F)

25. True or False: According to Erikson, you must make these three choices by the age of 18 to achieve identity: choice of values, choice of career, and choice of sexuality.

   True (T)   False (F)

26. You are unsure of what to major in at college, so you sign up for three different introductory classes and decide to do a few exploratory

internships before declaring your major. According to Erikson, you are using this process to define your identity.

    a. introspection b. fidelity c. role experimentation
    d. autonomy

27. Soft-boiled detective fiction often contains which of the following characteristics?

    a. the characters are frequently from the middle and upper classes b. the detective is often dismissed by the police c. there is little explicit violence d. the clues are readily available to the reader but difficult to fathom because of red herrings and false leads e. all of the above

28. True or False: In soft-boiled detective fiction, the plot is puzzle-oriented and operates within the rules of fair play between the author and the reader, and is often referred to as a whodunit.

    True (T)   False (F)

29. True or False: Soft-boiled detective fiction is most similar to the behaviorist approach to psychology.

    True (T)   False (F)

30. True or False: Hard-boiled detective fiction relates to the behaviorist approach to psychology because the stories often portray people influenced by their situation and group affiliations.

    True (T)   False (F)

31. Who is often considered the most influential psychologist of all time and who developed operant conditioning, where behavior is dependent on consequences or reinforcement?

    a. Sigmund Freud b. John Watson c. B.F. Skinner
    d. Philip Zimbardo

32. Which of Agatha Christie's detectives lives in St. Mary Mead and is a great observer of human nature.

    a. Miss Jane Marple b. Mr. Parker Pyne c. Hercule Poirot

33. Which of Christie's detectives uses their little grey cells to solve crimes.

    a. Mr. Parker Pyne b. Mr. Harley Quin c. Miss Jane Marple
    d. Hercule Poirot

34. True or False: The two leading psychologists associated with the humanistic movement were Sigmund Freud and Erik Erikson.

    True (T)   False (F)

35. True or False: The humanistic model of mental illness states that unconscious conflicts cause abnormal behavior.

  True (T)   False (F)

36. Tom was in a plane wreck and was lost in a heavily wooded area for two weeks. Although he was not hurt badly, he was hungry, thirsty and tired. According to Abraham Maslow's hierarchy of needs, Joe was motivated by which needs?

  a. love   b. safety   c. physiological   d. belonging

37. Which of the following correctly represents Maslow's hierarchy of needs (from the bottom to the top)?

  a. safety, love, esteem, actualizing, interactional   b. physiological, safety, love, esteem, actualizing   c. physiological, safety, esteem, love, actualizing   d. actualizing, love, esteem, physiological, safety

38. Abraham Maslow suggested that those who fulfill their potential have satisfied this need:

  a. self-actualization   b. identification   c. esteem   d. reciprocal determinism

39. True or False: Compared to male hard-boiled detectives, the female hard-boiled detective is only violent herself when necessary.

  True (T)   False (F)

40. The branch of psychology that focuses on people's thoughts and how we process information as causes of behavior and personality is called:

  a. cognitive psychology   b. behaviorism   c. humanistic psychology   d. psychoanalysis

41. True or False: George Kelly's Personal Construct theory states that irrational thoughts undermine our behavior and prevent us from reaching our potential.

  True (T)   False (F)

42. A mental picture or mental representation we have about a person, event, or object is a:

  a. schema   b. personal construct   c. range of convenience

43. True or False: The self-concept is defined as a personal schematic system that organizes and guides our processing of self-relevant information.

  True (T)   False (F)

44. The self-concept guides the behaviors a person chooses to enact while also mediating and regulating this behavior—it is, therefore, active, forceful, and capable of change, which is also referred to as:

    a. dynamic   b. irrational   c. permeable   d. self-actualizing

45. True or False: The main character in Sue Grafton's alphabet series is named Sharon McCone.

    True (T)   False (F)

46. True or False: Bullet matching is a type of forensic evidence technique.

    True (T)   False (F)

47. In the 1930s, detective novels began to imagine a new kind of sleuthing technique or technology that could distinguish an ordinary person's moments of deception. In other words, these novels introduced:

    a. geographical mapping   b. criminal profiling   c. lie detection

48. True or False: Because of new knowledge and better technology, psychologists now increasingly focus on links to the brain as potential causes of mental illness and abnormal (and normal) behavior.

    True (T)   False (F)

49. True or False: Patricia Cornwell pays careful attention to the scientific method and scientific instruments in her books and often goes into many details when describing lab equipment.

    True (T)   False (F)

50. True or False: If a killer takes a pair of underwear from the dresser drawer of a woman after killing her, that is their MO.

    True (T)   False (F)

Key Terms and People
- **industrial and organizational (I/O) psychology:** an applied area of psychology that focuses on the use of psychological theories and concepts in the workplace
- **radical candor:** a leadership style that stresses challenging others while also displaying empathy, care, and transparency

CHAPTER NOTES

1. Quiz answers: 1 F; 2 a; 3 a; 4 b; 5 T; 6 Dupin; 7 Wilhelm Wundt; 8 F; 9 T; 10 T; 11 c; 12 c; 13 d; 14 T; 15 T; 16 c; 17 d; 18 T; 19 T; 20 c; 21 T; 22 a; 23 d; 24 F; 25 T; 26 c; 27 e; 28 T; 29 F; 30 T; 31 c; 32 a; 33 d; 34 F; 35 T; 36 c; 37 b; 38 a; 39 T; 40 a; 41 F; 42 a; 43 T; 44 a; 45 F; 46 T; 47 c; 48 T; 49 T; 50 F.

Index

A Is for Alibi (Grafton) 118–119, 122
A Man Lay Dead (Marsh) 13, 41
accommodation 98–99, 124
The Achievements of Luther Trant (Balmer & MacHarg) 6–7
actor-observer effect 112, 126
actual self 84, 93–94, 113
adaptation 98, 101, 122, 124
Adler, Alfred 51, 76, 78
aha moment 40, 120
Allport, F.H. 160
American Psychological Association (APA) 23, 76, 82, 85, 94, 161, 171
Anaya, Rudolfo 154–156
Angel Dance (Beal) 116
anima/animus 34, 49
applied research 6–7, 22
archetypes 33–34, 36, 45, 48–49
Aristotle 5, 10–11, 21, 23
Armand Gamache series (Penny) 187
Ask the Cards a Question (Muller) 117
assimilation 98–99, 124, 139, 157, 159
Austen, Jane 20, 23
autobiographical memory 175, 186
autopsy 180, 186
availability heuristic 113, 123, 126

Bandura, Albert 60, 65–66, 68, 71–72
Bartlett, Frederic 130
basic anxiety 35, 45, 49, 69
basic hostility 35, 49
basic research 6, 20, 22
HMS *Beagle* 166
Beal, M.F. 116
Beatrice Bradley 42
Beckham, Dr. Albert Sidney 160
Beckham, Dr. Ruth Winifred Howard 160
Behavioral Science Unit (BSU) 187
behaviorism 54–68, 71, 75–76, 91, 97, 168, 170, 194
Benson, Mildred Wirt 50, 68
big reveal 40, 50, 113, 120, 150
Biggers, Earl Derr 149
Billy Beale 19, 120–121, 151
Birds of a Feather (Winspear) 121

The Black Lives Movement 155
Blanche on the Lam (Neely) 144–145, 156
Blanche White 144–148, 156–157
Bobo doll experiment 65, 72
body farm 179, 186
The Body Farm (Cornwell) 179, 182–183
Bones 178
Botswana 146–147, 156, 161
The Body in the Library (Christie) 41, 43–44, 46
Boston University 169
Bowen, Rhys 89–90
Buhler, Charlotte 77–78, 92

Calkins, Mary Whiton 27–28
Canady, Dr. Herman George 160
case study 7, 21, 94, 184, 196
Castle 89
The Castle of Otranto 23
The Cater Street Hangman (Perry) 88
C. Auguste Dupin 11, 21, 23, 50, 67, 177
The Celebrated Cases of Judge Dee: An Authentic Eighteenth-Century Chinese Detective Novel (van Gulik) 150
Chandler, Raymond 67–68
Charcot, Jean 28–29, 31, 50
Charlie Chan 149
Charlotte and Thomas Pitt series (Perry) 88, 90–91
Chazin, Suzanne 152–154, 156
Chomsky, Noam 97, 106
Christie, Agatha 10, 12, 39–41, 44, 50, 66, 86, 94–95, 118, 143–144, 150, 181
Claire Washburn 180
Clark, Kenneth and Mamie Phipps 28, 161
classical conditioning 55–59, 64, 70
client-centered therapy 84–85, 93
Cocaine Blues (Greenwood) 88
cognitive miser 112–113, 123, 126
cognitive psychology 60, 97, 111, 115–122, 124, 168
collective self 136
collective unconscious 33–35, 48–49
Collins, Wilkie 50

Index

complex(es) 33, 40, 45, 48, 51
computerized axial tomography (CAT scan) 168, 184
Conan Doyle, Sir Arthur 11–12, 20–21, 32, 39, 44–45, 50–51, 73, 95
concrete operational stage 100, 124
conditioned response (CR) 55–59, 70
conditioned stimulus (CS) 55–57, 59, 70
conditioned taste aversion 57, 70
conditions of worth 85, 91, 93
confirmation bias 113, 126
confounding variables 12, 23, 32
conscious(ness) 26–27, 29, 33, 47–48, 50, 54, 57, 67, 77, 82–83, 106, 176, 186
conscious ego 33, 48
The Consequences of Fear (Winspear) 121–122, 178
conservation 100–101, 124
control group 8–9, 22–23, 66, 72
Cooley 130
Cordelia Gray (James, P.D.) 89
Cormoran Strike series (Galbraith) 69, 89
Cornwell, Patricia 179–180, 183–183
corpse buffet 179
correct rejection 172–173, 185
correlational study 8, 21–22
Cortez, Sarah 152
cozy mystery 39, 43
Criminal Minds 171, 187
criminal (offender) profiling 171, 173, 177–179, 185, 187, 192–193
Cross, Amanda 40, 89–90
cross-cultural psychology 130–135, 142–156, 158
cross-situational consistency 108, 125
Crossing Jordan 178
Crossroads Between Culture and Mind (Jahoda) 160
cultural awareness 134, 158–159
cultural beliefs 131, 158
cultural display rules 142, 160
cultural intelligence 134, 156, 158
cultural psychology 130–135, 158
culture 3, 35, 81, 103–104, 130–142, 145–160, 195
culture shock 131–132, 158
curanderas 154
Curtain (Christie) 87

"Daisy Bell" (Mitchell) 42, 44
Daly, Carroll John 66
A Dangerous Place (Winspear) 89
defense mechanisms 30, 35, 37, 45, 47, 49
defensive pessimism 111–112, 123, 126
deficiency needs 80, 92
Dead Time (Taylor Bland) 122, 148, 156
Death Du Jour (Reichs) 180–181
Death on the Nile (Christie) 13, 44
Déjà Dead (Reichs) 179–180, 182
denial 30, 47

dependent variable 8, 22
Detective Shan 9, 152
discrimination 56, 64, 70, 145, 153, 155, 158
disorganized self 84, 91
disorganized serial killer 174, 183, 185
displacement 30, 47
Dr. Jekyll and Mr. Hyde (Stevenson) 33, 51
Doctor Thorndyke (Freeman) 11, 13, 177, 187
Dookhan, Annie 172
Douglas, John E. 187
dream analysis 31–32, 48
dynamic self-concept 115, 126

Ebbinghaus 97
Edwin of the Iron Shoes (Muller) 116–117
ego 29–30, 37, 47, 49, 51, 77, 82, 133
The Ego and the Mechanisms of Defense (Freud, Anna) 37
ego psychology/psychologists 37, 49, 51
egocentrism 99, 124
Ekman, Paul 141–143, 159
Electra Complex 51
Elegy for Eddie (Winspear) 121
Elements of Folk Psychology (Wundt & Schaub) 132
Elements of Psychophysics (Fechner) 25
emic 133–134, 158
encoding 176, 186
Erikson, Erik 32, 37–38, 45, 49, 77, 138–139
esteem needs 79, 87, 89, 92
ethnic identity 138–139, 157, 159
ethnocentrism 131, 158
ethnographic research 133, 158, 195
etic 133–134, 158
exclusion 172, 184
experiment 6, 8–9, 12, 21–23, 25, 32, 50, 55, 57–62, 65–66, 71–72, 130, 132
experimental group 8, 22
extinction 56, 64, 70
The Eye of Jade (Liang) 150–151, 156

facial feedback theory 141, 160
false alarm 172–173, 185
false beliefs 100, 126
"The False Burton Combs" (Daly) 66
false self 145
Farewell, My Lovely (Chandler) 67, 69
Fechner, Gustav 25, 50, 97
femme fatale 67, 72, 118
fingerprint 13, 171, 177, 187
1st to Die (Patterson) 180, 182
fixed interval 64, 72
fixed ratio 64, 71
flashbulb memory 175, 186
focus of convenience 106, 123, 125
foil 91, 93–95, 150, 196
The Fore 142
forensic anthropology 180, 186
forensic entomology 178–179, 186
forensic odontology 180, 186

Index 221

forensic psychology 6, 18, 22, 27, 171–182, 184, 193
formal operational stage 61, 73, 100–101, 125
free association 31–32, 39, 48
Freeman, R. Austin 11, 13, 177, 187
Freud, Anna 37
Freud, Sigmund 7–8, 26, 28–35, 37–48, 50–51
Fromm, Erich 51, 76
frontal lobe 167, 184
Fu Manchu 149
Fuller, Dr. Solomon Carter 160
fully functioning person 83–86, 88–89, 93
functional magnetic resonance imaging (fMRI) 169, 184
functionalism 26–28, 47, 75
fundamental attribution error 112, 123, 126, 137

Galbraith, Robert 69, 89
Gaudy Night (Sayers) 44–45, 87, 89–90, 94
generalization 56, 59, 64, 70
genome 170, 184, 187
Gerritsen, Tess 180–182
Gestalt psychology 60, 72–73, 76
Gilligan, Carol 104–105, 123, 125
Glaspell, Susan 116, 122
Golden Age of Detection 1, 13, 39–43, 51
Gothic novels 11, 20, 23, 42, 51, 117, 191
Grace Makutsi 147, 161
Grafton, Sue 117–120, 122–123
Great Mother 34, 49
Greenwood, Kerry 88, 90
growth need 80, 92

Hall, G. Stanley 28, 160
Hammett, Dashiell 67–68
hard-boiled detective fiction 66–69, 72, 115–123, 148, 182, 196
The Hardy Boys (Dixon) 68–70, 90–91
Harlow, Harry 76, 94
Harriet Vane 44–46, 87–90, 94
Hartmann, Heinz 37
hedonistic serial killer 174, 183, 185
the Heinz dilemma 102–105, 116
Her Royal Spyness (Bowen) 89–90
Hercule Poirot 1, 10, 12–13, 41, 44, 46, 67, 86–87, 95, 118, 145
hero 34, 45, 49
heuristic 113, 123, 126
hierarchy of needs 78–83, 86–87, 90–92, 183
hindsight bias 113, 126
History of Cross-Cultural and Cultural Psychology (Jahoda & Krewer) 160
History of Psychology (course) 1–2, 4
hit 172–173, 185
homo erectus 167
Hopkins, Pauline 42, 44
Horney, Karen 32, 35–36, 45, 49, 51, 69, 76
Hull, Clark 60–61, 71
Human Genome Project 170, 187

humanistic psychology 36, 75–93, 194, 196
hypnosis 29, 31, 48
hypothesis 7, 11, 14, 19, 22, 142
hypothetico-deductive reasoning/theory 61
hysteria 28–29, 47

the I 27
id 29–30, 40, 44, 47
ideal self 84, 93–94, 113
identity 36–38, 77, 87, 133, 136, 138–140, 157, 159, 161
inclusion 172, 185
An Incomplete Revenge (Winspear) 121
inconclusive 172, 185
incongruence 84, 93–94
independent self 135–137, 140–141, 156, 159
independent variable 8, 22, 72
individuation 172, 185
industrial and organizational (I/O) psychology 27, 195
The Industrial Revolution 26, 50
inferiority complex 45, 51
information processing approach 105–109, 115, 117, 119–122, 125, 176–177, 183, 186
The Innocence Project 175, 187
instrumental conditioning 57–58, 69–70
integrated/bicultural identity 139, 159
interdependent (collective) self 135–137, 140–141, 146, 151, 154, 156, 159
The Interpretation of Dreams (Freud, S.) 31
introspection 5, 26, 38, 45–46, 49–50, 58, 66, 68
Irene Adler 36

Jack Robinson 88
James, P.D. 40, 89–90
James, William 26–27, 34, 47, 106–107, 110, 161, 167
Jane Eyre (Bronte, Charlotte) 10, 20
Jimmy Vega 152–154, 156
Jonah complex 82, 92, 94
Judge Dee 150
Jung, Carl 31–36, 44–45, 48–49
"A Jury of Her Peers" (Glaspell) 116

Kat Guerrera 116–117
Kate Fansler 89
Kay Scarpetta 171, 179–180, 182–183
Keene, Carolyn 32, 50, 69
Kelly, George 106, 125
King, Stephen 23
Kinsey Millhone 117–121, 123, 148, 157
Kitayama, Shinobu 135–137, 140–141
Kohlberg, Lawrence 101–105, 123, 125

Land of Careful Shadows (Chazin) 152–154, 156
Langer, Ellen 11–12, 23
latency period 32, 51
latent content 31, 48

Index

law of effect 58, 71
Leipzig, Germany 25, 46
Liang, Diane Wei 150–151, 156
Lindsay Boxer 180
Little Albert experiment 58–59, 71–72
little grey cells 10, 41, 67
Little Peter experiment 72
Loftus, Elizabeth 175–176, 186
logical positivism 60, 71
logos 5
looking-glass self 130–131, 158
Lord Peter Wimsey 44, 87, 89
love and belonging needs 78–79, 86–87, 92
Loveday Brooke 42, 45
Luther Trant 6–7

Maisie Dobbs 7, 18–22, 88–90, 119–122, 151, 157, 171, 178, 192, 196, 211
The Maltese Falcon (Hammett) 67–68
manifest content 31, 48
marginality 139, 157, 159
Markus, Hazel 108–110, 113, 115, 125, 135–137, 140
Marti MacAlister 122, 148, 156–157
Maslow, Abraham 75–83, 86–87, 90–92, 94, 183
McCall Smith, Alexander 146–148, 156
the ME 27
medial prefrontal cortex (MPFC) 169
Mei Wang 150–151, 156–157
Miller, George 97
mindfulness 11–12, 21, 23, 86, 121
mindlessness 12, 21, 23
mini-mystery 14–18, 21, 192
The Minor Adjustment Beauty Salon (McCall Smith) 147
miss 172–173, 185
Miss (Jane) Marple 10, 41–44, 46, 67, 90, 118, 144–148, 157, 181, 195
mission-oriented serial killer 174, 183, 185
Mitchell, Gladys 42, 44
modus operandi (MO) 173, 183, 185
Moonlighting 89
The Moonstone (Collins) 50
morality 101–105, 115–116, 125, 144
morality principle 30, 47
Moriarty 63, 73
moving against people 36, 49
moving away from people 36, 49
moving toward people 35, 49
Muller, Marcia 116–117, 122–123
Munsterberg, Hugo 6, 22, 27
The Murder at the Vicarage (Christie) 42–43
"The Murder at Troyte's Hill" (Pirkis) 42
Murder on Astor Place (Thompson) 43
"The Murders in the Rue Morgue" (Poe) 20–21, 23, 40
The Mysteries of Udolpho 20, 23
"The Mystery of Marie Roget" (Poe) 23

Nancy Drew (Keene) 1, 32, 50, 68–70, 90–91, 150–151, 157
natural selection 166, 184
need 30–36, 45, 48–49, 51, 78–83, 89–92
Neely, Barbara 144–146, 156
negative reinforcement 62, 71
neopsychoanalytic theorists 32, 51
neuropsychology 166–168, 182, 184, 194
neurotic trends 35–36, 45, 49
neutral stimulus (NS) 55–57, 59, 70
New England Psychological Association (NEPA) 76
Northanger Abbey (Austen) 20, 23
The No. 1 Ladies' Detective Agency series (McCall Smith) 146–148, 156

object permanence 99, 124
observational learning 60, 65–66, 68, 71, 134
Oedipus complex 51
On the Witness Stand (Munsterberg) 6, 22
operant conditioning 61–65, 68–71, 73
organismic valuing process 83–85, 93
organization 98, 124
organized serial killer 174, 185
The Origin of Species (Darwin) 166

paradigm 1–3, 21, 26, 40, 44, 46–47, 54, 58, 60, 65, 67–69, 75–76, 83, 86, 88–89, 91, 93, 97, 117, 123–124, 132, 166, 194, 196
Paretsky, Sara 117–119, 122
Patterson, James 149, 180, 182
Pattison, Eliot 9, 81, 151–152, 156
Pavlov, Ivan 54–57, 61, 70
peak experience 80–82, 92
Penny, Louise 187
permeability 106, 123, 125
Perry, Anne 88, 90
person-centered therapy 84–85, 93
persona 33, 49
personal constructs 106, 123, 125
personal unconscious 33, 48
Philip Marlowe 67, 70, 120
Phineas Gage 167–169, 184, 187
Phinney, J.S. 138–139
Phryne Fisher series (Greenwood) 88, 90
Piaget, Jean 61, 71, 73, 97–101, 108, 123–125
Pine Manor College 14, 192, 196, 199–212
Pinkerton detective 66
Pirkis, C.L. 42, 45
A Place in the Wind (Chazin) 153–154
pleasure principle 29, 47
Poe, Edgar Allan 11, 20–21, 23, 39–40, 50
popular culture 1, 191, 194
positive psychology 86, 94
positive regard 84–85, 91, 93
positive reinforcement 62–63, 71
positron emission tomography (PET scans) 168, 184
Postmortem (Cornwell) 179
power-oriented serial killer 174, 183, 186

Index

preconscious 29, 33, 47
prejudice 131, 145, 152-153, 155, 158
preoperational stage 99-100, 124
Precious Ramotswe 1, 146-148, 151, 156-157, 161
The Principles of Psychology (James, W.) 26, 47
private self 111, 113-115, 119, 125-126, 136
process of becoming 83, 88, 93
projection 30, 47
Prosser, Dr. Inez 160
psyche 5, 21, 33
psychic determinism 29, 47
psychoanalysis/psychoanalytic 26, 28-45, 47, 69, 75-76, 78, 84, 91, 194, 196
Psychoanalytic Social Psychology 35
psychosexual stages of personality development 32, 50-51
psychosocial development/stages 37-38, 45, 49, 77, 138
public self 111, 113-115, 119, 125-126, 136
punishment (in conditioning) 58, 62-63, 69, 71
"The Purloined Letter" (Poe) 23
putrefaction 179, 186

Q-sort 84, 91, 93-94
Quincy, M.E. 178

radical candor 195, 217
random assignment 8, 23
range of convenience 106, 123, 125
rationalization 30, 48
Rayner, Rosalie 58-60, 71
reaction formation 30, 48
reality principle 30, 47
red herring 32, 48, 50
The Red Thumb Mark (Freeman) 11, 13, 177, 187
regression 30, 48
Reichs, Kathy 179-182
reliability 2, 20-21
representativeness heuristic 113, 126
repression 30, 47
Ressler, Robert 187
retrieval 176, 186
retrieval inhibition 176, 186
Rizzoli & Isles series (Gerritsen) 180-183, 187
Roderick Alleyn 13, 41, 45
Rogers, Carl 36, 75, 83-86, 88, 91, 93-94
Rohmer, Sax 149
role experimentation 38, 49
Rowling, J.K. 69

safety need(s) 35, 45, 49, 69, 78, 80, 86, 92
Sarah Brandt 43
satisfaction (need) 35, 45, 69, 77
Sayers, Dorothy 39-40, 44-45, 87-90
A Scandal in Bohemia (Conan Doyle) 20-21, 36, 45, 51

schedules of reinforcement 64, 71-72
schema 98, 108-110, 113, 119, 122-123, 125, 131
scheme 98, 108, 124
scientific method 5, 7, 9-12, 19-22, 28, 42, 45, 55, 179
"The Scream" (Munch) 84
self 27, 34, 36, 47, 49, 80, 83-86, 93-94, 97, 104-123, 125-127, 130-131, 135-143, 146, 148, 150-152, 154, 156-159, 161, 167, 169-170, 183
self-actualization 79-83, 85, 87, 89, 91-93
self-complexity 109
self-concept 91, 106-111, 113-115, 125-126, 130-131, 135-138, 159, 167
self-consciousness 127
self-esteem 6, 9, 79, 86, 92, 111-113, 126, 135-139, 159-161, 167, 169
self-handicapping 6, 111-112, 123, 125-126
self-monitoring 19, 89, 115, 121-123, 126-127
self-presentation 6, 111, 114, 125
self-protection 6, 111, 114, 125
self theory (Rogers) 83, 93
sensorimotor stage 99, 124
separation 139, 157, 159
serial killer 29, 171, 173-175, 178-181, 183, 185-187, 193
shadow 33-34, 44, 49
Shan Tao Yin 152
shaping 63, 71
Sharon McCone series (Muller) 116-117, 122-123
shelf research 6
Shell Game (Paretsky) 118-119
Sherlock Holmes 1, 10-12, 20-21, 23, 32, 36, 45, 51, 61, 67, 73, 95, 145, 149-150, 171, 177
signature 173-174, 183, 185
The Silence of the Lambs (Harris; Demme) 171, 178
Skinner, B.F. 61-66, 71, 73, 106, 170
The Skull Mantra (Pattison) 9, 81, 151-152, 156
sleuth 41, 44, 50, 68-69, 90, 144, 148, 151
social-learning theory (Bandura) 60, 65-66, 71
social psychology 11, 112, 125, 130, 135, 160, 168, 175
soft-boiled detective fiction 39-41, 46, 50, 66, 120, 122
sojourners 131-132, 158
Sonny Baca 154-156
spontaneous recovery 56, 64, 70
Steele, Dr. Claude 161
stereotype 131, 139, 145-146, 148, 157-159, 161
stereotype threat 139, 157, 159, 161
stimulus 25-26, 46, 50, 54-63, 67-68, 70-71, 106, 167, 170
storage 176, 186
The Strand Magazine 51
Stratemeyer, Edward 50, 68
structuralism 25-26, 46, 50, 75, 194, 196

A Study in Scarlet (Conan Doyle) 32
Sumner, Dr. Francis Cecil 28, 160
superego 29–30, 47
The Surgeon (Gerritsen) 180–183
syllogism 10–11, 21, 23

"Talma Gordon" (Hopkins) 42, 44
Tatum, Dr. Beverly Daniel 161
Taylor Bland, Eleanor 122, 148, 156
Temperance/Tempe Brennan 179–182
test batteries 168, 184
theory of mind 99–100, 126
third-force psychology 75, 91
third-variable problem 8, 22
Thompson, Victoria 43
Thorndike, Edward 57–58, 60–61, 70–71, 76
Titchener, Edward 26, 50, 59
token economies 64–65, 72
Tolman, Edward 60–61, 71
trace evidence 16, 172, 184–185
transpersonal psychology 82, 92
Tridimensional Theory of Feeling (Wundt) 26
Trifles (Glaspell) 116, 122–123

unconditional positive regard 85, 91, 93
unconditioned response (UCR) 55–57, 70
unconditioned stimulus (UCS) 55–57, 70
unconscious 28–35, 40, 42–43, 45, 47–49, 111, 125
unexamined ethnic identity 139, 159
An Unsuitable Job for a Woman (James, P.D.) 89–90

validity 2, 20–21
Van Gulik, Robert 149–150
variable interval 64, 72
variable ratio 64, 72
ventral anterior cingulate cortex (vACC) 169
vicarious learning 65, 71
Victorian Era 1, 10, 20, 46, 88
visionary serial killer 174, 183, 186

Watson, Dr. John 12, 23, 32, 51, 95, 150
Watson, John Broadus 58–61, 71–72, 76
Weber, Ernst 25, 50
Weber-Fechner law 50
White, Dr. Joseph L. 161
whodunit 18, 31, 48, 113, 149, 177
William James College 161
Williams, Dr. Robert Lee 161
Wilson, Edmund 143, 155
Winspear, Jacqueline 7, 18–20, 22, 40, 88–89, 119–122, 178, 192, 196, 211
Wirt, Mildred 50 (*see also* Benson, Mildred Wirt)
Wise Old Man 34, 49
Women's Murder Club series (Patterson) 149, 180, 182
word association test 31, 48
working self-concept 110–111, 125
Wundt, Wilhelm 25–26, 38, 46, 50, 132, 168

You Don't Have a Clue: Latino Mystery Stories for Teens (Cortez) 152

Zia Summer (Anaya) 154–156
Zia symbol 161

www.ingramcontent.com/pod-product-compliance
Lightning Source LLC
Chambersburg PA
CBHW032040300426
44117CB00009B/1128